ATLANTIC STUDIES ON SOCIETY IN CHANGE

Editor-in-Chief, Béla K. Király

Associate Editor-in-Chief, Peter Pastor

No. 60

Politics in Hungary:
For a Democratic Alternative

by

János Kis

Translated from the Hungarian Original by
Gábor J. Follinus, Ph.D.

With an Introduction by
Timothy Garton Ash

Social Science Monographs, Boulder, Colorado
Atlantic Research and Publications, Highland Lakes, New Jersey

Distributed by Columbia University Press
1989

ISBN 0–88033–963–2
Library of Congress Catalog Card Number 88–62292

Acknowledgements

Atlantic Research and Publications, Inc. conducts research, organizes conferences, administers scholars' exchange projects, and publishes books in the series "Atlantic Studies on Society in Change." The Open Society Fund, Inc., a New York-based organization, has generously contributed funds in support of the various projects of ARP. The Central and East European Publishing Project at Oxford, England, contributed to the costs of translation.

One of the essays was originally published by *East European Reporter*. Their reprinting was authorized by Dr. György Schöpflin, the editor of the journal. Dr. Schöpflin is also the translator of the essay on the 1956–57 restoration. The rest of the text was translated from the Hungarian original by Dr. Gábor J. Follinus. The copy editing was done by Ms. Jane C. Clancy, and the preparation of the manuscript for publication by Mrs. Patricia Stracquatanio of the staff of ARP.

To all these institutions and personalities, I wish to express my sincere appreciation and thanks.

Highland Lakes, NJ   Béla K. Király
March 15, 1989   Professor Emeritus of History, CUNY
       Editor-in-Chief

Preface to the Series

The present volume is a component of a series that, when completed, will constitute a comprehensive survey of the many aspects of East Central European society.

These volumes deal with the peoples whose homelands lie between the Germans to the West, the Russians to the East and North, and the Mediterranean and Adriatic Seas to the South. They constitute a particular civilization, one that is at once an integral part of Europe, yet substantially different from the West. The area is characterized by rich variety in language, religion, and government. The study of this complex subject demands a multidisciplinary approach and, accordingly, our contributors represent several academic disciplines. They have been drawn from universities and other scholarly institutions in the United States, Western Europe, as well as East Central Europe. The author of the present book is a distinguished philosopher, a leading personality in the Hungarian democratic opposition, and the editor of *Beszélő*, the samizdat journal published in Budapest.

The Editor-in-Chief, of course, takes full responsibility for ensuring the comprehensiveness, cohesion, internal balance, and scholarly quality of the series he has launched. I cheerfully accept this responsibility and intend this work to be neither a justification nor a condemnation of the policies, attitudes, and activities of any of the persons involved. At the same time, because the contributors represent so many different disciplines, interpretations, and schools of thought, our policy in this, as in past and future volumes, is to present their contributions without modification.

B. K. K.

List of Abbreviations Used

AVH   Allamvédelmi Hatóság(State Security Authority)
CPSU   Communist Party of the Soviet Union
CWC   Central Workers' Council (Központi Munkástanács)
HDIM   Hungarian Democratic Independence Movement (Magyar Demokratikus Föggetlenségi Mozgalom)
HSWP   Hungarian Socialist Workers' Party (Magyar Szocialista Munkáspárt)
ICC   Interim Central Committee (Ideiglenes Központi Bizottság)
IEC   Interim Executive Committee (Ideiglenes Intézö Bizottság)
NWC   National Workers' Council (Országos Munkástanács)
RCHI   Revolutionary Council of the Hungarian Intelligentsia (Magyar Értelmiség Forradalmi Tanácsa)
RCI   Revolutionary Committee of the Intellectuals (Értelmiségi Forradalmi Bizottság)
RWPG   Revolutionary Worker-Peasant Government (Forradalmi Munkás-paraszt Kormány)

Table of Contents

Acknowledgements v

Preface to the Series vii

List of Abbreviations Used viii

Bibliography on the First Publication of the Essays xi

Introduction 1

The End and the Beginning 7

Can 1956 Be Forgotten? 23

The Restoration of 1956-57 in a Thirty-Year Perspective 31

The Present Crisis and its Origins 85

From Reform to Continued Development 97

On Our Limitations and Possibilities 113

"Troops of Weary Seekers . . . " 127

Kádár Must Go 141

After the Fall Session of the National Assembly 153

What Should We Fear? 175

After Kádár 187

Hungarian Society and Hungarian Minorities Abroad 197

A Program of Action in Favor of Hungarian Minorities Abroad . . . 209

Once More on Mandatory Labor 221

On Ways of Being a Jew 231

Letter to the Signatories of the Prague Appeal 245

Yalta Problem in the Mid-Eighties 257

Volumes Published by Atlantic Research and Publications 271

Bibliography on the First Publication of the Essays

The End and the Beginning, in *Beszélő*, No. 19, 1987. Can 1956 Be Forgotten?, in *Égtájak Között*, No. 3, 1986.

The 1956–57 Restoration in a Thirty Years Perspective, in János Kis et. al., *Magyarország 1956*, [Hungary 1956]. AB Független Kiadó,Budapest, 1986. The Present Crisis and Its Origins, in *Századvég*, Nos. 3–4, 1988.

From"Reform" to "Continued Development", in *Beszélő*, No. 10, 1984.

On Our Limitations and Possibilities, in Ferenc Donáth et al., *A Monori Tanácskozás* [The Monor Conference], Vol. 1, Samizdat, Budapest, 1985.

"Troops of Weary Seekers . . .", in *Beszélő*, No. 16, 1986.

Kádár Must Go, in *Beszélő*, No. 20, 1987.

After the Fall Session of the National Assembly, in *Beszélő*, No. 21, 1987.

What Should We Fear?, in *Beszélő*, No. 23, 1988.

Hungarian Society and Hungarian Minorities Abroad, in *Beszélő*, No. 7, 1983.

A Program of Action in Favor of Hungarian Minorities Abroad, in *Beszélő*, No. 20, 1987.

Once More on Mandatory Labor, in *Beszélő*, No. 12, 1985.

On Ways of Being a Jew, in *Beszélő*, No. 11, 1984.

Letter to the Signatories of the Prague Appeal, in *East European Reporter*, 4/1986.

Yalta in the Mid-Eighties, in *Hírmondó*, 11, 1985.

Introduction

Introduction

On June 16, 1989, in one of the most remarkable ceremonies of recent European history, the leader of the Hungarian revolution of 1956, Imre Nagy, and his closest associates, were finally given decent, public burials, just thirty-one years after they were executed. Three weeks later, on July 6 János Kádár died—on the very day when Hungary's Supreme Court declared the conviction of Imre Nagy to be null, void, and illegal. Shakespeare would not have risked such a cruel tragic irony.

The essays collected in this volume treat what we can now see as a distinct, closed era in Hungarian history: the Kádár era. Although in day-to-day politics that era may be said to have closed already when Kádár was ousted from the post of Party leader in May 1988, the events of June-July 1989 furnished an essential, and fitting, historical epilogue.

One of the particular strengths of János Kis's essays is that he, unlike most contemporary analysts, never lost sight of this historical perspective. Throughout, he insists that the revolution of 1956 is unfinished business, and that the Hungarian politics of the nineteen-eighties cannot be understood without reference to what he calls, in carefully chosen terms, the 'restoration' of 1956–57, and the subsequent 'consolidation.' In 1989 this may seem like a commonplace, but a glance at contemporary political analyses in the early nineteen-eighties shows that most analysts had forgotten this, just as most of Hungarian society had accepted Kádár's invitation to forget. In his detailed analysis of the 1956–57 restoration, moreover, János Kis offers a significant piece of careful and original historical research.

Most of these essays, however, concern contemporary developments in the years 1983–88. They were mainly written for the *samizdat* quarterly

Beszélő (a word which means both 'the speaker' and visiting hours in prison)—of which Kis was the leading editor. *Beszélő* was the first major *samizdat* journal to appear regularly in Budapest (the first issue appeared in 1981) and it will have a place in the political history of Hungary at that time. The influence of such journals is always difficult to assess, but many would agree that it performed a 'vanguard' function: addressing themes and advancing propositions that were subsequently taken up in academic, journalistic, and eventually even in official political discussion. *Beszélő* was, for example, the first place in which the demand 'Kádár must go' was plainly and publicly stated, although, as the author himself emphasizes in that essay, it had been in the air for some time.

Within this vanguard journal Kis was a vanguard voice. These essays show why. Their lucidity, breadth, and combination of detached, sober analysis with strategic (and tactical!) political thinking, suffice to explain the author's intellectual authority. A philosopher by training and inclination, a Lukács pupil who has more recently immersed himself in Anglo-American liberalism, Kis here ranges, where necessary, far beyond his philosophical home ground. Recognizing the centrality of the economic crisis to Hungarian political developments in the 1980s, he does not shy away from detailed economic and even industrial analysis. His concern for social justice does not rest at the philosophical level, but finds expression in detailed examination of social injustices: whether the effects of proposed tax changes, new laws on compulsory labor, or the situation of minorities inside the Hungarian state borders.

The author of an original short book on human rights, he also tackles the fraught and sensitive issue of the large Hungarian minorities beyond the state borders (e.g. in Transylvania and Slovakia), seeking answers in terms of universal rights and practical action rather than in nationalist rhetoric. Ranging further still, he makes two exceptionally clear and thoughtful contributions to the debate about the meaning of 'Yalta,' the paths to 'peace,' and the possibilities of reducing or overcoming, by peaceful means, the East-West division of Europe. These two essays, in particular, should be read by Western policymakers as well as by peace and human rights activists in East and West.

His central subject is, however, as the title indicates, politics in Hungary. One particular strength of his political analysis is that he is almost equally good on all elements in the political process or 'game': on the Party as well as the democratic opposition to which he belongs, on the parliament, and on the vital intelligentsia groups—writers, journalists, economists, lawyers, sociologists, political scientists—which came together precisely in these five years (1983–88) to form a growing, albeit still heterogeneous pressure group for change. This is a rare quality, since very often those who write well about the opposition write poorly (if at all) about the Party, and vice versa. He is perhaps slightly less illuminating on the wider public, beyond the intelligentsia, which figures in these essays as a somewhat undifferentiated 'society' or 'people' about whose mood generalizations are tentatively ventured. Yet to some extent this was inevitable, since in this period other social groups did not have any clear political articulation; workers, for example, just did not belong to the 'political nation,' in the English sense of that term; and the object and achievement of Kádárism was precisely that they should not.

A fine example of Kis's sophisticated political analysis of developments inside the existing power structures is the chapter headed 'From "Reform" to "Continued Development".' Starting from the less than riveting text of the April 1984 resolutions of the Central Committee of the Hungarian Socialist Workers' Party, Kis explains not only the 'missed opportunity' for embarking on radical economic reform, but also why, in the logic of historical developments since 1956, this Party—under this leader—was almost bound to miss that opportunity. The dramatic worsening of Hungary's economic predicament over the next four years—rightly predicted by the radical reform economists—was then the fundamental cause of Kádár's ouster and the rapid changes that followed. In this sense, Kádárism prepared its own nemesis.

This book does not cover the period since Kádár's resignation, in which developments have gone further and faster than anyone—including János Kis—predicted. Thus it is striking to find Kis writing as late as early 1988 that 'the time has not yet come, even outside the Party, to revive the 1956 demand for a multi-party system. *Just one year later* the Party itself formally embraced the goal of moving towards a multi-party system. In this new political situation, in 1989, Kis is present both as a leading activist of the Alliance of Free Democrats (SZDSZ), an opposition party whose program owes much to the ideas advanced and discussed in these essays, and as an editor of *Beszélő*, which is due shortly to appear as a fully legal publication. At the time of writing, the 'democratic alternative,' for which János Kis was one of the first publicly to argue, seems more possible than at any time in the last forty years. But also, perhaps, more necessary.

With this volume, the Western reader has a chance to sample the work of an outstanding East Central European political essayist: a *spectateur engagé*, at once analyst and actor; and one who belongs in the company of Václav Havel and Adam Michnik.

Timothy Garton Ash   Oxford, July 1989

The End and the Beginning

The End and the Beginning

M
ore than a quarter of a century separates us from the watershed of 1956–57, but the revolution's defeat and the *ancien régime's* restoration[1] are not yet history. Hungarian society has yet to come to terms with the total defeat it suffered at that time, and those in power have yet to overcome the burdens of their victory. The economic and political crisis which in the '80s overwhelms Hungary is the crisis of the restoration regime which came into existence thirty years ago.

The restoration banished to the realm of utopias the revolution's fundamental demands: neutrality, a multi-party system, and economic self-government. Consequently, Hungarian society was forced back into the orbit imposed on it around 1947[2] which does not allow it to catch up with the main trend of European progress. We now begin to pay the price of this, thirty years later.

But what good does it do to point out this connection? No matter how much the internal and external conditions of the Soviet empire have changed since 1956, the revolution's fundamental demands cannot yet be placed on the agenda as short-term goals. A neutral, self-governing Hungary with a multi-party system is still a distant dream.

---

1 The Soviet army launched its concerted attack on Budapest and the provincial centers on the morning of November 4, 1956. Armed resistance was smashed in less than two weeks. The suppression of the peaceful social self-defense required months of terror and manipulation. By June 1957, the Communist party-state was largely restored. See "The 1956–57 Restoration in a Thirty-Year Perspective" in this volume.
2 In the fall of 1947 the Kominform was created. It was at its founding session that Andrey Zhdanov, the second man in the Soviet leadership after Stalin, told representatives of East European Communist parties that they must accelerate the establishment of the "dictatorship of the proletariat" in their countries.

The crisis of the '80s, however, is linked to the 1956–57 restoration in other ways as well. The prevailing political style of those in power was established at that time. János Kádár[3] and his entourage drew conclusions from those political struggles which they never revised—not during the consolidation era, nor the 1968 economic reform, nor the retreat of the '70s, nor even at the time of the economic recession and the new reform attempts at the beginning of the '80s. The present crisis is not simply that of the regime; a closer look reveals that it is a crisis of the rules, established in 1956–57, concerning the way in which power is to be exercised.

A speech and its antecedents

Kádár summarized his lasting political wisdom at the national Party conference in June 1957. His keynote speech and his closing remarks carried on a polemic on two fronts: He reproached Imre Nagy[4] and his associates for taking the Party's internal disagreements to the streets and for trying to appease the anti-Communist forces through negotiations. At the

3 János Kádár (1912-89), General Secretary of the Hungarian Socialist Workers' Party (HSWP) from October 31, 1956 through May 1988, joined the then-illegal Communist Party in 1932. From 1945 he was a member of the ruling Politburo, and was Minister of the Interior at the time of the Rajk trial. In 1950 he was arrested and tried under false charges, but was freed by the first Imre Nagy government in 1954 and returned to the party apparatus. In a radio speech made as General Secretary of the newly formed HSWP, he greeted the revolution on November 1. The same day, he disappeared from his office, fled to the Soviet Union, and returned behind the attacking Soviet army as head of a self-designated "Revolutionary Worker-Peasant Government." He presided over a particularly harsh terror between 1956 and 1961. In the '60s, he gradually transformed his rule into a kind of benevolent post-totalitarian authoritarianism. He supported the 1968 economic reform and in the early '70s made compromise with anti-reform hardliners. Unable to cope with the challenge of the economic and political crisis of the '80s, Kádár lost popularity and support at an accelerating pace after 1985. An extraordinary conference of the HSWP relieved him of his post of General Secretary, creating for him the prestigious but ineffectual title of Party President. In May 1989 he was stripped even of this title and excluded from the Central Committee.

4 Imre Nagy (1896–1958), was Prime Minister between 1953 and 1955 and from October 24 through November 4, 1956, and a Communist Party member since 1918. From the late '20s until the end of World War II, he was a political émigré in the Soviet Union. In 1948, he protested against forced introduction of the "dictatorship of the proletariat" and forced collectivization. As a consequence, he was dismissed from the Politburo to which he returned only in 1951. Nominated as Prime Minister in July 1953, Nagy initiated the first attempt to reform the Communist system in Hungary. In 1955 he was deprived of all of his party and government posts and excluded from the party, but was reintegrated in the party in the early days of October 1956. Prime Minister during the revolution, he recognized the revolutionary forces, he declared a cease-fire on October 30, and declared a return to the multi-party coalition government. On November 1, reacting to Soviet preparations to invade the country, Nagy declared Hungary's withdrawal from the Warsaw Pact and its neutrality. After the Soviet invasion, he fled with his collaborators to the Yugoslav embassy. He was kidnapped and deported to Romania on November 22, after he left the embassy with a

same time he condemned Rákosi[5] and his clique for ignoring the masses' limit of tolerance and thus driving them into the hostile camp. According to Kádár, in the absence of these two factions' misguided policies, the October catastrophe need never have happened. In his view, people show interest in politics only if they are not left in peace; the average persons who are satisfied with the conditions of their lives are indifferent to politics. But even if the populace is dissatisfied, the Party is in no real danger so long as it is outwardly unified and does not display its internal discord nor seek political conciliation. If the neutralization of the masses is successful and the Party retains its unity, it can easily isolate those political groups which claim to represent the public against it and thus retain the monopoly of political decision-making.

Around this time many people still knew—even if they were no longer permitted to say it publicly—that Kádár was also passing judgement on his own earlier political conduct: In the first months of the occupation it was out of the question for him to follow the recipe he would come to promote in June 1957. In November '56 he had but a few hundred followers. The overwhelming majority of the population considered him a traitor to the fatherland, since he had crushed the revolution with foreign tanks. The Rákosists who were gathering in the political apparatuses (especially in the militia) also considered him a traitor to the Party, since before becoming the prime minister of the Szolnok counter-government,[6] he had identified himself with the achievements of the revolution. Thus, his fate depended on the rather uncertain support of the Soviet leaders. He was desperately trying to break out of his isolation.

Kádár's hasty moves revealed an attempt to make progress in two directions: Within the Party he was trying to counterbalance the Rákosist camp by winning over all the non-Rákosist forces of the old Hungarian

---

safe-conduct signed by Kádár. In April 1957 he returned to Hungary under arrest, was tried, and was executed in June 1958. Buried in an unnamed grave, he was publicly reburied in 1989 after the fall of Kádár.

5 Mátyás Rákosi (1892-1971), was a founding member of the Hungarian Communist Party and Vice-People's Commissar under the 1919 Republic of Councils. Imprisoned in 1925, he was liberated and sent into exile to the Soviet Union in 1940. Between 1940 and 1956 he served as General Secretary of the Communist Party (since 1948 called the Hungarian Workers' Party, HWP). From 1949 through 1953, he commanded virtually unlimited power. Responsible for the Stalinist crimes committed in Hungary in these years, he was forced to resign after Khrushchev's denunciation of Stalin at the 20th Congress of the CPSU (February, 1956) and to return to the Soviet Union.

6 The Kádár government was claimed to have been formed between November 2 and 4 in Szolnok, a provincial city east of Budapest.

Workers' Party,[7] including the reform Communists who had followed Imre Nagy. Outside the Party, he was trying to counterbalance the revolutionary leadership of the workers' councils;[8] he was seeking partners, who—in exchange for workers' self-government at the factories—would be willing to give up the movement's regional structures and political demands.

The attempt, however, turned out to be a dismal failure. Kádár failed to prevent the kidnapping of Imre Nagy and his associates and did not even have the strength and courage to dissociate himself from this shameful act.[9] Thus he lost his already-remote chance of widening the Party's base toward the reform Communists. In the workers' councils, those elements which were willing to negotiate on the basis of his program were extremely weak. The Hungarian workers' council leadership of 1956 showed a great deal of flexibility, acumen for political realism, and a willingness to negotiate; but they could not go as far as abandoning the political arena altogether. The councils should have been offered a different, more daring bargain: On the one hand, their regional organizations should have been unequivocally recognized and their role in the new power structure clearly defined; on the other hand, the arbitrary abuses of the militia should have been halted, and negotiations about the schedule of Soviet troop withdrawal should have been initiated. But once again Kádár did not have either the strength or the courage to do that.

As a result of this, the situation deteriorated. By early December, Moscow was already considering the dismissal of the irresolute premier. In order to save himself Kádár gave in to the pressures by the Soviet leaders and by the Rákosist faction. There followed a wave of mass arrests; in several provincial cities the militia fired at the demonstrators; martial law was announced; the regional workers' councils were liquidated; and summary jurisdiction was introduced. As the resistance movement crum-bled under these blows, so did the Rákosist elements become stronger in the apparatus.

7 HWP was dissolved on October 30, 1956. On the same day a new Communist party was formed under the name of Hungarian Socialist Workers' Party. Its General Secretary was János Kádár and its most influential leader was Imre Nagy, the revolutionary Prime Minister.

8 Organizations of workers' self-management during the revolution and in the aftermath of the 1956 Soviet military invasion. The first workers' council was created on October 22, and the last was liquidated in September 1957. See "The 1956–57 Restoration in a Thirty-Years' Perspective" in this volume.

9 On November 21, Kádár gave a written warrant to the Yugoslav government's envoy to the effect that neither Nagy nor any of his associates were to be arrested, tried, or persecuted in other ways if they left the embassy's territory. Nevertheless, all the refugees were kidnapped and deported to Romania when they left the embassy on November 22. Kádár covered up the action, declaring on the radio on November 26 that Imre Nagy and his associates asked for asylum in Romania. In the same speech, he promised the none of these people would be tried for their activities between October 23 and November 4.

Nevertheless, Kádár survived his failure because he knew how to flow with the tide: He gave his name to the growing terror; he attacked Imre Nagy in increasingly harsh terms; he branded the October insurrection as a clearcut feudal-capitalist counterrevolutionary attempt; and one after the other he broke all the promises he had made in November. The shift of power in the Soviet Communist party leadership also helped him (In June 1957 the most ferocious Stalinists fell).[10] However, the major stabilizing factor of Kádár's position was the fact that the country's pacification curbed the Rákosists' chances of gaining ground. The paramilitary militia was first withdrawn and then discharged. The Party membership gradually became diluted: Flocking to the Hungarian Socialist Workers' Party were those people who—when the outcome of the struggle became clear—wanted to secure their careers with their membership cards. Due to them, in June 1957 Kádár could act not as representative of a defeated Party wing pushed into the corner, but as a centrist mediating between the Rákosist minority which was mad for revenge, and the majority which wanted tranquility.

From that time on, Kádár would always keep the balance of power. And he would always retain his mediating role with the same technique which he had used at the Party conference: Neutralize politically the larger social strata; do not allow internal Party disputes to become public; and do not recognize any group outside the Party as an independent negotiating partner.

From restoration to consolidation

In the summer of 1957 Kádár was not yet strong enough to get rid of the Rákosist elements. He needed them because somebody had to do the dirty work of reprisal and "ideological purges": The staging of trials was assigned to Rákosist investigative officers, prosecutors, and judges. But their jurisdiction was circumscribed. They could treat the past facts of the revolution and resistance as they saw fit, but they were not allowed to manufacture new cases out of thin air. They could maltreat the prisoners, but they were not allowed to use systematically the AVH's methods of torture. And without official permission they could not touch members of the elite. The result was an exceptionally cruel terror—which, however, left the populace's passive members unaffected.

The Rákosists played a leading role in the ideological campaigns as well, especially in the fields of philosophy and economics, where a "debate" had

10 After their abortive coup against Khrushchev in June 1957, Molotov.

already started in 1957. The later "debates" on literature and history, however, were already dominated by people who were not motivated by a fierce desire for vengeance, but by the feeling that the regime was stable. There were even a few participants who, in the guise of an ideological attack on 1956, actually criticized the Stalinist regime's official interpretation of history and its conservatism in literature. What really mattered, however, was not these secondary gains, but the fact that the leadership had these campaigns firmly under control and made its own decisions as to when stigmatization was to be followed by administrative consequences: Anyone who did not fall victim to the 1957–58 purges could be relatively sure that subsequent public attacks on him would not lead to imprisonment or loss of job.

In the background was the new approach to the economy. The reform proposals which had been prepared at the beginning of 1957 were, of course, rejected as revisionist; there was a return to a centralized planned economy, and investment cycles were resumed once again. But when this policy led to tensions, the leadership did not allow alleviation at the expense of real wages. In order to maintain a stable standard of living the regime was willing to tolerate temporary trade deficits instead of curbing consumption.

These were the main features of the restoration regime until 1962–63, when consolidation got underway. The 22nd congress of the CPSU[11]—which condemned Stalin once again, this time publicly—paved the way for the gradual removal of Rákosist elements from the apparatuses. Finally the terror abated; the ideological campaigns came to an end; the majority of political prisoners was released; the persecuted writers, artists, and scientists returned to the official culture; and everyday life was made more bearable through a host of relaxing measures. Kádár created a new, far more comfortable political balance. While the Rákosist elements' influence gradually decreased in the apparatuses, the weight of those elements which took the position of benevolent neutrality vis-à-vis the regime increased in every social stratum.

The leadership gained a comfortable leverage in managing society politically: It could experiment with minor changes without losing the reins of control. It could afford to allow people to discover the cracks and side doors in the wall of official regulations, since it did not have to fear that those who circumvented them would attempt to secure their position with demands of rights. Instead of constantly giving orders, correcting excesses and defining rules sufficed. It was at that time that Kádár's formula which he had put forward at the 1957 Party conference was realized: The masses

11 October 17–31, 1961.

were neutralized; the differences within the Party faded.

Nevertheless, the success of the consolidation depended on a host of favorable circumstances which proved to be temporary. It was of pivotal importance that in the defeated society there were no political groups which could criticize the rules of consolidation, determined from above, and could counter them with a proposal of reconciliation, coming from below. After 1956 the remnants of earlier democratic parties vanished for good, their continuity was broken, and their intellectual legacy fell into oblivion. The former reform Communists were decimated by the terror. The intellectuals who had participated in politics between 1953 and 1957 were glad that they were at least allowed to return to their professions. Their most prominent representatives disavowed their public role in 1956 as an immature adventure and celebrated consolidation as the pinnacle of *Realpolitik*. Consolidation went smoothly, far too smoothly: There was no one to isolate, no one to subdue.

It made the regime's job easier as well that after Rákosi's paroxysmal reign and the cruel oppression following 1956, the leadership was able to make several minor, politically costless concessions which visibly improved the quality of life. In addition, these measures were introduced at the time that first-generation commodities of consumer society arrived in Hungary: the refrigerator, washing machine, television set, and automobile. Their accessibility provided the people's withdrawal into private life with goal and meaning, fundamentally altered the way of life, and made it appear as if this was the achievement of the consolidation policy itself.

A continuously increasing supply of consumer goods depended, however, on one additional condition: There was a need for hitherto untapped labor resources and for cheap raw materials and energy, without which the extensive growth of Soviet-style economies could not be sustained. The mobilization of these resources made it possible for the Gross National Product to grow at a relatively fast rate (in spite of wasteful production practices), for the irrationally high level of investments to be maintained, and for mass consumption to be increased, all at the same time. As long as this was possible, the regime did not have to face those political conflicts which are the result of allocating scarce resources. It could give to everyone as much as was necessary to ensure that the very definition of interests remained the domain of those in power.

That these conditions gradually came to an end led to the regime's present crisis.

Advance in 1968, retreat in the '70s

First to be felt, in the mid-'60s, wsa the depletion of cheap economic resources. The consolidation regime was trying to defuse this danger by introducing the economic reform of 1968. This step was free of political risk, both internationally and domestically. A precedent had been set by the 1965 reform of the Soviet economy, and a parallel reform was emerging in Czechoslovakia at the same time. The domestic scene also appeared to be stable: the economy was not overburdened and substantial reserves of goods and money could be put aside to alleviate the tensions of the transition period. The expectation—which was soon proved right—was that the reform would bring an immediate improvement in the standard of living. The Party's status was untouched by the reform; the reorganization of the economic bureaucracy was postponed; and a variety of safety valves were built into the New Economic Mechanism. Not only did the reform not endanger the continuation of the policies which Kádár had announced in 1957 but also it promised their true realization.

Sooner or later the leadership had to face the dilemma of whether to complete the reform and accept responsibility for increasingly sharp political conflicts, to freeze the situation as it had been in 1968, or to return to the pre-1968 status quo. This dilemma could not have been sidestepped, even had the occupation of Czechoslovakia not occurred. August 21, 1968, however, made the need for the decision imminent. From 1969 on, the Brezhnev leadership's rhetoric encouraged the reform's natural opponents to go on the offensive. The executives of large companies who felt threatened by market competition, the regional Party apparatuses, the industrial ministries, and the trade union leaders stepped up their attack on the reform. Kádár did not enter a battle with this anti-reform coalition; he continued to avoid confrontation, sacrificed leaders who identified with the reform, and gave up reform policies one after the other. The conservative coalition, however, was so weak that it was unable to formulate a coherent policy and fell apart immediately after its 1972–74 victory. Due to this, Kádár was able to solidify his position and control the balance of power once again.

The reform's opponents were satisfied with the loosening of monetary regulations, with a program of major capital investment in industries closely aligned with the Soviet economy, and with a sprinkling of planned-economy rhetoric. Even the defeated reformists received something, however, since there was no complete return to the physical production quotas of the earlier command economy, and the economy's indirect control, through monetary policies, remained in effect. The blue-collar workers received the gift of an unscheduled pay raise. And while collective farms received the blow of consolidation into larger units, they were allowed, as a consolation, to move toward an organic linkage of household plots and collective farms. The leadership turned a blind eye to the proliferation of the second economy.[12] Although a short-lived campaign was launched against the critical intelligentsia within the fields of philosophy and sociology,[13] it soon became apparent that the regime wanted to interfere with the evolution of depoliticized science and culture even less than it had in the preceding decade. Thus, every significant social stratum received something; they could all reassure themselves that politics could best be left to the Party leadership.

Nevertheless, by the end of the '70s it became noticeable that the resources of Kádárist policies were running out. The return on the ranking of concessions diminished. As the second economy began to grow, it became increasingly clear that its benefits would sooner or later be undermined by human limits of self-exploitation. It became apparent that for some important social strata this option was, by definition, an unworkable proposition. The proliferation of uncontrolled economic activities increased individual autonomy, but the destructive effects of limitless self-exploitation were frightening. The evolution of culture also reached the point where its organization into movements was inevitable, and the opportunity for open debates without official tutelage could no longer be postponed. A new generation emerged for whom consolidation was not an unexpected gift, but a natural point of departure. Thus, it is no wonder that, following the Polish and Czech examples, there were people in Hungary who felt the necessity for a new start in politics, and who began to experiment with the exercise of human rights as guaranteed by international treaties. A few minor groups came forward who defiantly ignored the rules of the consolidation game, and by the end of the decade an embryonic opposition was formed.

But these developments could not be more than disturbing side effects as long as there were resources substantial enough to finance an economic policy which would neutralize the populace—more precisely, as long as the government was able to subsidize deficit-producing large companies,

---

12 Second economy was a network of non-declared, untaxed, economic activities. It played a particularly important role in the services sector.
13 In 1973, at the peak of an ideological campaign, several philosophers and sociologists (including the author of the essays collected in this volume) were expelled from their jobs and banned from publishing. In the same year Miklós Haraszti was tried for his book *The Red Star Factory*. In 1975, György Konrád and Iván Szelényi were detained for a week for their book, *The Road of the Intellectuals to Class Power*. Szelényi was forced to emigrate.

continue its large-scale investment program, and raise the population's level of consumption. In the '70s, however, the regime no longer had the internal resources for such a policy of virtually unlimited spending. The economy's expansion, which was continued in order to maintain political stability, had to be financed from outside sources. The loans which were received from Western creditors between 1973 and 1978 were spent on this, and on this alone.

By the end of the '70s the country was saddled with a six- to seven-billion-dollar debt and a backward economy of lopsided structure; it was unable to compete in the world market and, thus, to restore its balance of payment. In 1978 the National Bank of Hungary sounded the alarm bell.

For whom does the bell toll?

The time came when the populace's political neutralization could no longer be financed through further indebtedness. From that time onward, those in power have faced a hard choice: That of acquiescing to the erosion of their authority or of opting for a turn towards radical reforms. The second option, however, could be carried out only by facing up to political opposition and by mobilizing political support. Such policies involve risks; and if they succeed, they alter not only the technique of economic management but also the very relationship between the state and the society. As Gorbachev's experiment shows, it is not impossible that when faced with a regime's decline, the leadership of a ruling Communist party at least attempts to introduce such radical reforms. But the Kádárist leadership has always accepted and introduced every reform solely to *avoid* political conflicts or a revision in the accepted mode of exercising power. It is still willing to adopt reforms which are dealt out incrementally and can be easily kept under control. After 1978 it quietly rehabilitated the reform of 1968 and decided on a series of small reforms in that spirit.

The Party likes to look upon Hungary since the mid-'60s as a country of continuous (albeit moderate) reforms. Apart from the fact that this is not true—half of the twenty years in question was spent in a state of complete stagnation—the affirmation of the past process of piecemeal reforms serves no purpose but to justify the rejection of those radical reforms which have become inevitable: "We got by without them so far; they are not needed now, either." So, there is nothing left but to turn the old coat inside out. Earlier the leadership was trying to distribute the results of growth among the populace in such a manner that no group would feel the necessity for political action; now it tries to distribute the burdens of stagnation in the same way.

However, the tactics of neutralization are not equally successful during an economic expansion and during a decay. For two to three years the population can be mad to accept belt tightening. But the less people believe that austerity measures indeed prepare for a new recovery, the more impatient they become. And the leadership, which builds the stability of power on the neutralization of groups potentially capable of action, is less and less able to resist the increasing pressure on the budget. In my article "Troops of Weary Seekers" I explained the Kádárist leadership's political weakness by this fact—and by this weakness, the illusory promises of the seventh five-year plan.

The emptiness of this optimistic propaganda became apparent right in the plan's first year—to be more precise, right in its first quarter. The chances of recovery did not improve; on the contrary, they dramatically worsened. Production stagnated, productivity indicators fell even lower, indebtedness and the budget deficit increased. The trouble is not simply that nothing was achieved by the 1986 plan, and not even that we came closer to declaring insolvency. By now, the deterioration of economic indicators is overshadowed by the confusion of the leadership—and by the fact that its inability to deal with the crisis became obvious to large segments of the population. Thus, even before the worst consequences of the economic crisis have become full-blown, we are in the very midst of a political crisis.

True, the people are not ready for action yet. But the signs of growing anger and despair can be felt everywhere: at the workplaces, in the stores, and on the streets. And the discontent is not exclusively of an economic nature. The less the government is capable of keeping its promises, the more the people grumble over the lies of official propaganda, the more furious they become that the country's leaders have no better ideas than to prod them to work harder. As it is, most people already toil 10 to 12 hours just to make ends meet. And all this at a time when their work is of less and less value, public services deteriorate, public safety is on the decline. This is no longer simply a bread-and-butter issue. What the people question is fundamental: How does the state treat its subjects?

The confidence of those who govern is decreasing even faster than the patience of those governed. Governmental technocrats are grumbling because they are aware that if things continue as they are, bankruptcy will become unavoidable, as will its catastrophic consequences: the sudden fall in consumer supplies, lines at the stores, unheated homes, rotating blackouts, and disrupted production. The political apparatuses are grumbling at having to be the representatives of all unpopular measures. The Party rank-and-file is complaining about being sandwiched between the apparatus and the populace; Party meetings frequently turn into grievance days or group therapy sessions to vent pent-up frustrations. The military and the police are discontented because their privileges are being steadily devalued, and their social prestige has sunk to a low unprecedented since the mid-'50s. Those prominent cultural figures who have been acting as mediators between the regime and the intelligentsia (and society at large) are on their way to dying out or abandoning a public role.

The growing anxiety and discontent have drawn important intellectual groups away from the discredited behavioral patterns of the consolidation era. True, the machinery of oppression did succeed in preventing the numerical increase of the opposition, but it failed to isolate the opposition, which defiantly exercises its constitutional rights. There is a lively exchange of ideas and models of conduct between the dissenters and those intellectual groups which have not yet left officialdom. And in this gray zone new groups keep emerging which experiment with intermediate behavioral strategies: They stop short of embracing openly oppositional conduct, but exceed the officially-sanctioned modes of behavior. These groups tend to be short-lived; and since the Danube Circle's[14] crisis, no intermediate movement has come forward. At the same time, however, a significant shift has taken place in the behavioral patterns *within* the official institutions. This may be the most important development of recent times.

There are three important areas which resist traditional official control: The first one is literature. At the November 1986 assembly of the Writers' Union[15] the populist writers reproached the government for ruining the country's economy, culture, and public mores, and for leaving Hungarian minorities abroad to their fate. At the subsequent re-election of the Union's officers this group scored a sweeping victory. In response, Party headquarters summoned the faithful to resign their membership in the Writers' Union and took steps to charter a new one. More than two months after the assembly, only 27 people listened to this admonishment; at least four-fifths of those Union members who belong to the Party refused to resign.

14 Environmentalist movement opposing the project of the Bős- Nagymaros hydroelectric station. It came into existence in 1983 as a result of continuous official harassment, but was less active in 1985–86. In 1988, however, it resumed its activities on a spectacular scale: In September, 30,000 people followed the environmentalists' call to demonstrate in defense of the Danube, and by January 1989 more than 100,000 signatures were gathered on a petition demanding a plebiscite on the Bős- Nagymaros project.

15 On November 29 and 30, 1986 a scandal erupted in the general assembly of the Hungarian Writers' Union: The participants severely criticized the country's leadership and refused to elect as their officers most of the HSWP-backed nominees.

Another area where the regime faces mounting troubles is the mass media. What makes this more remarkable is the fact that journalists were left out of consolidation's bargains: Even in the late '70s they were treated as mere propaganda tools, with a social status of intellectual pariahs. The '80s, however, produced a new generation of journalists unwilling to accept the role assigned to them. The reporters, commentators, and publicists have their own ideas about the problems of Hungarian society and want to become spokesmen of independent opinion. But the Party demands from them dissemination of optimism and of propaganda lauding success and achievement. The Party leadership is more and more irritated because this breed of journalists does not deliver. The journalists themselves are becoming increasingly frustrated and angry because they feel that they are gagged and that the fraction of the truth they manage to tell is still considered a lie by the population at large.

The third troublesome area is economics. Hitherto Hungarian economists have given two assignments: theoretical analysis and advising the leadership. Some of their most prominent representatives are becoming dissatisfied with their limited roles, for serving as a prompter to the government which balks at radical reform is not a promising enterprise. To retreat into academic research seems, in today's critical situation, irresponsible. Thus, reform-minded economists have started to experiment with a third role: Along with advancing reform proposals to the government they also try to enlighten the public about the economic situation and prospects, to suggest alternatives for action, and to enter a dialogue with the leadership as independent partners representing a program of their own.

Writers, journalists, economists: In looking at the symptoms of disobedience within these three groups, who would not think of the years of 1954–56? It was not the opposition press, but *Népszabadság*, the most official organ of all, which first stated that the country's present atmosphere recalls the mood of the pre-1956 period. There are marked differences between the two eras, however. It took only three years for the crisis to undermine completely the Rákosi regime; the crisis of the Kádárists is in its ninth year. Against the Rákosists the whole country rose in a united front; the cohesion of the Kádárist politics is being tested by more divided forces which are frequently hostile to each other. As an antipode to Rákosi there was Imre Nagy whom the Hungarian people considered their political leader after his fall in April 1955;[16] as an alternative to Kádár, no one has

16 In April 1955, the revivified Rákosi wing of the party launched an all-out attack on Imre Nagy: He was denounced as right-wing, dismissed from the Politburo, relieved of his post as Prime Minister, and finally expelled from the Party in December.

yet emerged as the symbol of a democratic solution. Within Rákosi's Party there was a growing political opposition; in Kádár's Party, only the grumbling and discontent is growing. The Rákosi regime was pushed into political crisis by external events: Its convulsions were direct reflections of swings on the barometer in Moscow such as the transition after Stalin's death, the fall of Beria, the dismissal of Malenkov, and the 20th congress of the CPSU.[17] The crisis of the Kádár regime is of internal origin. It quietly started in Brezhnev's last years, continued in Andropov's year, then in Chernenko's, and has nothing in common with Gorbachev's acceleration policy except that its acceleration coincided with the turn Gorbachev is signalling in the Soviet Union. It is an irony of fate that the Kádárist politics has entered the depths of stagnation and decay when Soviet politics is in the process of leaving them.

Back to the origins

Since the beginning of consolidation there has been almost no one in Hungary who did not wish to forget the circumstances of the post-'56 regime's origins. The regime asked for forgetfulness in exchange for concessions; but its subjects had to forget, in order to be able to love the hand which just a few years before had so cruelly whipped them. Only a tiny minority wanted to remember. Their resistance to the collective amnesia was fueled by faithfulness to the ideals of the revolution and by an unwillingness to forgive, in exchange for rewards of any kind, its bloody suppression and the subsequent terror. But they could not be a political alternative either: What could they have offered, and to whom? They were left with nothing but their moral testimonial to the defeated cause.

Still, the crisis of the consolidation regime justifies them, the moral few. It also points beyond them. Today we must remember the restoration not just in order to regain moral integrity, but in order to understand the present political crisis of the regime. We have to revive the tradition of resistance in order to overcome the political decay of our society. We have to analyze former (failed) proposals of conciliation in order to find a more effective compromise to our present and future (perhaps less hopeless) situation. The events of 1956–57 developed from a moral issue into a political one.

17 The 20th congress of the CPSU met on February 14–25, 1956. Khrushchev (General Secretary of the CPSU between 1953 and 1964) delivered his secret speech about Stalin's crimes on the night of February 25 after the congress had officially closed.

Can 1956 Be Forgotten

Can 1956 Be Forgotten?

Almost exactly 30 years ago when the march of demonstrators set off from the statue of Sándor Petőfi[1] to the statue of Jósef Bem,[2] neither the authorities nor the students—who initiated the demonstration[3]—were in control of the events. Hundreds of thousands poured into the streets taking hold of the city. The crowd got a sense of its own strength and the weakness of those in power; it became daring and demanded more and more. The first slogans had cheered the renewal of the Party and Soviet-Hungarian friendship based on equality; by evening, the streets demanded an end to the one-party system and foreign occupation. The demonstration did not come to an end; something had to happen. Groups of marchers went to Stalin Square to tear down the monument of the hated dictator. Other groups gathered at the central radio station in an attempt to force the station to broadcast the sixteen demands which were adopted the previous night by students of the Polytechnical University. As the crowd tried to make its way into the building, the guards fired. News of the shooting spread throughout the city like wildfire and the hunt for guns began. People took rifles from depots of factory militias, police precincts, army barracks, and paramilitary sports clubs.

1 Sándor Petőfi (1823-1849), Hungary's national poet, initiator of the 1848 democratic revolution, died at 26, in a battle against Russian invasion troops.
2 Jósef Bem (1794-1850), army general of Polish origin, emigrated after the fall of the 1830 anti-Russian uprising in which he actively participated. In 1849, he was one of the military leaders of the Hungarian war of national liberation. He died in the Russo-Turkish war.
3 The October 23, 1956 demonstration was initiated by students of the Budapest Polytechnical University as a gesture of solidarity with the Polish reform movement.

At that moment, the time bomb which had been placed by Party leaders under their own edifice detonated. After midnight Soviet tanks entered Budapest. Earlier that afternoon, the panicking leadership called upon tanks to disperse a then-peaceful demonstration by their mere presence, as they had in Berlin in June 1953. But by the time the tanks appeared on the streets of the capital, they found themselves face to face with armed resistance.

Until that moment the insurgents had not really known what to do with their guns. They were limited in number, unorganized, and lacking in leadership and strategy. The Soviet army's intervention provided them with a clear target and made the populace take their side decisively. Isolated shots suddenly escalated into a war of national liberation.

As the moral strength of the revolution grew, so did the Party-state become demoralized. Calling in the foreign army turned a substantial segment of the Hungarian officer corps and the government and party apparatus against the leadership and fatally undermined the self-confidence of its remaining partisans. The leaders of the Hungarian Workers' Party[4] in effect notified the world that they considered themselves unable to rule; and for that very reason, they had to vanish from the scene. The Soviet army units ordered to Budapest did not only not prevent the spreading of the insurgency; on the contrary, they provoked it, and soon themselves became infected with the spirit of the people's movement. The State collapsed in a couple of days and had to find reconciliation with a few thousand poorly-armed insurgents. By that time, however, order and calm could only be restored by fundamental changes that a few weeks before would have been unimaginable: representational democracy in national politics, self-government in public administration and at the work place, and neutrality in foreign affairs. A classical revolution took place, and only another military invasion of sweeping force could reverse it.[5]

The Hungarian October, like all revolutions, had as midwife numerous accidents. If on the evening of the 23rd the Soviet tanks had not been called in, and if the armed intervention had not been justified by the Warsaw Pace, the people probably would have calmed down even without declaring neutrality. If on October 24 a national unity government had been formed under the aegis of the People's Patriotic Front,[6] the renewal of the

---

4 HWP was the Communist Party's name between 1948 (year of the forced merger of the Social Democrats with the Communists) and October 1956.

5 See note 1 of "The End and the Beginning" in this volume.

6 PPF is a façade organization through which the Communist Party presents its candidates at local and national elections and maintains some communication with non-party elites.

multi-party system perhaps would not have become inevitable. Had the government firmly held public administration in its hand, probably the spontaneous process of forming regional organs of self-government— National Committees—would have faltered. But, as in the case of every true revolution, the summary effect of accidents helped a birth of changes which had been in labor for a long time. The people's desire to shake off the dictatorship of the Communist Party, police despotism, and humiliating national subjugation could come as a surprise only to those who felt content during the reign of terror which Rákosi & Co. imported into the country. Far more remarkable is how quickly the overwhelming majority reached a consensus on how to replace the fallen regime. It is paradoxical but true: Hungarian society was prepared for some common goals to be effected by the Stalinist dictatorship, which forced a swift and profound transformation on the country. Between 1948 and 1956 a big industrial spurt overcame the country's economic stagnation, a large-scale cultural revolution took place, and the social structure underwent unprecedented equalization. The new industry was lopsided and inefficient; the new culture was shoddy; the people lived in want and their mobilization was hastened by coercion. The young working class and intelligentsia, however, wanted more than healthier industrial development, freer culture, liberties, and higher standard of living: They wanted to gain commanding positions in the management of the workplace, their communities, and national politics— that is, to play a role in society which matched their new economic and cultural status. As the Workers' Council movement demonstrated, this aspiration was a major moving force of the revolution.

An earlier but not less important forerunner of the agenda of 1956 was the half-revolution of 1945. The intent of filling the power vacuum with National Committees—organs of self-government—started from the grass-roots and moved up; the demand for free elections and the return of collectivized small farms was, indeed, the heritage of 1945. The reorganized former coalition parties were driven by the aspiration to salvage and continue the betrayed and expropriated democratic transformation of 1945.

And 1945 was but one in a long line of fallen revolutions, lost wars of independence, and aborted reform movements which all aimed to return Hungarian society to the mainstream of European evolution. In October 1956 it seemed for a moment that the historical struggle had arrived at a triumphant end. Imre Nagy[7] was not exaggerating when, in his radio speech

---

7 See note 4 of "The End and the Beginning" in this volume.

of November 1, he spoke of the realization of the Hungarian people's century-old dream.

With this we arrive at the question in the title: Can the Hungarian people forget 1956? After the crushing of the revolution the new authorities did everything possible to erase the events of 1956 from the collective memory of Hungarian society. More than 16,000 people were convicted for their participation in the revolution; at least 350 people were executed;[8] tens of thousands were interned without trial; countless others were placed under police surveillance and fired from their jobs. Then the '60's brought consolidation, with its unexpected bargaining proposal: "We will not punish you any more for '56 if you also let bygones be bygones." For the most part the surviving victims of the reprisals were let out of jail; those who had been expelled from their professions were allowed to steal their way back into their field; the writers whose works had been purged could publish again; the ideological crusades came to a halt; and everyday life was made more bearable by a number of minor adjustments. This was real improvement, and the country—drained of its blood and energy—was eager to enjoy its modest pleasures. Only a tiny minority abstained from the bargain; those few who were not willing to forgive in exchange for concessions of any kind, but who did not present any meaningful political alternative. They were left with nothing but their testimonial to '56 and their moral posture.

The "pact of forgetting" functioned almost flawlessly for a generation. Why not suppose that it could be extended *ad infinitum*? That would be possible only if the regime could offer to Hungarian society a future which would compensate for the irrevocable departure from the path of European evolution: compensate for relinquishing lawfulness, representational democracy, independent trade unions, liberty, market economy, and experimentation with self-government. Even the most enthusiastic partisans of consolidation believed only for a short time that this was possible. And now, even among them, the prevailing sentiment is that the politics of consolidation has exhausted its potential. The situation in the country is stagnating, and in certain areas deteriorating. It has become less and less worthwhile to forget.

But what is to be done with the memory of the revolution in a non-revolutionary era? Of course it enhances the self-respect of any people

---

8 First official data with a claim of comprehensiveness about executions was published only in 1989 (*Magyar Nemzet*, May 11). The number given is 277. The estimation in this article, published three years earlier, was based on a careful analysis of data made by Elek Fényes (pseudonym of a Hungarian historical statistician) in his article "Reprisals After the 1956 Revolution," *Beszélő*, 19, 1987.

if they know that the power of their masters comes from them—an understanding which becomes direct experience in revolution—and if they are aware of their dormant creative forces which become liberated in and by revolution. The central issue nevertheless remains whether the demands of the revolution have any *practical meaning* for the *present*. It is beyond doubt that the Soviet Union still does not tolerate either the neutrality of the small Eastern European states or the pluralization of their political systems and the introduction of self-government. The examples of 1968 and 1980–81 serve as warnings that events less extreme than the Hungarian revolution might prompt violent showdowns. On the other hand, the Soviet empire is not the same in 1986 as it was in 1956. Its economic cohesion is shaken. The ever-growing internal problems of the Soviet Union and the increasing complexity of Eastern European societies undermine the effectiveness of its day-to-day policing. The technological backwardness of the region calls for the expansion of foreign relations. As a nuclear superpower the Soviet Union is forced to seek orderly relationships with the United States. In return for the guaranties of European status quo the Eastern bloc had to sign the human rights statutes of the Helsinki Agreement. This action did not bring about its anticipated results, but it was not without consequence. We live on the western fringe of a declining and increasingly isolated empire; it is not hopeless to seek new paths to an evolutionary approach to the agenda of '56.

It is not only society which has to face this task, but the rulers as well. The regime has already squandered too much of the popularity it enjoyed in the '60s. If it does not take stock of the fact that it has become impossible to satisfy the people in the old way, it will find itself very soon in the same position as the leadership of the neighboring countries: except for brute force it will be without support. There is no sign that the Hungarian leadership has recognized the unequivocal imperative of renewal. It is unwilling to make even the most elementary humanitarian gestures if they might raise the question of '56. It still does not allow those executed between 1956 and 1961 a decent burial by their relatives; furthermore, the surviving victims of the trials still suffer discrimination.[9] On this 30th anniversary the regime turned once again to the same old outrageous slanders. Publication of a literary periodical was suspended because

---

9 Reburial of Imre Nagy and his associates was only made possible 31 years after the execution, in June 1989. In the same year, the government promised that decisions of the post-revolution trials would be revised.

allusions to '56 could be read into one of its poems.[10] A writer of national repute was blacklisted because on his American tour he called 1956 a revolution. A young artist was threatened with expulsion from Budapest because he intended to mount an exhibition in his apartment of artworks dedicated to the memory of '56.[11]

But the writing is on the wall. Lately the walls of the Budapest subway have been sprayed with red graffiti in English: "I love '56," "Remember 1956." This message is not sent by grayhaired former revolutionaries; it is sent by today's teenagers.

10 *Tiszatáj*, a literary magazine published in a provincial city, was suspended and its editorial board dismissed because it published, in June 1986, a poem by Gáspár Nagy ("From the Diary of the Boy") which was interpreted as making allusion to the treason of Kádár and the execution of Imre Nagy. After the fall of Kádár in 1989, the old editorial board was reinstated.
11 The police first warned Tamás Molnár of *Inconnu*, a political art group, not to hold the exhibition. Then, on the morning of October 23, 1986 the apartment of Tibor Philipp, another *Inconnu* member, was raided and all the collected artworks confiscated.

The Restoration of 1956–1957 in a Thirty-Year Perspective

The Restoration of 1956–1957 in a Thirty-Year Perspective

T he period following the suppression of the revolution has vanished from the collective memory of Hungarian society. People are reluctant to think about the fact that the same rulers who pacified their subjects with such generous concessions in the 1960's had dealt with them ruthlessly just a few years previously. They do not even like to remember their own resistance. The population, which began to enjoy the sober pleasures of the consolidation some five to ten years after the revolution, regards the nation's rearguard action as the immature adventure of its adolescence. It takes the view that it should have known that the Soviet state would allow nothing in its suzerainty over Hungary and would regard any changes in the system as a maneuver directed against its influence. It takes the view that it should have known that a decade earlier the Western powers had agreed that Hungary belonged to the Soviet sphere of interest, so it could accept the rulers' offer of reconciliation with an easy conscience. It endeavors to remember events as if nothing had happened between the destruction of the uprising by force of arms and the consolidation, and as if János Kádár had made his declaration, "He who is not against us, is with us," in December 1956 and not, as actually happened, in December 1961.

But he did not declare it in December 1956 and this coy reticence about the truth has not been to the advantage of political thinking. The nation corrupts its self-respect by trying to conceal under a veil of shame an act unparalleled in its 20th century history. It also harms political realism if one does not give a proper account of the origins of the regime in the aftermath of 1956. The unquestionable benefits of the consolidation should not allow us to forget that today's Hungarian regime is the child of the 1956–57 restoration. The monocentric party-state system restored at that time is not the only thing to survive to our days. The practices of power which the restoration leadership adopted while breaking the back of the resistance still retain their validity. These could be forgotten during the time of improvement in the consolidation, because the exercise of power was offering palpable improvements. Nowadays in a period of decline no realistic policy is possible without reckoning with the historic burden of the restoration. A renewal is only possible if the country can move beyond the political preconditions common to the restoration and the consolidation. And this requirement casts a new light on the post-1956 resistance. Instead of hiding its memory, one should learn from it.

These thoughts comprise the background to this history of the restoration. The period begins on November 4, 1956 and essentially closes with the June 1957 conference of the party. Although a few final steps in the reconstruction of the system took place after this date,[1] the political battle was decided by the summer of 1957. Hence, I intend to look at later events only exceptionally.

The eight months of the restoration were divided fairly clearly into four shorter phases by a few critical events. The first began with the Soviet attack and lasted until the point when the political struggle took the place of armed fighting. Strictly, this is where my analysis begins. I shall not be dealing with the story of the street fightings. In Budapest, the resistance of the last significant fighting unit, in Csepel, was broken by the Soviet army on November 11. But by November 7, it was sufficiently in command of the situation to relocate the Kádár government to the capital. On this day, the group which presented itself as Revolutionary Worker-Peasant Government (RWPG) held its first sitting and issued its first decrees. On the other side, the outlines of non-violent resistance were already being drawn up. Thus the beginning of the second phase can be put at November 7. Its end was marked by the dissolution of the Greater Budapest Central Workers Council (CWC), the arrest of its leaders, the promulgation of martial law, and the suppression of the nationwide unrest which had erupted in

---

1 The legal liquidation of the workers' councils was completed in November 1957; the refilling of the party membership can be regarded as completed in December 1957 when the exchange of party cards took place; the Writers' Union was only reorganized in October 1959; and repression was still continuing in 1960–61.

response. This took place between December 9 and 12. During the third phase resistance was in retreat but still had organized structures at its disposal. After January 8 to 11, 1957, it can be regarded as ended. This was the point when the workers' council of the Csepel Iron and Metal Works resigned and when the last major clash between demonstrating workers and the militia erupted. From then on until the June 27 to 29 national Party conference, the only remaining question was to decide where the struggle between the various forces determined to effect restoration would come to rest.

I.

At dawn on November 4, the Soviet army attacked Budapest with firepower that would have been enough to annihilate an entire national army, let alone a few anti-aircraft batteries and a few thousand civilian insurgents. If this demonstration of force was senseless from the military viewpoint, it had its impact in terms of mass psychology. Unceasing artillery fire for days beat into the heads of Hungarians that everything was in vain, that the Soviet Union with its military superiority would always do what its leaders wanted in this small country. The first response after the shock and the indignation was a sense of helplessness.

When, however, the roar of weapons ended, it was soon clear that the Soviets had gained only a military success; politically they were not masters of the situation. The RWPG, entering behind the tanks, had neither a functioning state machinery nor a party it could mobilize nor even a police force at its disposal. And it was opposed by the decisive majority of the population. Even a month later, the Kádár leadership was unbelievably weak. They had a 23-member central committee, the composition of which they thought it better to keep secret; they had a national party newspaper, whose contributors used pseudonyms and were even paid pseudonymously; they had a party with 38,000 members, which met away from workplaces, in maximum secrecy; they had a police force of a little more than 10,000, which was incapable of maintaining order without Soviet backing; and they had a hesitant, unreliable public administration, which was quite incapable of competing with the revolutionary national committees and the territorial workers' councils for the offices of power, especially in the provinces.[2]

2 Regarding the journalists on *Népszabadság*, see the statement by Zoltán Horváth at the Writers' Union general meeting of December 28, 1956. (AB Independent Publishing House, Bp. 1983) On the party membership, see István Szenes, *A kommunista párt újjászervezése*

These forces would have been worth precious little had the invaders not regarded the Kádár leadership as the government of Hungary.

To counter the second Soviet invasion, the national unity which had begun to fragment into different political currents during the consolidation of the revolution between October 31 and November 3 once again re-emerged on an even broader basis. Total strangers stopped each other on the streets, the queues in front of food shops became impromptu political meetings. Handwritten, typed, and stenciled leaflets covered the walls. The principal demands were repeated as if ritually: Soviet forces should be withdrawn at once; Imre Nagy's last cabinet should be returned to office; the multi-party system should be restored (and free elections held)

And while the government had virtually no organized apparatus behind it, the resistance movement had the organizations inherited from the revolution and those brought into being after the dying away of armed fighting. It was true that the national leaders of the parties newly formed between October 28 and November 3, with a few exceptions, withdrew from the struggle immediately after the Soviet attack, so that the local party organizations which still functioned were unable to assume much significance.[3] The organization undertaken by the ex-Communist opposition was all the more important. They had been in the vanguard of renewal up to the autumn of 1956, but were left behind by the speeding-up of events in September-October; now with the loss of momentum on the part of other parties, they again became a leading force. On November 13 they were the ones to bring into being the illegal grouping known as the Hungarian Democratic Independence Movement (Magyar Demokratikus

---

Magyarországon 1956–57 [The Reorganization of the Communist Party in Hungary 1956–57], (Budapest, 12976) p. 54. On the police, see Arpád Szabó, *A magyar forradalmi honvéd karhatalom—November 1956–June 1957* [The revolutionary armed forces of the Hungarian National Defense, November 1956 to June 1957], (Budapest, 1977), p. 51. On the struggle between the old public administration and the new organs of self-government, see János Molnár, *A Nagy-Budapesti Központi Munkástanács* [The Greater Budapest Central Workers' Council], (Budapest, 1969), pp. 93ff. Several leading coalition politicians took part in the discussions about a settlement as private persons. But only the two State Secretaries of the Petöfi Party (the National Peasant Party), Ferenc Farkas and István Bibó, issued a declaration in their party's name when they appeared as signatories to a compromise proposal in early December. To my knowledge, Bibó attempted to persuade representatives of the other coalition parties to sign the memorandum, but without success.

3 The leaders of the Movement were the economist György Adám, who had been through Rákosi's prisons, and the journalist Miklós Gimes. The first number of the papers appeared on November 15. Altogether ten numbers were prepared, seven edited by Gimes and a further three after his arrest edited by Péter Kende. Sándor Geréb & Pál Hajdú, *Az ellenforradalomn utóvédharca*, [Rearguard Actions by the Counterrevolution], (Budapest, 1983), pp. 183ff.

Függetlenségi Mozgolom), with the goal of integrating all democratic national political forces. They published the paper *Október Huszonhar-madika* (October 23) as the Movement's organ.[4] After the end of the fighting, several insurgent groups became the centers of peaceful resistance. The most influential of these, the Tüzoltó St. group, was under Communist guidance. It members found refuge in the Péterfy Sándor St. hospital, where they issued leaflets, launched mass protests, and published an illegal paper with the title *Élük* (We are alive).[5] The Revolutionary Committee of Intellectuals (Értelmiségi Forradalmi Bizottság), set up on October 28, sought to harmonize the political positions of the professional bodies under the influence of the Communists close to Imre Nagy. It continued its activities and then, on November 21 it reorganized itself on a broader base under the name the Revolutionary Council of the Hungarian Intelligentsia (Magyar Értelmiség Forradalmi Tanácsa).[6] The Writers' Union once again became an important center of opinion formation. Its programmatic declaration of November 12 was supported by every artistic union, the Hungarian Radio, the Hungarian Telegraphic Agency (MTI) and the Hungarian Academy of Sciences. In the majority of public offices, including a number of the key ministries, the revolutionary committees set up at the end of October and the beginning of November were on top. The factories were everywhere in the hands of self-managing bodies and the regional organization of the workers' councils was launched.[7]

The government did not even have the strength to defend its own people. After November 4 the removal from factories and offices of elements labelled as pro-Rákosi continued—in many places it began in earnest only at this point. Party organizations were banned from places of work. Already during the last days of the revolution the workers' councils had sought to enforce the principle that political parties should not organize within the factories, but,

---

4 The Tüzoltó St group was headed by István Angyal, condemned to death in 1957. Six numbers and one special number of *Élünk* appeared, edited by the writer József Gáli and the journalist Gyula Obersovszky. Geréb & Hajcú, op. cit., p. 136.

5 RCHI was led by the economists György Ádám and György Markos; it held under its influence the Writers' Union, the Journalists' Union, the University Revolutionary Committee, the Hungarian Academy of Science, etc. President of RCHI has become Zoltán Koddly, and its general secretary György Markos. (*Népakarat*, November 27, 1956.

6 J. Molnár (op. cit. p. 54) affirms that Budapest Workers' Councils held their first territorial meeting on November 12, in the districts of Kispest and Obuda.

7 István Bibó, "Tervezet a magyar kérdés kompromisszumos megoldására," [Draft Plan for a Compromise Solution to the Hungarian Question], in *Bibó István összegyüjtött Munkái* [The Collected Works of István Bibó], (Berne, 1983), Vol. 3, pp. 881–884. An English version of this appeared in (ed) István Kovács, "The Bibó Plan," *Facts about Hungary*, (New York, 1956), pp. 100–116.

whereas at that time their object was to exclude party political struggles, now the ban was aimed at restricting the power of the newly organized state-party. The armed factory guard remained in being even after the destruction of the insurgent groups. The workers's councils took decisions in all matters, including the distribution of scarce food supplies. Above all, it depended on the councils whether work, which had in practice been suspended on October 24, would resume or whether the general political strike would continue. It would seem that the government was incapable of restoring order even under the protection of thousands of Soviet tanks.

This gave hope that not everything was lost, even in the face of the oppressive superiority of military power. István Bibó, the last minister in office in the Imre Nagy government, probably summed up the views of the majority when he wrote in his Draft Plan for a Settlement, dated November 6, that Soviet forces had occupied Hungary on the grounds that they had wanted to restore order, but no accommodation was possible as long as they remained in the country. Given that the international situation urgently prompted the Soviet Union to withdraw its forces, a compromise solution was in the interest of all parties.[8] Hence the country regarded the fundamental demands it made after November 4 not as a heroic gesture, but as a starting point for a negotiated settlement. But even those who had given up hoping for the departure of the Soviets and the return of the coalition government—observing the awesome strength of the resistance and near total isolation of the Kádár government—formed the opinion that the pre-October situation could not be restored and, whatever might happen, it was inconceivable that the Hungarian people would have no power over their own affairs.

Resistance by society, however, was hampered from the outset by what might be called a strategic weakness. The demands, the programs and the compromise proposals all presupposed that the Soviet government now controlling the situation militarily would sooner or later enter into negotiations with the politically dominant Hungarian resistance movement.

8 For what it is worth, there was only one serious attempt at mediation. At the beginning of December, K.P.S. Menon, the Indian ambassador to Moscow, was allowed into Hungary. At Nehru's behest, he offered his good offices. He stayed in Budapest from December 2 to 7 and met several representatives of the opposition. He accepted a proposal for a settlement, which subsequently appeared as the Memorandum of the Hungarian Democratic Independence Movement [Magyar Demokratikus Függetlenségi Mozgolom], See *Beszélő* 1, (1981). By then, however, the time for compromise was over. While Menon was holding discussions in the Grand Hotel on the Margitsziget (Margaret Island), mass arrests were underway and the government was preparing for the crushing of the Central Workers' Council.

The Soviet side, however, never appeared at the negotiating table.[9] It insisted on the fiction that Hungary had a sovereign government, viz. the RWPG, and that all questions must be discussed with or through it. The attitude of the Moscow leadership immediately raises the question: was it not inherently an illusion to believe that some kind of a compromise could be wrested from it by the resistance? Answers to this question can be put forward on the basis of the political position of the Soviet leadership, particularly after an examination of its perceptions regarding its situation, its possibilities and its constraints. I shall return to this in the final part of this paper, which should be regarded as an appendix. But even at this point it can be noted that the behavior of the Soviets posed a grave dilemma for the Hungarian resistance movement. It could choose to boycott the Kádár government that it viewed as illegal and to persist with total non-recognition until the Soviet side was forced into negotiations. Alternatively, without recognizing the legality of the Kádár government it could enter into talks with it. The first course would have risked the complete ruin of the country and the exhaustion of the people, and no one could be certain whether it might not have prompted the Soviet army to take even bloodier measures. Choosing the second course meant at least the *de facto* recognition of the RWPG. But this held a danger. The RWPG could go through the motions of looking for a settlement and, using this as a lever, disarm the resistance step by step, separating the radicals from the moderates, until the eroding resistance movement was finally maneuvered into accepting the status quo. this dilemma become particularly acute when, with the formation of the Central Workers' Council (CWC), a body representing the entire resistance and capable of exercising overall political leadership, came into being. But before looking at the contradictions of the CWC, some time should be spent in examining the initial position of the RWPG; that, too, was contradictory.

The Kádár leadership, as long as force of arms was its sole effective instrument, was constrained to promise unusually daring concessions. Partly this was because they were trying desperately to widen the circle which would at least passively accede to their supremacy; partly, however, this was because they had to offer radical concessions even to their supporters in order to consolidate their positions on a very narrow basis.

---

9 No data has been made public on the composition of the party membership in November and December. However, it emerges from Szenes, op. cit., p. 129, that even as late as the spring of 1957, at a stage when the party membership had increased five-fold, the proportion of pre-1946 members was strikingly greater than a year previously.

The few thousand Communists who joined them at the outset were mostly former functionaries of the Hungarian Workers' Party, as well as party members of pre- and post-1945 vintage.[10] Their political behavior was strongly polarized. Some took fright for their future even at the 1953–56 ferment or, fearful of the anti-Communist atmosphere during the revolution, committed themselves to the Stalinist restoration. These people wanted bloody revenge for their terror at the end of October and wanted it not just on the few dozen perpetrators of the occasional lynchings, but also on those who removed former party secretaries and informers from their jobs, and even on those Communists who eased the way for the popular movement and were reluctant to oppose it. Many in this category joined the reestablished regional organizations of the Hungarian Socialist Workers' Party and flooded into the new semi-regular militia. The other group of party members from this initial period consisted of those who oscillated with the party leadership between 1953 and 1956, were increasingly in favor of renewal from the spring of 1956, and by the October 20 resolution of the Central Committee accepted the revolution as a national democratic movement. At that point, they experienced a serious crisis of conscience triggered by the occupation and its consequent social upheaval. The excesses of October, the anti-Communist atmosphere of the masses and, indeed, the *fait accompli* of November 4 placed them firmly on the side of Kádár, but they did not thereby become the unconditional adherents of occupation and restoration. Their inner need was for the HSWP to differentiate itself unmistakably from the "Rákosi-Gerö clique." Equally, it was to regard the sweeping away of the Imre Nagy government as justified by reason of being conciliatory towards the "counterrevolution." At the same time they wanted to be able to maintain the continuity of the goals of October 23. They wanted to attract to themselves the vanguard of the Party renewal movement, viz. the Communists supporting Imre Nagy, and to be able to persuade others, as well as to believe themselves, that the Soviet forces would shortly leave the country. It was no wonder that the struggle between these categories of party members was almost as desperate as that between the party and society and that the party leadership could not avoid adopting a stance in this conflict.[11]

---

10 On intra-Party conflicts see Szened: op. cit., p. 52. On vacillation within Party ranks see the protocol of the November 8 meeting of the IEC of the Budapest Party committee in: MSZMP Budapesti Pártbizottság *Valogatott dokumentumok és források a budapesti pártmozgalom történetéből, 1956, november–1957 junius.* [Selected Documents and Sources from the History of the Budapest Party Movement]. Budapest, 1982, p. 12.

11 The most vocal representative of this tendency was, in mid-November, *Népszabadság.* See, p. ix., its November 11 editorial.

The Kádár group had the greatest personal interest in eliminating the pro-Rákosi forces that were gathering strength within the party. There was hardly a person in a leading position in the party or government who did ont have reason to fear the Rákosists gaining the upper hand (the only one that comes to mind is Imre Dögei, who appeared out of nowhere to become Minister of Agriculture). In the eyes to the supporters of the *ancien régime*, Kádár himself was the principal traitor—after all, he remained with Imre Nagy until November 1, he recognized the multi-party system and the workers' councils, he hobnobbed with insurgents, and he voted in favor of leaving the Warsaw Pact and the declaration of neutrality. But Antol Apró, Káoly Kiss, and Ferenc Münnich had equally little ground to expect sympathy because they had given their blessing to the dissolution of the AVO and the Hungarian Workers' Party. György Marosán and Gyula Kállai did nothing much in October, but as former prisoners of the Rákosi era, they could hardly be certain that a Stalinist takeover would not cast them back into the dungeons. Béla Biszku belonged to the circle around Imre Mezö which had been looking for alliance with Imre Nagy. Lajos Fehér had been deputy editor-in-chief of *Népszabadság* during the revolution and his post-1954 career overlapped at several times with the reform Communists supporting Imre Nagy. Sándor Gáspár and Jenö Fock took the Hungarian trade unions out of the World Federation of Trade Unions under Moscow's control. István Kossa had protested at the July 1956 Central Committee meeting against the election of Gerö as first party secretary. Thus the leadership that took the political stage at the beginning of November thought it a better idea to make common cause with the hesitant elements against the Rákosists and to broaden its platform towards the supporters of Imre Nagy.[12]

The Interim Executive Committee (IEC) [Ideiglenes Intézö Bizottság], which simultaneously played the roles of secretariat and politburo, made its first task the compilation of the list of those former leaders who would no longer be permitted to hold high office.[13] They instructed the county interim committees to put together similar blacklists in their own areas. This actually happened in a few places, and even where no formal list was published, a purge was launched.[14] In the guidelines on recruitment to the party accepted

12 The public was informed of this decision by Kádár's November 11 radio speech. For names, see the November 16, 1956 issue of the Veszprém Party committee's daily.
13 The IEC of the Szolnok department published its own blacklist in the early days of November. See *Népszabadság*, January 29, 1957. *Népszabadság* reports on purges in Veszprém department on November 25, Szenes (op. cit., p. 96.) mentions Nógrád and Vas departments among those leading the anti-Rákosist campaign.
14 On the officers' declaration, see Szabó, op. cit., p. 38. According to this source, 80% of army officers in Budapest signed the pledge of loyalty by November 14.

on November 22, the IEC excluded applicants from three categories: those whom "the leadership does not regard as worthy of membership by reason of the serious political errors they committed during the rule of the Rákosi-clique"; those who "committed crimes against the people and the party under Rákosi leadership"; and those who "murdered Communists or other progressive people as participants in the uprising or incited others to this end, by plundering, engaging in financial speculation or generally taking part in arbitrary acts of terror" (*Népszabadság*, November 23, 1956). While the first two categories were significantly wider than the "Rákosi-Gerö-clique" proper, the third did not extend to the supporters of Imre Nagy at all, however narrowly defined.

The choice of the political base within the party had its effect on the choice of policies towards those outside it. The Kádár government was in a hurry to demonstrate by deeds that it regarded as its own "the noble goals of the mass movement launched on October 23," to use the formulation in its earliest declaration (*Szabad Nép*, November 6, 1956). Initially it only hinted indirectly that it regarded two basic measures taken by the revolutionary government—the return to the multi-party system and the declaration of neutrality—as invalid. On the other hand, it promised that in its relations with socialist countries, there would be "complete equality of rights" and "respect for Hungary's internal affairs." It even held out the prospect that "once order and tranquility are restored," negotiations would be started about the withdrawal of Soviet troops and that non-Communists would be offered government portfolios (ibid). One of its earliest decrees reaffirmed the dissolution of the AVH (*Népszabadság*, November 13, 1956), the freedom to take up employment (*Népszabadság*, November 17, 1956), and it was quick to lay down the rights of the workers' councils, first by government decree and then by law (*Népszabadság*, November 14 and 22, 1956).

On the other hand, the leadership had to take steps to assure its power and its consolidation. It banned the revolutionary councils of armed units at its very first meeting (*Népszabadság*, November 8, 1956) and it obliged army officers to sign an oath of loyalty.[15] In practice, executive power was placed in the hands of local council chairmen, who were appointed, not elected; the revolutionary committees operating in offices were stripped of their competence and, accordingly, all public officials were reconfirmed in the office that they had held on October 1, irrespective of whether or not the workers' council or other organ of self-government had dismissed them

15 This demand was made public on the very first occasion that Kádár met delegates of the workers' councils in the parliament building. (*Népszabadság*, November 14, 1956).

(*Népszabadság*, November 8, 1956). The government refused to recognize the right of enterprise councils to elect managers (ibid., November 22, 1956). And from the very outset it insisted that the party's organizational hierarchy would extend to places of work.[16] It made no secret of its view that it intended to downgrade the workers' councils into non-political organs, functioning at the enterprise level only and concerned with workplace matters,[17] and that it wanted to purge the councils of the leaders who had emerged during the revolution and whom it regarded as unbiddable.

The struggle, then, was not merely about who was the government, but, at a lower level, who had the right to decide personnel questions, who had the competence to fill leading posts, and who would decide on the composition of workers' councils and revolutionary councils. While the Kádár group could retain the power to govern, thanks to Soviet arms, they lost battle after battle in the struggle over personnel. The resolution abolishing the competence of the revolutionary councils remained a dead letter, and the removal of Rákosists from public office continued apace. Far from having any success in eliminating the political pacesetters from the workers' councils, party members lost out in the new elections even in those places where, towards the end of October, they had taken the initiative to found the councils as a way of preempting the situation.[18] The dismissal of managers and other enterprise leaders continued undisturbed; seeing that the majority of the offices were controlled by the revolutionary committees, they had no difficulties in acquiring the official stamp needed for the resolution determining the sackings. The remaining or newly-appointed managers, on the other hand, did their best to remain on good terms with the real masters of their places of work, the new self-governing bodies. In such circumstances, the restoration of the hierarchical chain controlled from above could make nest to no progress.

The government found itself in a confused situation. Relying on the resolution invalidating the dismissals, the most hated Stalinists started to drift back to their places of work.[19] The workers' councils protested, of course, and

16 Miklós Sebestyén, "A Nagy-Budapesti Központi Munkástanácsról" [Concerning the Greater Budapest Workers' Council], *Szemle* (Brussels), No. 3, 1961, p. 54.
17 Szenes, op. cit., p. 24.
18 A few cases were described by the press. *Népszabadság*, November 13, 1956, detailed how the workers' council of the Budapest Press Enterprise protested against the return to office after November 4 of Ernö Gáll, who had been sacked as leader of the printers' trade union on November 2. *Népakarat*, November 29, 1956, announced that Gabriella Andics, who had been forced to resign by the workers of the Bajcsy-Zsilinszky hospital, wanted to resume as director. *Népakarat*, December 8, 1956, told the same story of Béla Kruzslák, the dismissed director of the Technical Translations Office [Müszaki Forditó Iroda].
19 See the *Bulletin* of the Greater Budapest Workers' Council, November 30, 1956.

the Kádár group could not do much against this, because they themselves had taken up the stance of being the most determined enemies of the Rákosists.[20] By the same token, by condemning the Rákosi period and publishing the prohibited lists, it was as if the Kádár group was justifying the wave of dismissals sweeping through offices and factories. However, this triggered off protests in their own camp. Those sacked frequently turned to the militia for help; indeed, Kádárists joined up in fair numbers.[21] Their complaints received a sympathetic hearing in the party leadership not least because it was easy enough to explain the weakness of party recruitment by the "excesses" of the anti-Rákosi campaign.[22]

These were the contradictions with which the Kádár leadership was struggling when, on November 14, the Central Workers' Council (CWC), the directing body of the Budapest workers' councils, was founded. The emergence of centralized structures was a dangerous challenge for the government. It made it inherently impossible to foresee how the workers' councils could be domesticated into non-political administrative bodies in the near future and then be reined in one by one. It rapidly became evident that the CWC was not just capable of harmonizing the resistance of the factories, but that through its existence the illegal resistance groups, the legal organizations of the intelligentsia and even the restive peasantry could establish connections with the striking workers.[23] A center capable of

20 The ranks of militia included more than 1,300 former party employees (Szabó, op. cit., p. 56). At the National Party Conference, Kádár declared that party functionaries were sent to join the militia only because the central party apparatus had been dismantled (*Az MSZMP országos értekezletének jegyzökönyve*, [Minutes of the National Conference of the HSWP], Budapest, 1957, p. 217). One case which disproves this contention: Géza Timári had been secretary of the Party's Youth Organization [DISZ] in the Ganz Shipyard until October 30, when he was expelled from the enterprise; after November 4, when he was not permitted to return, he joined the militia (*Népszabadság*, November 27, 1956).

21 "We cannot allow the shelving of those who did no more than hold office . . . because this would hinder the reorganization of the party," declared Károly Kiss, the Organizing Secretary of the HSWP, at a meeting of the Kispest aktif, (*Népszabadság*, November 27, 1956).

22 The CWC was in contact with the legal Writers' Union, the semi-legal Revolutionary Council of the Hungarian Intelligentsia [Magyar Értelmiség Forradalmi Tanácsa], and the illegal Hungarian Democratic Independence Movement [Magyar Demokratikus Függetlenségi Mozgalom], as well as the *Élünk* circle. It requested Gyula Obersovszky to edit its planned paper. On contacts with the countryside, see KMT *Tájekoztatója*, [CWC Bulletin], No. 3, December 5, 1956.

23 The formation of the Budapest Central Workers' council was initiated by the Ujpest Revolutionary Workers' Council in its declaration of November 12. On November 13, armed police occupied the council buildings of the 4th district of Budapest where the body was actually meeting and arrested those present. Hence the CWC only came into being a day later, at the Egyesült Izzó [United Lamp Factory]. See Sebestyén op. cit., p. 50.

coordinating the non-violent resistance of the entire nation had come into being. The Kádár group—old Communists raised on Lenin—immediately recognized the danger of dual power.

At first, they tried to use force to prevent the establishment of the CWC.[24] When, a day late, the joint organization of the Budapest workers' councils did, after all, come into existence, they experimented with the creation of a parallel counter-center. But after this attempt failed as well, they were obliged to accept that they would have to come to terms with the CWC.[25]

It was in the government's vital interest that production begin. This was not simply or even primarily a question of avoiding economic collapse. The prolongation of the strike was proof that Kádár and his cabinet were not in command of the situation, while the resumption of work would be the first sign that the country accepted them at least *de facto*. Besides, the managements could only be taken over once work had actually begun—as long as production was at a standstill, the constraints on managers allowing the government to enforce obligations on them would not come into play.

On the other hand, the RWPG lacked the power to break the strike by force. The occupation forces could be deployed only in the streets; they never entered the factories. The Hungarian militia was too small to force several million people back to work. (One could see in December 1981 what a sizable and well organized military-riot police force would have to be mobilized for this.) There was no solution for the Kádár group other than to have the CWC declare the strike ended.

Kádár first received the delegates of the Budapest Workers' Council on the evening of November 14, on the day of its foundation, and then met them again on November 15 and 16. The representatives of the CWC took the main demands of the revolutionary movement with them—at the top of their list of eight points were the return of Imre Nagy to office and the restoration of the multi-party system. Kádár could not negotiate on questions of this kind, even if he had wanted to. Consequently, he could not accept that the workers' councils—which inherently negated the legitimacy of the RWPG—were

---

24 The founding meeting was convened at the headquarters of the Metalworkers' Union [Vasas]. The story of this was recounted in great detail by Sándor Rácz in his interview "A munkástanács mint egy pecsét, hitelesitette a forradalmat" [The workers' council validated the revolution, as a seal of office might], *Beszélö*, no. 7 (1983)

25 Most harshly in his radio address of November 26: "In offices, in factories there are many people, who became prominent in recent times, who had not been seen before, who call themselves democrats, but who, if they are looked at more closely, can be seen never to have been workers or democrats, but are factory owners or mill owners, maybe professional officers of Horthy's days and are, on top of all this, Fascists." *Népszabadság*, November 27, 1956.

transmitting the popular will from below. He had to persist with the proposition that the CWC's list of points had been spread among the masses by a reactionary minority. Hence, while using every means to persuade the delegates of the Workers' Councils to call off the strike, the same delegates were subjected to harsh attacks[26] and their proposed demands met with evasive answers.[27]

It would be inaccurate to describe the meetings between November 14 and 16 as negotiations. Kádár kept the CWC delegates for five to six hours, while his associates took them aside one by one, interrogated them and lectured them.[28] The discussions had no agenda, each side repeated its own standpoint. Eyewitnesses spoke of shouting and table-banging. The delegates left the parliament building on November 14 and 15 empty-handed.

The government's behavior forced on the CWC an extremely hard decision. They could persist with the strike until their demands were met, but at its meeting on November 16 only a minority took up this position. The majority thought the suspension of the strike unavoidable; they were conscious that the tolerance of the tired population was not infinite. Some remember that they were also afraid that, if the confrontation did not ease, the Soviet army might have been tempted to launch a massacre. The question really was how the strike could be called off if they received no concessions in exchange. After a heated debate, it was decided that they would inform the government that work would resume on November 19, but if the main demands were not met, the CWC would call for a new strike.[29] That same evening a delegation was sent to the parliament and, although, as before Kádár promised nothing,

---

26 While Imre Nagy is on the sovereign territory of a foreign state, one cannot negotiate with him; Soviet troops will leave when there is order and tranquility; the government wants a multi-party system and honest elections, but this can only be discussed when it is certain that Communists would not be forced out of the parliament, because without them "the people's democratic state order" would come to an end; work should be resumed first, then political questions could become a matter for negotiation. In this instance, contemporary press sources and personal reminiscences are absolutely identical. See *Népszabadság*, November 15, *Uj Ut*, November 15, 1956, Sebestyén, op. cit., p. 50, Rácz, op. cit.

27 See Rácz, op. cit.; Ference Tőke, "A Nagy-Budapesti Központi Munkástanácsról," *Szemle* (Brussels), no. 3, 1961, p. 60. Marosán, writing on the tactics of the government, noted, "There was a division of labor between Kádár and myself; we agreed that I would talk to the workers' council first and would tell them whatever came into my head; then, when everything was stood on its head, Kádár would come in, sit down and tried to calm things down." ""Az élet újra indul" [Life Begins Again], interview with László Rapcsányi, *Jel-Kép*, No. 1, 1982, p. 90.

28 Sebestyén, op. cit., p. 52.

29 See the CWC pamphlet, *Felhívás valamennyi üzemi, kerületi és megyei munkástanácshoz*, [Appeal to All Factory, District and County Workers' Councils], Budapest, November 27, 1956.

(*Népszabadság*, November 17, 1956), Sándor Rácz, the newly-elected second chairman of the CWC, announced the Council's decision on radio shortly thereafter.

It is not clear how far the participants at the November 16 meeting of the CWC were conscious of the shift in their policies. Despite the threats, a nationwide strike for the immediate departure of the Soviet troops, for the return of the Imre Nagy government to office, or for the restoration of the multi-party system was never again launched. The CWC maintained its basic demands, but they slipped down the list of priorities and, during the weeks that followed, it made efforts only where it could hope to achieve something. In part, its attention was concentrated on those tasks which it could undertake without the cooperation of government—to build up and strengthen its organizational structures, to establish regular contact with workers' councils in the provinces, to encourage the creation of district and territorial councils, and to work on the formation of a National Workers' Council (NWC) [Országos Munkástanács]. Somewhat later, it began to encourage the workers's councils to constrain the official trade unions to begin their renewal from below. In its contacts with the government, it sought to place in the forefront those demands which could form the basis of negotiations in the existing situation, eg. that postal and railway workers also be allowed to found workers' councils (which the Kádár leadership rejected, probably because of the strategic significance of communications and transport); or that the CWC have the capability of informing the country through the media of its agreements with the government; or that the workers' councils have their own press.

It is noteworthy that the first clash between the government and the CWC, on November 21 and 22 did not reverse this trend towards Realpolitik, but strengthened it. The Budapest workers' council announced a grand assembly for November 21 in the Sport Hall [Sportcsarnok] for the founding of the National Workers' Council. The Kádár group, on the defensive after its failure to halt the establishment of the CWC and in effect content with not meeting any political demands, now launched a counterattack. This time, it was successful. By deploying Soviet armor and the Hungarian militia, the Kádár group frustrated the plans to set up the NWC. The government decree on the workers' councils appeared on the same day and the amendments proposed beforehand by the CWC were systematically ignored. On the 22nd, after word of the dispersal of the meeting to set up the NWC became known, the majority of factories and mines ceased work, the CWC declared a 48-hour strike, and it sent a delegation to Kádár with a list of demands. The delegation, announced for 8 p.m., was received at 2 a.m. An agreement was reached by dawn. The government recognized the CWC as a "deliberative body" [tanácskozó testület]; the issue of managerial appointments was again taken to the Council of Ministers for revision; the CWC would be permitted to make public its declarations in the press and radio; and in exchange the CWC would call off the strike (*Népakarat*, November 23, 1956, 2nd edition).

This, however, did not bring the crisis to an end. At dusk on November 22, Soviet armed units ambushed and kidnapped Imre Nagy and his associates as they were leaving the Yugoslav embassy where they had taken refuge. By the time the agreement between the CWC and the government was broadcast, the CWC had heard the news of the kidnapping. On November 23, they set up a committee to clarify the whereabouts of the former Prime Minister and to demand a meeting with him. But they decided not to rescind the agreement with the government. After a heated debate, they decided that work should continue.[30] The plan to establish a NWC was postponed; for the time being, they sought instead to transform the more or less recognized CWC into the national center of the movement.

This should not be understood as having been a thought through, unequivocal, political move. The negotiations with the Kádár government meant its *de facto* recognition, but this in turn unwittingly brought the legitimacy of the CWC into debate. After all, the legality of the workers' councils sprang from the revolution, whereas the RWPG derived its existence from the destruction of that revolution by military intervention. Furthermore, the CWC was so recent an organization that its members had not had time to become used to each other. Lacking lengthy experience in shared struggles, mutual trust rested on the assessment of the behavior of the moment. One badly formulated sentence could bring failure with it.[31] In exactly the same way, the CWC itself had continuously to prove to the workers' councils fighting their local battles that it was worthy of their trust. At all times, it had to struggle against the not-altogether-unjustified climate of opinion that Kádár leadership was using the negotiations as a pretext for delay, even while a reckoning was being prepared. Anyone who might have said in November 1956, "let's recognize the Kádár government, let's see where we get with it," would have been finished at once. It was no wonder that Rácz and the others had to insist that even if they were talking to Kádár, even if they were giving

---

30 This was how Jósef Dévényi, the first chairman of the CWC, lost his mandate. See Rácz, op. cit.

31 "Even if the results achieved to date are not satisfactory for a moment," stated the CWC's appeal of November 27, "all the same, . . . in our negotiations we did not deviate for one second from the outstanding goals and basic demands of the national revolution of October 23."

way in some things, they were not surrendering the principles of October 23.[32]

This is how it becomes understandable that precisely in the very days when the CWC was embarking on a policy of concessions, it also launched a policy of symbolic confrontations. In the afternoon of November 23, between 2 and 3 p.m., the streets of Budapest were deserted at the request of the CWC. On December 1, the country boycotted official papers. On the 4th, at the initiative of *Élünk* and with support from a section of the CWC, a silent mourning procession of women placed wreaths at the Tomb of the Unknown Warrior; in the evening candles were lit in the windows of the capitol. The purpose of these collective gestures was partly to demonstrate the mass influence of the CWC and partly the unity and attachment of the nation to the ideals of October 23. But they had another more covert function as well. The CWC, precisely because it had entered on a bargaining process leading towards taking cognizance of the status quo, needed to experience its adherence with the country to the revolution again and again through these symbolic acts. Nevertheless, behind the smoke billowing from the burning newspapers, the curtain of candle flame, and the heaps of flowers there began an exploration to discover the possibilities of an agreement.

Whether anything would come of it would depend on the attitude of the authorities. After November 21 and 22, one or two things pointed towards the conclusion that perhaps Kádár also was being pushed towards a compromise by the lessons of the crisis. In the last week of the month a few minor concessions were made. While insisting that no workers' council could operate at the railways and the postal service, he held out the prospect of recognizing councils in "production units" [termelöi részleg]. The application by the CWC to launch a newspaper was—temporarily, it was said—rejected, but it was noted that the Council was publishing an Information Bulletin, using stencils. István Kossa, the Minister of Finance, and Jenő Fock, the secretary of the trade unions, were entrusted with working out the draft version of the law on workers' councils together with representatives of the CWC. Although harsh exchanges were frequent, and more than once discussions were broken off without any result, the form of contacts—to judge by the CWC's Bulletin—was beginning to resemble regular negotiations. An agenda was agreed; the questions to be decided were so marked; and other "general questions" were the subject of exchanges of opinion.

What explains the greater flexibility of the Kádár leadership? They probably took fright at the Soviet kidnapping of Imre Nagy and his associates. It is

32 Personal communication from István Eörsi.

unlikely that Kádár would have no idea of Soviet intentions at the time when he gave his written guarantee that all the Hungarian citizens at the Yugoslav embassy could return home in safety. After all, this took place on November 21, three days after the kidnapping of György Lukács, Zoltán Szántó, and Zoltán Vas, who had departed from the same embassy of their own free will. The outside world was informed of this kidnapping on the same day[33] and Kádár could have come to know of it. Even if the fate of the Nagy group was no surprise, to him, we can certainly assume that it presented him with a *fait accompli*. If he believed until then that he had some time for maneuver, he now had to recognize that this was not so. He either consolidated his power in a very short time or anything was possible, including finding himself together with Imre Nagy, under arrest in Romania. Besides, it was at this very time that they came to understand what a powerful opponent the CWC was. After November 16, the Budapest Workers' Council demonstrated that if it so decided, factories and mines would resume working; now it proved that its call for a strike would be acceded to as well. One could see how quickly the territorial network of workers' councils around the CWC was being organized throughout the country and that a center for this structure did not depend on the formal act of bringing a National Workers' Council into existence. The tactics of delay and evasion were not adequate to dismantle this powerful force. The government had to choose—either it tried for an agreement or it opted for a settling of accounts by force which would play into the hands of the Rákosists. I would not say that after November 21 and 22 the Kádár leadership did so decide unequivocally, but it did take a few small steps in the direction of a settlement by negotiation.

They were also driven in this direction by the spread of the workers' councils movement and how this unsettled political control over the running enterprises. Party organizations had not been reintroduced into places of work and the ferment in the official trade unions had already begun. At the initiative of the workers' councils, enterprise committees were reelected one after the other, in some places including even the higher union organs. Printers and textile workers opted out of the trade union council and there was a serious possibility that this Council [Szakszervezetek Országos Tanácsa, called Szabad Szakszervezetek Országos Szövetsége between November 1956 and January 1957] would disintegrate.[34] Trade union leaders left over from

33 A fairly-detailed picture of the process of disintegration in the trade unions is given by Molnár, op. cit. p. 82.
34 In the CWC the general idea was that the hierarchical command planning system should be replaced by one of industrial chambers [iparkamarák] to coordinate matters from below. See the document *A magyar népgazdaság önkormányzati tervezete* [The Self-Management

the early 1950s tried to escape upwards, to avoid being swept away by the avalanche. The secretariat of the trade union council declared that the unions were independent of the party and the government; it promoted recognition of the right to strike; it co-opted one or two old Social Democrat trade union leaders who had been demoted or imprisoned in the 1949–53 years; and, unprompted, it announced the general renewal of officials in order to take these elections to the enterprise councils and out of the hands of the workers' councils (*Népakarat*, November 28, 1956). In the meantime, Gáspár and his lieutenants sought to convey the idea that the unions were loyal partners of the CWC's—that they supported the demand to amend the projected law on worker's councils, that they agreed with the CWC's proposals to transform the economic planning system,[35] and that they adopted as their own the proposal to create a Producers' Council as the second chamber of parliament (*Népakarat*, November 29, 1956). The Trade Union Council, then, tried to respond to the pressure from outside by taking controlled initiatives for renewal from above. Thereby it pulled the government towards compromise as well, offering itself as intermediary between the RWPG and CWC.[36]

Another development must be mentioned here which, though less significant, likewise influenced the disposition of the government to negotiate. In the second half of November, some of the economic ministries were entrusted with working out a new reform concept for the running of industry. The motives for this initiative were complex. During these weeks, every renewal plan not linked with the twelve-day revolution was welcome to the government. The idea of economic reform was in this category. Direct planning had been largely discredited in the state administration and few believed that it was capable of resolving the aggravated economic problems deriving from the destruction after the fighting and the wave of strikes. In several ministries, the revolutionary committee was strong and determined in its opposition, so that the request to work out an economic reform plan was an ideal spur to cooperation. But in a situation where the internal structure of industrial enterprises was to undergo a revolutionary transformation, the

Plan for the Hungarian Economy] discussed by Iván Petö and Sándor Szakács, *A hazai gazdaság négy évtizedének története*, [The History of Four Decades of the Hungarian Economy] Vol. I, Budapest 1985, p. 347.

35 At the outset, the relationship between the CWC and the Trade Union Council was decidedly hostile. The workers' leaders had not the least intention of having anything to do with the Gáspár group. Early in December, however, relations between the two bodies improved somewhat. The CWC was having problems in finding a headquarters and preferred to accept the offer of the Trade Union Council to that of the Government.

36 The Petö & Szakács book discusses the projects of the Ministries of Finance, of Steel and Engineering Industries, Chemical Industry, Light Industry, and Construction Industry, at p. 344.

reform of the economy would unavoidably become linked with the workers' councils. Willy-nilly the question would arise: in what way could the method of industrial management be adapted to the method of enterprise self-management? The ministries themselves, in the grip of a revolutionary ferment, were inclined at all costs to make this the center of gravity of the entire reform.[37] Thus the government was pushed in the direction of taking the workers' councils seriously by the discussions it was having with its own apparatus.

All the same, pressure in the opposite direction was also intensifying. The kidnapping of Imre Nagy put an end to the hope that within the Communist party, the reform camp might be extended by taking the oppositionists; thereby, the Rákosists began to gain in strength. At the top, the leadership was terrified by the nightmare of dual power, while at the bottom the conflict between the workers' council, management cadres, and the militia was intensifying. Here, a sacked Rákosist would try to get back with armed help, there a party committee expelled from a factory would insist on returning. Elsewhere a forged leaflet issued in the name of the workers' council would provoke the workers or, relying on these, the militia would appear to arrest the chairman of the workers' council. In some other place still, the workers' council's duplicators and distributors would be taken away. The first steps were taken to wind up the illegal groups, and this also lessened the room for compromise. The activity of the militia more and more assumed the nature of a vendetta. People began to disappear in large numbers and often no one knew why. Every such conflict could become an occasion for the eruption of a strike, and every local strike became the source of newer conflicts.

The situation grew particularly acute in the provinces. Away from the capital, the local organs of state power and the new local government organs paid less heed to the nascent, though uncertain, ground rules emerging between the government and the CWC. In many places, there was open fighting between the territorial workers' council and the old local authority over positions of power.[38]

37 See J. Molnár, op. cit., pp. 92ff. Among the larger conflicts, he mentions Salgótarján (Nógrád ary activities in the Gyula district], Gyula, 1958. The new militia only entered Gyula on December 17; until then the national committee ruled, in cooperation with the local police.

38 "The arrests will cease immediately," the Kádár government declared at the consultations with industrial managers and the workers' councils in the parliament on November 25, "when they stop the banditry and stop threatening those miners and workers who want to go on working." (*Petöfi Népe*, November 27, 1957). The head of the RWPG also warned the leaders of the resisting workers' councils at this meeting "to pull in their horns." Cited in *Tiltakozás* [Protest], a leaflet issued by Workers' council of Budapest 20th district, November 27, 1956.

Towards the end of November, representatives of the CWC could still manage to have arbitrarily arrested members of workers' councils released, though the effectiveness of their intervention was declining. But they could not prevent the government from persecuting the illegal groups nor have the excesses of the militia condemned and its activity and organization brought under regulated control. The Kádár group made no secret of it—there would be no question of bringing the armed detachments to heel.[39] In the struggle with resistance movement, they could hold solidly only to this one position: thus, they resisted with utter determination all suggestions that the militia be disbanded and a workers' guard be organized in conjunction with the CWC. They just could not give up their sole source of strength. But they had to pay a price for this, by becoming more and more defenseless in the face of the Rákosists thirst for revenge.

The conflict grew increasingly venomous. The question of the militia became the key issue in the conflict. First among the demands made by the Nógrád county workers' council in its strike call on December 3 was the reorganization of the militia.[40]. A three day strike in support of dissolving the militia, which ended in disorder, began at Tatabánya on December 6 (*Népszabadság*, January 2, 1957, *Magyarország*, March 6, 1957).

Street clashes were more frequent. The protest movement in Tatabánya was dispersed by arms. On December 5, the militia dispersed the crowds demonstrating outside the British and American embassies in Budapest,[41] just as they did with the passersby who attempted to prevent a house search of the Technical University hall of residence in Bercsényi street. On December 6 and 7, the militia forcibly ended the demonstration in several communes in Békés county.[42] On the 6th, at the behest of the Interim Central Committee (ICC) [Ideiglenes Központi Bizottság], the Budapest Communists tried their strength in a street demonstration for the first time since October. The not sizeable demonstration, though under militia guard, had to called off when it

---

39 Valéria Bozsik, *A nógrádi kommunisták harca az ellenforradalom ellen*, [The Communists of Nógrád in their fight against the counter-revolution], Budapest, 1957, p. 116. The demand for the reorganization of the militia had appeared in the resolution of the county workers' council on November 30, ibid., p. 111.

40 Geréb and Hajdú, op. cit., p. 144.

41 [n.a.] *Ellenforradalmi események a gyulai járásban*, [Counter-revolutionary activities in the Gyula district], Gyula, 1958, p. 53.

42 During the clashes, there was shooting. According to the press, a worker, Janka Szakács from Lánggyár, called "a peaceful passerby" (so not a demonstrator!), was killed. Two otherwise unnamed army officers are also mentioned, one of whom was shot dead and the other wounded by snipers firing at the demonstrators. According to the official statement, the police captured the perpetrators (*Népszabadság*, December 7, 1956). However, since neither the two officers nor the allegedly captured perpetrators were ever named, it

was attacked near the Nyugati [Western] railway station by workers going home from the factories.[43]

In the first week of December hundreds of workers from the councils and intellectuals cooperating with them found themselves in prison. The compromise process between the government and the CWC came unstuck. A bad omen, on December 4, was the banning of the revolutionary committees in offices and nullification of dismissal notices they had issued (*Népszabadság*, December 5, 1956). Nor did the report of the resolution of the ICC, which met December 2–5, offer much ground for hope. This text was the first standpoint on the October events adopted by the party sitting collectively. While the initial declaration of the RWPG had accepted the demonstrations of October 23 in their entirety and only found aspects of the subsequent armed uprising culpable, the December resolution of the ICC shifted the emphasis, charging that the counterrevolutionary slogans had been heard even during the demonstrations. Earlier there had been no suggestion that the mass movement of October 23 might have been the outcome of a conspiracy; now it emerged that the course of the uprising implied conspiratorial preparations. This was the first official occasion for the accusation that the assault on the system had been covertly organized by Western states. And for the first time, Imre Nagy and his associates were attacked not merely for their behavior during the October events, but also for what they had done beforehand (*Népszabadság*, December 8, 1956).

Neither the few sporadic items cited from party archives nor the scanty memories of participants can provide the answer to the questions of what role was played in bringing about the changes in the leadership's standpoint by shifts in the internal balance of forces and of how extensive direct Soviet intervention might have been. The mention of "imperialist subversion" hints at Soviet preferences, and maybe it was at Soviet insistence that the strongest possible condemnation of the Imre Nagy group was included, as a way of justifying the kidnapping of November 22. Whichever way it was, the growing strength of the Rákosists and the intensified Soviet pressure both pointed in the same direction. The secret visit to Hungary mentioned by Khrushchev in his memoirs probably took place in the last days of November or the first days of December.[44] It emerged quite clearly from what he wrote that the CPSU

appears more likely that the militiamen accompanying the demonstrators fired at those attacking them and this was how Janka Szakács came to lose her life.

43 *Khrushchev Remembers*, (London, 1971), p. 424.

44 The meeting was originally summoned to debate the founding of a NWC, but in the confused situation this did not happen. Details of the preparations are in Tőke, op. cit., p. 64; how news of the provocation at Salgótarján was received, see Rácz, op. cit.

leadership was dissatisfied with the achievements of the RWPG; that it demanded a more determined attitude and was considering the removal of Kádár and replacing him by Münnich. The personnel change never took place, most likely because Münnich made a bad impression on Khrushchev, but it is very probable that the Soviet leader left unequivocal instructions that the resistance must be liquidated by all means available. It is not impossible that the intensified terror of the early days of December was a response to Soviet orders.

Quite independently of this, the situation was very tense. It needed only a spark to start an explosion. In its dramatic Memorandum of December 6, the CWC called on the government to desist from illegal force before it was too late. The declaration was joined by the RCHI a day later. That evening, the last meeting between the Budapest workers' council and government representatives broke up without any result. On the 8th, while the CWC was discussing the political crisis,[45] Hungarian and Soviet units at Salgótarján committed the ugliest provocation to take place after November 4. They fired into the crowds demonstrating against the arrest of two members of the workers' council, leaving, according to official accounts, 39 dead and about 100 wounded.[46] Was this a local excess? There is no direct evidence that the orders to fire came from Budapest. But the clashes of the following week are hauntingly similar to what happened at Salgótarján. Hungarian *and* Soviet armed units appeared at the scene of the demonstrations and fired at the crowd.[47] The parallel suggests that the militia received central instructions to use firearms against demonstrators and to make use of support by the Soviet military. Perhaps it was up to local commanders to decide on the size of the bloodbath, but it was unlikely in the extreme that, during a single week, the militia would fire independently into crowds in five different places (to these five may be added the pro-Communist demonstrations on December 6 in Budapest where the militia likewise used its weapons).

At news of the Salgótarján massacre, the CWC proclaimed a 48-hour strike for December 11 and 12, "for a life without fear and for personal freedom."[48]

---

45 Bozsik, op. cit., p. 128. It also emerges from the text that, following the bloodbath, several hundred were mentioned as dead in Nógrád county.
46 On Miskok see: *Népszabadság*, December 14, 1956 and February 10, 1957 as well as Ernő Déri—László Pataki. *Az ellenforradalom Miskolcon [Counter-Revolution in Miskolc]*. Budapest, 1957, p. 66–69. On Eger see: *Népszabadság*, December 23, 1956 and February 1, 1957. On Kecskemét see: *Népszabadság*, December 14, 1956. The militia had used arms against Tatabánya rioters, as it transpires through a May 16,1957 article of *Népszabadság*.
47 Quoted by Molnár, op. cit., p. 133.
48 Molnár, op. cit., p. 137, mentions the following towns where street clashes took place between December 10 and 12: Miskolc, Eger, Kecskemét, Gyula, Hódmezővásárhely, and

The government used this occasion to declare the territorial workers' councils illegal, to deport their leaders, and also immediately to institute summary jurisdiction. Over the next few days, public assembly was declared illegal and internment without trial was introduced.

The response to this challenge was an enormous outcry. The whole country went on strike. Clashes followed one after the other in provincial towns on December 10–12. Another four to five days were needed to restore order in smaller places.[49] For nearly a month, the country had avoided clashing with the occupying power by unprecedented self-discipline. It was hardly surprising that tens of thousands now felt that enough was enough and nothing worth swallowing one's pride for was left.

But by Christmas, the time of clashes was over. The government was the unchallenged master of the streets. This, perhaps, was less of a surprise than the fact that the territorial workers' councils could be liquidated without trace after just a few days of confrontation. The foregoing analysis, if it is correct, should help to explain why the final trial of strength between the government and the CWC became inevitable. But it does not give an answer to the question of why the CWC and the other likeminded territorial workers' councils could be eliminated from the political arena with such speed. Why was there not a single declaration in the name of the CWC after December 9? The sources at my disposal do not make it possible to offer a satisfactory answer. The most that I can do is to list a few explanatory factors and to raise a few more questions. First, the CWC did not prepare second and thirds lines in illegality, which could coordinate the work of the enterprise councils. Did they look at this at all? Was the time at their disposal too short to set up such illegal structures? Or did they consciously reject this possibility? The answers will be provided by specialist historians. Further research is also needed to answer the question of to what extent the terror loosed in mid-December fell on the workers' councils movement. Another point demanding clarification is how many members of the territorial workers' councils and their ancillaries were affected by the wave of emigration after December 9. Also requiring investigation is the role played in the rapid deflation of the resistance by the exhaustion of the masses. According to official accounts, several enterprise

---

Ozd. The militia put and end to the strike only on December 15 (*Népszabadság*, December 18, 1956). At Gyulavár, clashes continued even on December 17 (*Népszabadság*, January 11, 1957).

49 J. Molnár (op. cit., p. 133) affirms that the workers' councils of the Tungsram Works and of the Ganz Shipyard voted against the striking while workers' councils in MAVAG, DANUVIA, and FINOMMECHAVIKA remained divided on the issue. Molár recognizes, however, that at least MAVAG went on strike, the indecision of its leaders notwithstanding.

councils did not join the last strike call by the CWC.[50] The instances listed are not numerous and, looked at more closely, not wholly convincing. Nevertheless, it cannot be asserted that the desire for tranquillity and security did not have an effect. Finally, it is worth noting that the government, citing the danger of economic collapse, employed the threat of unemployment. Were not many people deterred by the fear that, if they did not behave themselves, they would soon find themselves on the streets?

Whatever the truth of this, workers no longer had the strength for protest action. The second phase of the restoration was over, the period when the structures of state power and the resistance movement were being built up in tandem, at the same time. The liquidation of the resistance had begun.

II.

For the moment, however, the fatal blow fell only on the territorial organizations of the workers' councils. The enterprise councils were still strong and their mutual links had not been broken. Even a kind of center could emerge from their informal contacts. After December 12, the central workers' council of the Csepel Iron and Metal Works grew into such an authoritative force. That Csepel temporarily gained this leading role after the banning of the CWC was attributable not merely to its industrial weight and to political mythology, but also to the earlier attitude of its workers' council. From the very beginning, the central workers' council at Csepel was the most moderate force in the CWC. Its leaders, the chairman Elek Nagy and his associates, did not consider it conceivable that a multi-party system could be restored or that Soviet forces might leave unconditionally. They began from the belief that what could be salvaged from the achievements of the revolution should be done within the status quo established by November 4. They disapproved of the November 22 strike call (*Népsza-badság*, November 23, 1956) and, indeed, relations between Csepel and the CWC leadership deteriorated, a fact the government, with its keen sense of tactics, sought to exploit. If the Csepel central workers'

---

50 On the setting up of the commission, see *Népszabadság*, December 11, 1956. On December 20, the paper announced that former members of the CWC, József Balázs, István Babai, István Kléger, Lajos Varga, István Ring and Imre Tóth, were invited to join the body; on December 22, that the leadership of the commission's secretariat was entrusted to István Babai, the onetime secretary of the CWC. The press did not mention that Elek Nagy, chairman of central workers' council at Csepel, also became a member of the commission.

council was forced to the sidelines of the leadership of the national movement, it was this that gave them prestige in the new situation. The defeat of the CWC, so it seemed, justified the moderation of Csepel, all the more so since the government was in a hurry to indicate that its measures of repression were aimed only at the workers' councils active in organizing political resistance and that it continued to recognize those functioning as organs of enterprise management (ibid.).

Government declarations gained a degree of credibility from the fact that it was in these days that the preparatory work on economic reform speeded up. The ministry projects were ready at the beginning of December and on December 10, the government's newly set up Economic Committee decided to call together a whole series of reform commissions. On the same day, a government resolution was issued concerning the establishment of a legislative commission which would work out the status of the workers' councils and the higher organs of industrial management (the various industrial chambers). A few former members of the CWC and the chairmen of several large industrial enterprises were invited to the commission.[51]

One aim of this step, undoubtedly, was to lower tension. The news of the legislative commission appeared on the same day as the dissolution of the CWC and the introduction of martial law. But this was more than a purely tactical device. One should bear in mind that the Kádár group was also on the defensive vis-à-vis the Rákosists, so they too had an interest in improving their political strength. They had good reason to believe that this might now be possible. What was left of the workers' councils was what the RWPG's initial statement had wanted: enterprise self-management. The blows the councils had suffered had unavoidably lowered their aspirations. There was a chance that they could be transformed from organs of political resistance into organs of enterprise management and be gradually integrated into the monocentric hierarchy. If this were to be successful, not only would the working class be pacified, but the shift in the bases of power would also be halted. Hence the economic reform commissions were not brought into being merely by impotence and by anxiety about the continuing deteriora-tion in the economy. The government wanted to institutionalize the workers' councils according to its own recipe of a more modest function and a more suitable composition.

---

51 József Minczér, a miner, was sentenced to death and Károly Minczér, a locksmith, received ten years on the ground that under their leadership the strike at the Kesztölc mine lasted until December 15 when the armed militia intervened. According to press reports, they forced other miners to stop work "at the head of a ten-member gang" (*Népszabadság*, December 18, 1956).

Csepel and the other likeminded councils tried to exploit the possibilities hidden in this. The CWC had been chasing fantasies, they believed, but all was not yet lost. What had to be defended from among the gains of October was what was still defensible after December 9: workers' councils integrated into a reformed economic order.

Neither the Kádár group nor the Elek Nagy group was correct in its calculations. Preparations for the reform took place in the quiet of offices detached from the political conflict, while a wave of terror was sweeping through the country. The first summary verdict was issued on December 17.[52] The remnants of the illegal political groups were disbanded and charges for the trial against *Élünk* were under preparation.[53] On December 11, the RCHI, the quasi-legal organ of the intellectuals' resistance, was banned. The activity of the completely legal Writers' Union was severely restricted and its journals, which had been suspended after November 4, were banned. The membership meting of December 28 convened in an atmosphere of doom. Áron Tamási's declaration "Concerns and Confessions of Faith" [Gond és Hitvallás] was voted through at the request of the praesidium, by the great majority of those present. Essentially, this was a pledge to adopt a morally suitable stand after the acceptance of defeat.[54]

The purges in the state administration, the procuracy, and the judiciary began. Factories were not exempt either. On December 10, the government decreed that factory guards must apply for permission to carry arms. From this point, the possibility of defending the workers' councils by arms ceased or became illegal. After the destruction of the CWC, the number of party members doubled,[55] and the party insisted with growing self-confidence on reestablishing its organizations within the factories (*Népszabadság*, December 15, 1956). Enterprise managers dismissed between October 23 and December 11 were gradually reinstated.[56] An ever larger

---

52 *Népszabadság*, January 9, 1957. The cases against Gyula Obersovszky and József Gáli were soon combined with those against the group operating in the Domonkos street clinic; Ilona Tóth, a final-year medical student who was in charge, and her companions were accused of murdering a police informer.

53 "We pledge allegiance to the flag which showed us that the nation was reborn out of the revolutionary unity of the people. We will pretend and protect the spirit of the Hungarian nation on the grounds of these confessions of faith. Let our work be based on morality . . . " See: Protocols of the December 28, 1956 meeting of the Writers' Union, AB Independent Publishers, Budapest, 1983. The declaration was accepted against 9 negative votes and 4 abstentions.

54 See Szenes, op. cit., p. 76.

55 I found the earliest instance of this in *Népszabadság*, January 2, 1957: the workers' council of the Tatabánya coal mines called a strike for January 1, in order to protest the reinstatement of István Gál as managing director.

56 The manager was to execute the directives of the government, and "at the same time, he

number of workers' council leaders were newly discovered to have had a Horthyist or Arrow Cross or capitalist past; curiously this seemed particularly to be the case among those who resisted state power (*Népszabadság*, December 17, 1956). There was no damming the flood of arrests.

The rapid worsening of the balance of power was also expressed in a new shift in the government's general line. The RWPG declaration of January 6 termed the October events counterrevolutionary without qualification. While in the December resolution of the ICC, the "Rákosi-Gerö clique" still headed the list of those responsible and the Imre Nagy circle appeared as one wing of a broad anti-Rákosi party opposition which had some merits until Rákosi's removal, now Imre Nagy was the chief culprit. There was not a word about his past merits and, indeed, he was charged with treason. The programmatic points of the resolution unmistakably indicated that the rulers regarded its November promises as concessions to be withdrawn. The primary goal of agricultural policy was once more collectivization. Instead of abandoning the command system in the economy, there was mention only of restraining "excessive centralization" and it was also stated that the factory managing director was in the first place the subordinate of the central authorities, whereas the workers' council had only a secondary and restrained role.

The ceaseless provocations and the complete inflexibility of government policy made the line adopted by the Csepel group untenable. Two days after the RWPG declaration was published, the praesidium of the central workers' council of the Csepel Iron and Metal Works recognized that it had failed. It had to decide between subordination and its original remit. Elek Nagy and his group opted for the latter.[57] We came into being by virtue of the events of October 23 being respected as a revolution by the Hungarian people," it challenged the government, which now called October 23 a counterrevolutionary movement. "For us, there is no other role left. We cannot implement regulations against our convictions, we cannot stand idly by while members of the workers' council are arrested without any particular grounds, are harassed and the entire council is, in effect, branded counterrevolutionary . . . in the present situation, incapable as we are of implementing the wishes of our fellow workers by our existence, so to this

---

validates the resolutions of the workers' councils in so far as these do not violate existing legal regulations" (*Népszabadság*, January 6, 1957). The same paper gave an account of the outcry caused by the declaration, ibid., of January 18, 1957.

57 The resignation statement of the central workers' council of the Csepel Iron and Metal Works is in *Szemle*, (Brussels), No. 3, 1961.

end we return our commission to the workers from whom we first received it."

The statement of resignation makes it quite unambiguous that the conflict between the CWC and the Csepel leaders derived from differences in assessing the situation and tactical considerations, and not from differences of political principle. One can ask whether the Csepel workers' council had been right to use Kádár's paper in which its decision condemning the CWC's strike call (or to permit it to published there, *Népszabadság*, November 23). It is also open to argument whether Elek Nagy and his group were right to join an official government commission at the very moment when the territorial workers' councils were being made illegal and the hunt against their leaders launched. But from a 30-year perspective these are secondary questions of detail. The essence is that every important current of the workers' councils movement sought the same goal—to bring pressure to bear on the government and the Soviet occupiers through organized working class action and to enforce the best possible compromise. By early January, however, there was no hope of reasonable compromise from either the CWC's tactics or those of the Csepel group. Anyone who still wanted to negotiate had to turn against the revolution. Elek Nagy and his group were unwilling to do this; they opted instead to withdraw from the political stage with dignity. (Several of them were arrested within days.)

The praesidium of the Csepel central workers' council was followed by the entire council, by the councils of all the Csepel factories and by the councils of several other enterprises. On January 11, Csepel went on strike. The workers marched to the main building and those at the head entered the office block. There they found two newly reinstated enterprise group managers and a government commissioner. Demanding the exclusion of the party leadership, they clashed with the militia defending the building. The militia opened fire and a worker, Imre G. Nagy, collapsed, dead; others were wounded. (*Népszabadság*, January 12, 1957). A riot followed, and the embattled militia had to flee the steelworks. The workers occupied the enterprise and erected barricades at the gates. In the afternoon, fresh militia units arrived under the protection of Soviet tanks. They began to machine-gun the unarmed workers from the floor of their vans. More than one hundred unarmed workers were slain before the militia could enter the factory courtyard.[58]

---

58 A rare exception: on March 3, 1957, *Népszabadság* was complaining that the workers' council at the Beloiannisz factory would not permit the party committee near the enterprise

III.

Just as the liquidation of the Greater Budapest Central Workers' Council terminated the opening stage of the peaceful resistance, so the second, retreat, stage was ended by the voluntary dissolution of the workers' councils at Csepel. From then on, the rearguard actions were scattered and almost invariably reactive. The remnants of the Hungarian Democratic Independence Movement continued its activities for awhile in deep illegality, but finally had to recognize that the chances of achieving anything by organized resistance were nil and that cooperation with the party of retaliation was impossible. So, gradually their activity was restricted to collecting money in support of the families of those arrested (subsequently, the régime was to take harsh revenge for this). In the enterprises, the goal was more and more to prevent the return, if possible, of those who had been expelled before December 9, as well as to prevent the sacking of managers who had cooperated with the workers' councils and the takeover of the workers' councils by Communists In the end, workers in many places concluded that it was better to have no workers' council than to have it taken over by the Communists—around April, the voluntary liquidation of the councils began. The local party apparats liked this and encouraged the idea.[59] The Trade Union Council hurriedly rejected the platform it had agreed to in November-December (*Népszabadság*, January 26–27). The Writers' Union was closed down on January 18; on the 20th the Journalists' Association was suspended. The Association of Hungarian University and College Students, the last legal organization which supported October 23 even in January, was smashed.[60]

The wave of arrests struck ever higher—well-known writers were thrown in jail and the number of death sentences multiplied.[61] People were

---

radio. But this was a long way from the time when the party had been banned not only from the studio but from the factory.

59 Kádár stated at the national party conference that "the offer to dissolve some workers' councils was made as a May 1 pledge" and he added "in a few places, it was indeed the workers who demanded this." He mentioned "some mining areas" as an example (HSWP, *MSZMP országos értekezletének jegyzökönyve*, [Minutes of the HSWP National Conference], p. 58.) János Kukucska, second party secretary from Borsod county, boasted on the same occasion, "in the majority of enterprises in Borsod, the workers' councils have died off," ibid., p. 130.

60 The press gave a full account of the subjugation and demoralization of this organization, see e.g. *Népszabadság*, January 3, 9, 13 and February 16, 1957.

61 Ferenc Nezvál, the acting head of the Ministry of Justice, stated at a national conference of chairman of tribunals that up to February 12, summary verdicts had been brought in against 208 persons including 31 death sentences, 21 of which had been carried out

interned in vast numbers. Many of them were taken away on the basis of lists compiled by enterprise party secretaries. The militia resorted to ever wilder acts of violence—on the pretexts of house searches, it beat its way up and down the student hostels; entire villages were surrounded, their inhabitants herded together and then beaten black and blue; there were instances of summary killings, which were never investigated.[62]

The anti-government mood could only be expressed in gestures and these were increasingly indirect, more remote from the previous year's political scene. The last nationwide affair was that of religious instruction in schools; parents demonstratively sent their children to religious instruction classes. The government responded by quickly withdrawing its concession in this respect. In the weeks before March 15, public opinion, unable to resign itself to defeat, persuaded itself by a last act of autosuggestion that only the winter was the government's, the spring would be the people's—"we resume in March" [márciusban újra kezdjük]. But in reality by then only the belatedly normalized villages could be mobilized. Only armed units demonstrated in the streets of the capital on March 15. True, during the preceding weeks the authorities resorted to unprecedentedly widescale campaigns of preventive arrests. It was also true that the march-past of the new party militia, the workers' guard, was treated in the streets with loud contempt; for this alone, at least 200 people were picked up.[63] But the facts remained; "We resume in March" was a dead letter and thereby it was universally clear that social resistance was at an end. From then, only ad hoc incidents can be documented.[64] From mid-January on, the most important political variable was no longer the conflict between the régime and the resistance, but the shift of power within the establishment. Even as the self-governing organs which had come into being in October-November were forced out of the political

---

(*Népszabadság*, February 16, 1957). According to János Berecz, 321 judgements were brought in political cases up to July 1 and 71 accused were sentenced to death. (János Berecz, *Ellenforradalom Tollal és Fegyverrel*, [Counter-revolution by pen and arms], Budapest, 1981, p. 180.) The writers Gyula Háy, Balázs Lengyel, Tibor Tardos, and Zoltán Zelk were arrested on January 25, 1957, as were the journalists Pál Löcsei and Sándor Novobáczky. Tibor Déry was arrested on April 11. István Bibó on May 23.

62 Folk memory recalls the killing of several village priests.

63 Lajos Halas, *Az R gárdától a Munkásőrségig*, [From the R Guard to the Workers' Guard], Budapest, 1986, p. 221.

64 Agnes Bakó, party secretary in the 8th district of Budapest, complained at the National Party Conference that in May, after the introduction of the new coat of arms, the mass of workers at the Aron Gábor Foundry wore the old Kossuth coat of arms and they even stuck it on the walls. (*Jegyzökönyv* [Minutes], p. 140.)

arena, so the middle level of the apparat, which had been the focus of attack until not long before, now consolidated its position. I have already mentioned that the dismissed officials were reinstated with a stroke of the pen by the December 4 decree which liquidated the revolutionary committees. In the second half of January, the IEC investigated the matter of the banned Rákosists and decided on a case by case handling of each individual proscription.[65] The effect of this was like an avalanche. The party committee in Szolnok county invalidated its own blacklist within days (*Népszabadság*, January 29, 1957). Following this demonstrative step, the sacked cadres regained their old status, even if they did not necessarily get back their former posts (most of the former territorial party leaders were appointed to high posts in the local administration of a given area).[66] In the interim, the removal of those leaders who had cooperated with the new organs of self-government after November 4 went ahead at full steam. The purge was extended to party organizations, to the whole of the state administration and industrial enterprises.[67] Pivotal in this were the changes in the personnel of the procuracy, the judiciary, and the political police, because of their impact on the machinery of retaliation. Thus in December the head of the Ministry of Interior's Department of State Security was a former political prisoner rehabilitated before October, a Communist called László Mátyás. He had been entrusted with investigating the records of AVH personnel. The investigation began in early December (*Népszabadság*, December 6, 1956), but rapidly fell into oblivion; Mátyás, for his part, resigned in mid-January, because he would not accept unlawful terror measures. The operational side of the state security department fell into the hands of persons who, though they may not have been with the AVH before 1956, had worked under Vladimir Farkas at some time in the Hungarian Association of Democratic Youth (MADISZ), from where a section of AVH

65 See Szenes, op. cit., p. 96.
66 Iván Szenes, "A párt újjászervezése, állandóság és változás," [The reorganization of the party—continuity and change], *Párttörténeti Közlemények*, No. 3, 1982, pp. 188ff asserts that 67 % of new members of the apparat had been party workers before October 1956. However, it must be taken into account that in 1956—57, there was considerable movement between the party apparat and the appropriate level of the state administration, which does not appear in this statistic. Károly Kiss declared at the National Party Conference that the reinstatement at higher levels of dismissed "old comrades" was largely concluded, but not so at lower levels. This too would make an upward revision of Szenes's figure justified. See *Jegyzökönyv [Minutes]*, p. 136.
67 "State and economic organizations are engaged in a major task, the cleansing of counterrevolutionary rubbish from their offices," wrote László Szabó, "The filthy flood," *Népszabadság*, May 5, 1957. From then on, the paper published a series of articles on the purges, eg. May 9, 15, June 1, 9, 11, 12, 20 and 22, 1957.

investigators had been recruited. In the investigative group, the interrogators of the pre-1953 show trials served together with those who supervised the rehabilitation process in 1954-56.

Essentially by June 1957, the pre-October situation had been restored for that part of the Rákosi-era officials who had made no serious concessions to public opinion either during the revolution or in the first stages of the restoration; the waverers who survived the purges increasingly gravitated towards them.

In November-December, the cadres were in a defensive position, fighting for sheer survival. By January, the middle level constituted a crucial political current. The first trend-setters were embittered old Communists—from the 1919 Hungarian Soviet Republic or Spanish Civil War veterans or "proletarian writers" pushed to the periphery, and the like—who rigidly rejected the slightest concession to the October events. Their grievances were helpful to their early role for they too had had problems with the "Rákosi-Gerö clique," even if they had not resembled those who, in their view, had supported the cause of the bourgeoisie. Their line was the mythicized "pure proletarian policy" of the Hungarian Soviet Republic. They condemned the Rákosi dictatorship for its alleged opportunism, in that it shelved "honest Communists," but failed to suppress "class alien elements" properly; that while nursing the tradition of national independence, it made concessions to nationalism and, as a by-product of this deviation, accepted "bourgeois" currents alien to Marxism-Leninism into official culture. Consistent ideological orthodoxy, the pitiless implementation of class considerations in culture and politics, the ruthless suppression of the "class enemy," but "socialist legality" for the adherents of the dictatorship of the proletariat—these were the main planks of the program which the supporters of the Soviet Republic line sought to have accepted by the leadership. From January on, this group had a political discussion club, the Táncsics circle, at its disposal. After March, it also had a paper, the weekly *Magyarország*.[68]

At the beginning of March, Jósef Révai who had returned from Moscow published an article in *Népszabadság* (March 7, 1957), thereby unfolding the banner of the Rákosi-Gerö camp. Révai, a Politburo member between 1945 and 1953, did not deny that the Rákosi group had committed "errors,"

---

68 After disbanding the Writers' Union, the government invited people close to the Táncsics Circle (György Bölöni, Béla Illés, Lajos Mesterházi, Kálmán Sándor, etc.) to run the affairs of the literature through the newly created Literary Council. The same persons published from March 1957, "Élet és Irodalom," the only literary magazine of those times.

but wanted the emphasis to fall on their "merits" when their record was assessed. For the moment, he only named the leaders of the Trade Union Council as declining from the "correct line of Marxism-Leninism," but through them he was evidently attacking the Kádár group for the political concessions of November and December. Pointing the finger at the leftovers of conciliation, he urged an unequivocal break with the policies of the early days, while pressing the unmistakable adoption of continuity with the 1948–56 period.

Révai himself became an institution. He played the role for the Rákosists that the Táncsics circle had for the protagonists of the 1919 line. Under his wings, lesser figures also began to mobilize. A campaign was launched for the moral and political rehabilitation of the AVH.[69] Using the impetus of the anti-revisionist campaign directed against Imre Nagy and his circle, the Rákosists simply attacked as revisionists everything that had made for the intellectual renewal of the party between 1953 and 1956. They had a particularly large role in branding in this way the last surviving progressive idea, that of economic reform, in the spring of 1957.[70]

During these months, the leadership retreated constantly in the face of the ideological offensive launched by the middle-level cadres looking to their own restoration. At the end of March, they were whitewashing Rákosi and attacking Imre Nagy as the demonic figure behind a conspiracy that stretched to include Cardinal Mindszenty.[71] In the name of the myth of 1919, the party youth movement was reorganized as the Communist Youth Alliance [Kommunista Ifjúsági Szövetség or KISZ]. The reform commissions had not even submitted their reports for discussion when the new economic mechanism was official condemned.[72] The international situation also favored the Rákosists. The CPSU partly retracted the anti-Stalin line

---

69 Révai himself speaks on behalf of the AVH at the National Party Conference. See: Protocols, p. 149.

70 Leaders of the anti-reform campaign are László Háy and Andor Berei; the daily work is made by younger Party propagandists including Endre Molnár and Géza Ripp.

71 Cf. the speakers at the grand meeting on March 29—Marosán, Münnich, and Béla Biszku. (*Népszabadság*, March 30, 1957.)

72 In addition to the ideological campaign, the prospects for economic reform were also weakened by the liquidation of the workers' councils, underway by this time. From January, the reformers sought to distinguish the case for the market from that for enterprise self-management, but this retreat helped only temporarily. When it emerged that, with the help of Soviet, Chinese, and East European loans, production could be raised to a much higher level than expected without structural change, the leadership lost all interest in the reform and joined the Stalinist assailants of the new mechanism with a light heart. See Berend, op. cit., pp. 108ff.

adopted at its 20th Congress,[73] Chinese leaders proclaimed ever more conservative views, antirevisionist campaigns were rampant in Poland and the GDR (this last had a direct Hungarian connection as the works of Gyorgy Lukács published in Berlin were condemned), and, most important, Kádár was told during a visit to Moscow at the end of March that Imre Nagy and his associates must be put on trial.[74]

In the weeks before the party conference it began to look as if the restoration wave would even wash away the leadership that had taken the stage in November. At the local preparatory meetings for the conference, speakers frequently reacted as if they regarded the leadership team as temporarily in office.[75] Here and there, there were demands that the party investigate "errors" committed in November. To buttress the symbolism of the break with the past, they proposed that the party abandon its new name of HSWP and resume the name that it had before 1948, Hungarian Communist Party [Magyar Kommunista Párt].[76] In the meanwhile, the political police was collecting confessions from onetime Communists now under arrest that would incriminate Kádár.[77]

The leadership felt the situation to be so unstable that it did not dare to entrust the election of delegates for the conference to the preparatory meetings. It only abandoned its intention of nominating them directly in the name of ICC at the last moment, following the cadres' protests.[78]

Yet the fear proved exaggerated. The unquestionable stabilization of the situation played into the hands of the leadership. By April-May, the demobilization of the semi-regular militia could begin and it could be replaced in the capital and the provincial centers by reorganized units of the police and the army.[79] The petering out of the strikes and protests made it possible to pull the armed forces—in any case diminished in number—out

---

73 The most visible instance of this was at the reception given by the Chinese embassy in Moscow on January 17, 1957 during a visit there by Chou En-lai. Khrushchev declared on the occasion, "According to our understanding, 'Stalinist' and Stalin himself are inseparable from the great Communist name itself . . . Stalin's name is inseparable from Marxism-Leninism." (*Népszabadság*, January 20, 1957.)

74 In my article "Kirakatper—zárt ajtók küzütt," [Show trial behind closed doors], *Beszélö*, No. 8, I sought to summarize all the facts on the basis of which it can be asserted with greater or lesser certainty that Kádár received his instructions to arrest and try the Imre Nagy group during his visit to Moscow in late March-early April.

75 Szenes, op. cit., p.158.

76 Marosán also referred back to the debate on the name change at the National Party Conference, see *Jegyzökönyv* [Minutes], p. 71.

77 Personal communications from Ferenc Donáth.

78 Szenes, ibid.

79 Szabó, op. cit., p. 142. The formal dissolution of the militia took place only on December 20, 1957, see ibid., p. 144.

of politics. Although the state security enjoyed great freedom in discovery and investigation, it was sufficiently under control that in materials transmitted to the procuracy individuals in power were not accused and arrests did not extend to party members and non-party members in senior posts without higher permission. By the spring of 1957, only one semi-regular unit was operating—the workers' guard brought into being by the IEC's January resolution. This voluntary body undoubtedly became the gathering point for elements dissatisfied with the leadership,[80] but as it failed to acquire any genuine function in the maintenance of order, it quickly became a kind of political backwater where the passionate dogmas excluded from the power struggles could grow into inanity.

But perhaps what was even more important was that in the first half of 1957, in tandem with the consolidation of the middle-level cadres, the party membership once more started to fill up. This offset the consequences of the revival of the Rákosists. Those who had not committed themselves in the political struggles or had not done so irremediably were returning to the party *en masse* and were now seeking to secure their personal futures by acquiring a party card. Some did it because they could foresee that they could not hold their jobs if they did not join the party, others because otherwise they would have been threatened with losing them. At the end of December, the party had barely more than 100,000 members; by the end of February nearly 200,000 members; and by the end of June some 350,000 members. By comparison with the membership of early 1956, the proportion of workers in April had fallen by some six percent, while that of employees and members of armed units had risen by some six percent, thereby indicating that the motivation for a very large number of the applications must be sought in career terms.[81] The party members of the earliest days could protest against this dilution in vain, (*Népszabadság*, February 16, 1957). It was a vital interest of the leadership's that the HSWP be a mass party of all social strata and be adequately represented in all institutions, even if it was not to be a mammoth party of the size that its predecessor the Hungarian Workers' Party [Magyar Dolgozók Pártja] had been. It needed to fill its ranks for the normal functioning of the party-state and also to counterbalance the growing pressure from the vindictive

80 Cf. József Hajdú, "A budapesti munkásörség történetéhez," [On the history of the Budapest workers' guard] in (eds.) György Fukász, Mihály Ruff, and József Vági, *Utban a szocializmus felé*, [En route towards socialism], Budapest, 1985, p. 169.
81 The comparative data refer to April 1957, cf. Szenes, op. cit., p. 129. The author expressly notes that after the collapse of the "we resume in March" action, employees flooded into the party at an extraordinary rate, p. 144.

sections of the middle cadres. Although the party members of 1957 were mostly a passive, demoralized mass and did not gather as a group, whether mustering around Révai or the Táncsics Circle, they could be used to fill positions and their presence modified the atmosphere within the party. At the National Party Conference Kádár could appear as the intermediary between the middle cadres looking for a total settling of accounts and the majority desiring peace and quiet.

Kádár's personal success is customarily explained by a favorable external circumstance—the majority in the Soviet praesidium attempted to oust Khrushchev during the third week of June, but the first secretary was able to convene the Central Committee and vote down those against him. The outcome of the putsch and counter-putsch was that those elements of the CPSU leadership—Kaganovich, Molotov and Malenkov—who were regarded by contemporary opinion as the most impatient backers of the Hungarian restoration, lost their positions. It is not impossible that this event did play a role in the outcome of the Party Conference. (The preparations for the Imre Nagy trial were suspended after the ousting of "the anti-party group.") It is conceivable that the postponement of the HSWP Conference by a week—it had initially been scheduled for June 20 but in fact convened on June 27—was connected with the showdown in Moscow. But even if the fall of Molotov and the others favored Kádár, without the restructuring of relations within the Hungarian party, its first secretary could at best have only consolidated his power temporarily. For all that Molotov and his associates were purged, the CPSU did not return to the anti-Stalin line of the 20th Congress for years, and Khrushchev continued with his policy of restoring order in Eastern Europe, ordering the leadership of the HSWP to execute Imre Nagy. Kádár remained because by June Hungarian political conditions had stabilized.

The policies proclaimed in the first secretary's report and in his concluding remarks were the child of this stabilization. Equally, though, they were Kádár's personal creation. It was he who, in looking back at the lessons of October and after in the more settled conditions of June, found the formulas to stabilize the balance of forces. He was summarizing the most fateful experiences of his career in this context. The ideas about the exercise of power that he reviewed at this point went far beyond the needs of the moment and, indeed, they illuminate his entire subsequent political leadership style. This was the point at which the unchanging features of Kádár's policies emerged and remained constant whether under consolidation or decay.

"The significant part of the working masses," he declared, "are not interested in the general problems of politics, but in the correct solution of the economic and cultural questions affecting their everyday lives. They do not form their opinions of the party or of the system . . . on the basis of political issues."[82] Kádár drew important rules from this not altogether democratic truism. Firstly, there was the rule that separated him from Rákosi's practice: There must be a stop to the limitless exploitation of the population and people must be offered tranquil, satisfactory conditions of living. This was not in itself an innovation, but more of a return to the 1953 government program, except that he could hardly admit this, in that the Prime Minister of the time was being condemned as the worst traitor in the party's history, someone who even in 1953 was already forging an alliance with reaction.

But Kádár's words also hid another rule, one foreign to Imre Nagy: that if the leadership does not harass or provoke the population, then it can hold onto politics for itself. It can shape the system as it likes on condition that it not cause chaos in the everyday lives of the people. Furthermore, another view is hidden in these words: that if the masses who are not normally political do line up behind political demands, then self-evidently they are not acting in their own best interests. Whereas an interest in politics can scarcely be aroused in satisfied people, nothing is easier than to *deceive* those who are dissatisfied.[83] In situations of crisis, doubtful elements seize the initiative and the *misguided* masses follow them.[84]

This is the view that separates Kádár from Imre Nagy, who already at the time of his first Prime Ministry tried a cautious experiment in providing a framework for mass political activity with his program of renewal for the People's Front. From October 28, 1956, he was prepared to go as far as the sharing of power in order to settle the political crisis. The main lesson of the events in the exercise of power for Kádár had been that deals of this

---

82 *Jegyzőkönyv* [Minutes], p. 50.
83 It is worth noting how Kádár justified his assertion that the party had had to behave with patience and tact during the liquidation of the workers' councils. The "less class-conscious workers" remember only "that at that time they got sugar, ham and double wages and did not even have to work for it. What they don't think about is that in reality this was not good for them, but bad." *Jegyzőkönyv* [Minutes], pp. 57ff. It never occurred to him that maybe the workers had regarded the workers' councils as their own achievement. The more doctrinaire Révai was much closer on this point to the original, democratic conception of Marxism, in saying that the question was "are there still working class strata, and if so how significant are they, that regard the councils as their own institution . . . we do not have the right to ignore their viewpoint." ibid., p. 152.
84 This idea was already evident in Kádár's thinking in November: "When the workers find that times are troubled, trouble-makers among them float to the top; many of them have not been workers for long." (HSWP, Budapest Party Committee Education Commission, *Document*, p. 14.)

kind were a fatal error. The everyday needs of the "masses" must be satisfied, thereby isolating the political trend-setters, who if necessary could be removed from the scene by force.[85] Concessions must never be made to groups making political demands. On the other hand, great care must be taken to preempt excessive dissatisfaction, because then the isolation becomes difficult. Finally, if transitional difficulties give rise to internal party debates, it cannot be tolerated that these are publicly ventilated by anyone, as Imre Nagy's supporters had done. Nothing is more dangerous than the party's inability to appear as a unified block towards the outside world. Discord of this kind has the result that, instead of taking a determined stand against its opponents, the party capitulates and tries to regain control over the crisis situation by making political concessions.[86]

This was the conception that was adopted by the Party Conference as its program of holding and consolidating power. Révai, the one delegate who openly stood out against the leadership, was called to order in the name of party unity; once and for all it was laid down that the retreat would not go so far as to include the rehabilitation of Rákosi and Gerö. The leaders of the Táncsics Circle were not even allowed to speak; in any case, by June the 1919 movement had run out of impetus and had started to change into a generational interest group (the Circle was dissolved in December by party resolution and its paper was closed down). From then on, every ideological campaign was strictly conducted from above. The IEC was transformed into the party's standing Political Bureau without any changes in personnel. It was decided that the new régime would be identical with the one that had taken over in November. In exchange, the new leadership left the restored middle-level cadres alone. The coexistence of the Rákosist functionaries and the political neutrals who had returned to the party gained permanent form.

This compromise over personnel determined the more immediate content of the practice of Kádár's program over the next four to five years. In the economy, the former hierarchical relations and command planning were entirely restored; allowances were made for the interests of the apparats and for ideological pressure, although care was taken that the operation of the system should be compatible with the security of real

---

85 This idea too was evident by November, cf. Kádár's speech on the radio, "I have learned the lesson for which the Imre Nagy government charged a pretty high fee—you don't fight counterrevolution by making concessions to it but by smashing it." (*Népszabadság*, November 27, 1956.)

86 See Kádár's concluding remarks at the National Party Conference, *Jegyzőkönyv* [Minutes], p. 221.

incomes and of consumption. On the one hand, the cycles of accumulation characteristic of command planning resumed, but on the other the planners reacted more sensitively to excesses than before and tried thereby to avoid resolving the tensions from over-investment at the cost of the consumer. Rather they resorted to temporary deficits in the balance of trade.[87] In the field of ideology, there were regular campaigns against currents alien to Marxism-Leninism. "Debates" directed from above were organized about revisionism, nationalism, the populist writers, post-1945 literature, the position of criticism, education, history, economics, and Communist culture. But the interests of the administration of culture often cut across those of the campaigns. So Gyula Illyés, who remained demonstratively silent, was not attacked during the anti-populist campaign, while the reentry of the much-abused László Németh to public life was gladly received and even while he was subjected to massive ideological onslaughts, his way back into official literature was smoothed from above, right up to his visit to Moscow in 1959. In general, it can be said that the stigmatizing and the banning during the post-June 1957 campaigns were not invariably parallel. As far as the terror machine was concerned, retaliation for 1956 assumed unprecedented dimensions and it was not clear even in 1959 where its limits would be and what would be punished by imprisonment or worse. But while punitive terror, aimed at the past, remained without limits, prophylactic terror, aimed at the present, was strictly circumscribed. This did not, as such, apply to the definition of a crime or the extent of the penalty—in this context arbitrariness remained the rule. If somebody did something, he would have no idea what his fate would be; but if he did nothing, he could be certain that he would come to no harm.

These were the main features of the system that crystallized in 1957. The régime that came into power in the wake of the revolution and the restoration was stable and continued to retain its main characteristics. Any tendency towards change was built solely and more or less automatically into the use of force. Since the brunt of terror fell on activity committed during months between the collapse of the system and its reconstitution, it inevitably had to decline with the passage of time. Society was paralyzed. Official violence could only have been sustained at the same level if the political police had been permitted to fabricate anti-régime conspiracies by the hundred, as its predecessor the AVH had done. And this would have been too dangerous for the balance of forces that came into being in June

---

87 Tamás Bauer, *Tervgazdaság, beruházás, ciklusok*, [Planned economy, investment, cycles], Vol. I, Budapest, 1984, pp. 149ff.

1957. Yet the diminution of the terror failed to initiate changes in other areas. Ideological campaigns continued without letup until 1960–62. The organization of the economy not only failed to adapt to consumer needs, but inclined more and more towards centralization. In 1959–61, the forced collectivization of agriculture was executed and in 1963–64, a massive campaign of mergers gripped the whole of industry.

The restoration régime could only start to change when, on outside impulse, the balance of forces within the machinery of power underwent significant change. Khrushchev's campaign of relaxation in about 1960 and, particularly, the second de-Stalinization campaign proclaimed at the 22nd CPSU Congress were necessary to upset the 1957 equilibrium and to exclude the most implacable Rákosists from the agencies of coercion and from the entire apparat. This restructuring led to the policy of consolidation in the 1960s.

On the upward trajectory of the consolidation, the country was happy—and correct—to see in János Kádár the man who used opportunities offered, who maneuvered skillfully to remove the worst Rákosists from the middle-level of the system, and who launched the process of reconciliation. In this period, the only people who wanted to remember the restoration of 1956–57 were those who would not forgive the smashing of the revolution and ensuing ruthless retaliation at any price. In the eyes of the majority, conjuring up the memory of 1956–57 appeared a kind of tactless moralizing.

After all, in exchange for its silence and for its collective forgetfulness, society gained palpable advantages. Those who survived the retaliation were largely free to leave prison; those who had been banished from their careers could drift back; writers expelled from literary life could publish again; ideological campaigns ceased; and everyday life was made more bearable by a series of minor gestures. And the consolidation did more than bandage the wounds left by 1956; it also pointed the way towards to a more far-reaching development. From the 1960's, the management of the economy and culture became more flexible; in the 1970's the pressure on the churches diminished; the secondary economy—from which state supervision had been withdrawn—experienced an unparalleled expansion; the international contacts of the scientific élite became freer; national traditions and the current concerns of the country gradually acquired the right of public expression. True, this evolution was the same as the consolidation which had served as its foundation. Society had not gained rights to be defended, but concessions which could be suspended at any time. Nevertheless, an evolution did take place and it was more organic than in any other country in the region.

By the mid-1970's, however, this evolution had exhausted its reserves. The economy, which had not fundamentally changed its Soviet-type nature after the 1968 reform, entered a crisis and could not emerge from the general deterioration that accompanied its stagnation without a radical reform which would terminate the hierarchical relationship between the party-state and the enterprises. Economic organizations would have had to acquire clearly determined rights to be able to function in a market and to establish a relationship with the state by means of taxation and contract. Under conditions of stagnation, it was increasingly difficult to satisfy each and every social group; legally protected interest groups would have been needed to resolve the conflicts of interest that were reaching the surface. Legal rights were required to allow those needing state support to oblige the state to shoulder its social-policy responsibilities and were needed, equally, to prevent redistributive policies from taking benefits away arbitrarily from one social category or economic unit and giving them to another. Legal rights were needed, too, for the newly emerging cultural currents, for strengthening of the status of associations, for the requisite level of press openness, for the initiatives of the environmental movement and much more. The country cannot escape the cul-de-sac where it has been led by the consolidation if it cannot transcend the consolidation itself. And this ineluctably takes one back to the beginnings.

Doing justice to the revolution and to the resistance that followed and looking for ways out of the current crisis of Hungarian society are two interdependent problems. Partly this is so because even today what is needed is something like what was attempted—with extraordinary political maturity—by the 1956 resistance movement, namely a series of compromises independently arrived at by society with the party-state. Partly this is so because the first obstacle in the way of the compromise is that selfsame firmly established style of the exercise of power which was sanctified, as the sum of the restoration, by the June 1957 National Party Conference. On the one hand this does not tolerate groupings within the party and on the other it neutralizes the masses, thereby safeguarding the monopoly of power for the system, never making room for experiments which might exert pressure on the leadership from outside. As long as society is not emancipated from this treatment and the party-state does not accept that it must approach society in a new way, nothing can reverse the long-established trend of decline in the consolidation era.

IV.

But what does it meant, to "do justice" to the 1956 resistance movement?
I believe that, above all, it will have to be established with maximum
emphasis that the November-December resistance was a popular movement. This is not just a way of saying that most of society became active,
that the factories went on strike and that the villages were in constant
ferment. The *leading forces* of this movement came not from professional
politicians nor from intellectuals used to public life, but from workers and
engineers in large industry. We do not diminish the significance of what was
done by an István Bibó, a Tibor Déry, or a Miklós Gimes if we say what they
said themselves at the time, that the leading organ of the resistance was the
workers' council, its leading figures were people like Sándor Bali, Sándor
Rácz, and Elek Nagy. These people and the entire workers' councils
movement provided a rare example of political dignity, wisdom and
resourcefulness. They proved that a modern society possesses the political
capacity for the practice of an effective democracy. This proof was provided
by the Hungarian people, and by the generation before ours, though mostly
still with us.

Was what looked like the quest for a sophisticated compromise at the
time no more than a romantic gesture? In the introductory part of this
essay, I cited the ruling idea of the consolidation period, according to which
the resistance should have known that there was no social force in Hungary
that could have constrained the Soviet Union to make concessions. But if
the reconstruction of events offered here is by and large acceptable, then
this consensus is false. When the Kádár government entered the parliament
building under the protection of Soviet tanks, no one knew what the
post-occupation order would look like. Nor indeed could anyone know
whether Kádár would stay in power at all. One could easily imagine that if
the political crisis dragged on, the Soviet Union would have brought back,
if not Rákosi or Gerö personally, some disciple of theirs—or they would
have made a deal, if not with Imre Nagy himself with some of the
Communist politicians close to him. The process of the restoration was not
decided by a predetermined plan, but by the amalgam of reciprocal moves
and countermoves. I have shown in this essay that the logic of the Kádár
government's situation dragged it towards ever more extreme neo-Stalinist
positions. It was neither strong nor independent nor determined enough to
satisfy the resistance movement; it was increasingly subordinated to the
Rákosists gathering at its back. I have not, however, dealt with the decisive
factor of the conflict, the behavior of the Soviet leadership commanding the
occupation forces. I merely put the question: Was it not inherently an

illusion to reckon with the readiness of the Soviet Union to reach agreement? I have left scrutiny of this problem to this final section.

We cannot provide a satisfactory answer to this question even today. All that we can assert is that on the basis of what we know now, there is no need to accept the proposition that the case of compromise was hopeless.

In the weeks before the invasion (and to some extent afterwards), the Praesidium of the CPSU gave numerous signs of its uncertainty. It was confused by the ferment in Eastern Europe which had been triggered off by the crisis of power in Moscow following on the death of Stalin and, chiefly, by the 20th Congress. It was flustered and had to improvise. Sometimes, it offered unusually generous concessions in order to save what it could; sometimes it sought to dominate the situation by force. On October 19, a high level delegation was dispatched to Warsaw to prevent Gomulka's rise to power. Khrushchev stomped, threatened military intervention. Soviet forces stationed in Poland left their barracks, but seeing the steadfastness of the majority of the Polish Politburo, Soviet leaders had second thoughts, gave their blessing to the nomination of Gomulka and flew back to Moscow.[88] Not a week passed and the Soviet leadership was improvising again. At the request of Gerö, they hurriedly ordered Soviet forces stationed in Hungary to send armored units into the streets of Budapest. By the next day they knew that the show of force had backfired and, although they were determined to hang onto Hungary even at the cost of fighting, they began desperately to look for a political settlement.[89] On October 24, Mikoyan and Suslov arrived in Budapest and, a day later, removed Gerö. They still believed that this would be sufficient. On October 26, they sat silently through the session of the Central Committee which in effect confirmed the catastrophic policies of the previous days and then flew back to Moscow. When it transpired that the available Soviet and Hungarian military forces were insufficient to put down the uprising, Imre Nagy agreed with Andropov on the morning of October 28 at the Soviet embassy in Budapest, that a cease-fire be proclaimed, and that the leadership of the Hungarian Workers' Party and the government recognize the insurgency as a national democratic movement. On the 30th and 31st, Mikoyan and Suslov were again in Budapest. They approved the multi-party system and the restoration of the coalition government and they acceded

88 Cf. the interview with Edward Ochab, in Teresa Toranska, *Oni: Stalin's Polish Puppets*, London, 1987, p. 76.
89 Cf. Velijko Micunovic's entry for October 25 about his talks with Khrushchev, *Moscow Diary*, London, 1980, pp. 126–127.

to the withdrawal of Soviet troops.[90] On October 30, the Soviet leadership went further than ever before. A government statement was issued which recognized that in the past the Soviet state had violated the sovereignty of the East European countries, and that it regretted the shedding of blood in Hungary. It announced the withdrawal of its forces from Budapest in the interests of diminishing tensions, and promised that, if necessary, it would hold negotiations concerning the evacuation of occupied Hungary, Poland, and Romania (*Népszava*, November 1, 1956). Yet the declaration had not even appeared when the possibilities of a new military intervention were already being weighed in the Kremlin.[91]

By the time that Khrushchev and the others made their final decision to invade—presumably on the evening of October 31 after having obtained the approval of Liu Shao-chi— it had already been decided that under no circumstances would they permit Hungary to be neutral and to adopt a multi-party system. That they were unwilling to make other concessions was far less certain. At their meeting on November 2 on Brioni, Khrushchev and Malenkov accepted Tito's arguments that the new Hungarian government must unmistakably differentiate itself from the Rákosists, that it must appeal to the workers' councils, and that it must promise to effect the evacuation of Soviet forces in the shortest possible time.[92] Kádár's initial freedom of maneuver derived from this concession, which he could hardly exploit without others, however. But the flexibility of the Soviet leadership did not cease completely even after November 4—in the middle of the month, they received Gomulka and approved the new line of the Polish party, the very steps that the restoration in Hungary liquidated or prevented from coming into being.[93]

---

90 A reporter of Igazság met them in the Parliament building on October 31. (Igazság, November 1, 1956.) Khrushchev says they spent a night in Budapest which means they had to arrive on the 30th, because on November 1 the Moscow leaders began their tour in Eastern Europe to make Hungary's second occupation accepted. See Khrushchev: op. cit., p. 417. On the contents of the Budapest negotiations of two envoys see Maléter's interview on the November 2 midnight news program of the free Kossuth Radio.

91 Khrushchev claims the decisive Praesidium meeting was held in the absence of Mikoyan and Suslov. That means it had to take place on October 30 at the latest because it was followed by a one-and-a-half day visit by Liu Sha-chi which could not be ended after November 1, the day when Khrushchev and Malenkov left to see Gomulka.

92 See Micunovic's entry for November 3, 1956, op. cit., pp. 135ff.

93 Gomulka, though on a single-list basis, revitalized the multi-party system, postponed the collectivization of agriculture *sine die* and made a compromise with the Roman Catholic Church (in the framework of which new Catholic journals and intellectual clubs were permitted and the formation of a club of lay Catholic deputies, called ZNAK was allowed). It is another matter why these concessions were withdrawn one after the other from 1957 onwards. In any event, they could not be entirely annihilated. *Op. cit.*, pp. 11ff.

Knowing what we do today, we cannot say that the hopes that kept the national resistance alive were irrational. If we do not regard *Realpolitik* as consisting exclusively of going for certainties,then it can be safely asserted that the 1956 resistance movement did pursue *Realpolitik*. It is much easier to say this than to reconstruct the process which ended the indecisiveness of the Soviet Praesidium and determined that Khrushchev would not be satisfied with anything less than the restoration of monocentric party-state obtained by deploying terror. But if we take the position that there was a chance of success, then something must be said about the factors which undermined those chances. To conclude, I would like to go through a few important historical details, without looking at interconnections and without offering serious assessments.

One of these was the unfavorable world political situation. I do not have only the Anglo-French Suez adventure in mind here, for all that it had the quality of a commercial offer: "You overlook our aggression; we'll overlook yours." A far more significant though less visible fact was that in October-November the United States rhetoric of containment and roll-back proved empty. Nor could it have escaped the attention of the Soviet leaders that neither the U.S. State Department nor the U.S. delegate to the United Nations responded to Imre Nagy's declaration of neutrality. This meaningful silence gave a new meaning to the official American statement at the end of October, to the effect that the United States did not regard Poland and Hungary as potential allies. At that time, the meaning of the formula was "you can withdraw safely, we shall not advance into the resulting power vacuum." Now, however, we interpret it as "you should feel free to invade, we shall do nothing." Nor did they, in fact, take any worthwhile diplomatic measures. What had not been decided at Yalta was decided for a long time to come in October-November 1956.

The second unfavorable circumstance was the rapid transformation of the relations among the socialist countries. Until the end of October, the Hungarian people could count on the conditional support of three ruling Communist parties. The Poles backed Hungary for the longest time—at the beginning of November, they strongly opposed the action planned by the Soviet army and even in January they were not willing to go to the Budapest meeting of East European party and government leaders, which had been summoned to condemn the Hungarian October.[94] The Gomulka leader-

94 On November 2, the day after the secret Polish-Soviet meeting, PAP reported the PUWP Politburo statement, which recognized that "Hungarian events are entering a new, dangerous phase. It has become increasingly clear that reactionary elements are gaining the upper hand. They are threatening the bases of the Socialist system. Reactionary bands are

ship, on the other hand, never counted for much on its own. The indications are that the CPSU leadership regarded the Chinese standpoint as the most important. Until the end of October, the Chinese party was the most powerful supporter of East European efforts towards autonomy. Mao condemned the Soviet Union's "great power chauvinism" in the harshest terms, warned the Soviet Union against the forcible removal of Gomulka and even supported the Imre Nagy government for awhile. At the end of October or beginning of November, there was a sharp turn. Initially, Liu Shao-chi, who was sent to Moscow by Mao at the request of the Kremlin, took the view that the Hungarian crisis had to be resolved by the Hungarians. However, on the afternoon of October 31, as he was leaving Vnukovo airport, he accepted the tenet that there was no alternative to invasion. The reorientation of China's policy had begun. The Mao leadership, once the scourge of Soviet "great power chauvinism," was transformed into the assailant of the "revisionist nationalism" of the small Socialist states and the protagonist of the restoration of order. By the time the new Chinese line emerged—from the end of December 1956 to early January 1957—the decisive phase of the Hungarian political struggle was already over.

Finally, the Yugoslavs. Hungarian developments during the weeks after November 4 were negatively influenced to an extraordinary degree by the sudden deterioration in Soviet-Yugoslav relations. Relations between Moscow and Belgrade were warmer than average at the beginning of October, but the events of Warsaw and Budapest cast a shadow over them. The Yugoslavs were actively involved in trying to promote de-Stalinization in Hungary, so it was no surprise that Khrushchev held Tito responsible for the intractability of the situation. When it emerged on November 2 that Tito would support the invasion of Hungary, it looked for a moment as if all the misunderstandings had been dispelled and that the former good relations had been reestablished. The Kremlin accepted Tito's personnel and political proposals, while Tito promised that he would endeavor to

---

lynching and murdering Communists in a bestial fashion." Up to this point, the Polish leadership's assessment of the situation closely resembled the Soviet Union's. But in the decisive question, the antithesis is complete: "It is our view that the Hungarian people, with the working class at its head, can defend the achievements of Socialism by its own forces." Quoted, without the final sentence, by Berecz, op. cit., p. 158. For the final sentence, see György Gömöri, "A magyar forradalom lengyelországi visszhangja," *Szemle*, (Brussels), No. 2, 1959, p. 30. The Budapest meeting was held on January 1–4, 1957 with the Bulgarian, Czechoslovak, Hungarian, Romanian, and Soviet leaders present. Hungary was represented by Kádár and Münnich, the Soviet Union by Khrushchev and Malenkov, *Népszabadság*, January 6, 1957.

persuade Imre Nagy to adopt a line that would secure the minimum loss of life for the military operation.[95]

Because of the shortage of time, the Yugoslavs made contact with the Hungarian Prime Minister only after the Soviet attack had begun.[96] They offered asylum by way of the Yugoslav ambassador in Budapest to him and to anyone whom he cared to bring with him. Once on embassy premises, Imre Nagy was handed Rankovic's cable in which he was called upon to recognize the rival government set up under the aegis of the Soviet army. Nagy insisted that he represented the legal government and party leadership. In Yugoslav eyes, the stratagem was at least half successful— even if Imre Nagy did not resign *de jure*, he had been withdrawn from political life and was *de facto* not the head of a functioning government.[97]

In Soviet eyes, it looked very different. Khrushchev expected Tito to persuade Imre Nagy to make some gesture favorable to him. Instead, at dawn on November 4, the Hungarian Prime Minister read on the radio a declaration which could be interpreted as a call to resistance. ("Our forces are fighting. The government is in place.") Then he appeared with his associates at the embassy of the Tito who had been trying by every means to influence events in Hungary since the spring of 1956. The leadership of the CPSU, brought up in Stalin's schools, sensed a conspiracy: If the *traitor* Imre Nagy was staying at the Yugoslav embassy, then this proved that he had always been acting on Belgrade's *instructions*. On the day after November 4, the script for the trial of Imre Nagy and others that took place nearly two years later, was already sketched in the minds of the Soviet leaders. First they made demands that the Yugoslavs hand over the Hungarian citizens who had taken refuge in their embassy. However distasteful a role Tito may have played in the liquidation of the Imre Nagy government, he would hardly go along with a manifest violation of international law. Then the Kremlin offered a deal—Imre Nagy and the others would be handed over to the Romanians who would give them asylum. The Yugoslavs would not accept this either. The Soviet side then broke off negotiations, arguing that the Kádár government should handle the affair. Then, once an agreement between the Yugoslavs and the Hungarians was reached, they kidnapped the Imre Nagy group.[98] It was probably at this point that Soviet-Yugoslav relations worsened so dramatically that the last chance for a compromise settlement was lost. On the

95 Cf. Micunovic's entry for November 3, op. cit., p. 137.
96 Personal communication by Ferenc Donáth.
97 Cf. Micunovic's entry for November 7, op. cit., p. 150.
98 Ibid. and entry for November 12, pp. 155ff.

other hand, the Kádár leadership was not aware of this on November 22. It made a final attempt to separate Imre Nagy from his entourage, to persuade him to resign, and to have him announce that he was going to Romania voluntarily.[99] This was the time when the Soviets showed the greatest flexibility towards the CWC. In all likelihood the consequences of the Soviet-Yugoslav conflict only became manifest to the Hungarians when Khrushchev arrived secretly in Budapest and ordered the extermination of the resistance movement with fire and sword.

This list of external circumstances does no more than explain why the rear guard action of the revolution was doomed. The facts and related events give no answer to the question of why Hungarian society abandoned its lost cause. After defeated revolutions and wars of independence, the majority of the people have little choice but to withdraw into private life, it's true. But the emptying of the political arena does not automatically bring about the abdication of political ideals. Whether a privatized society identifies with its defeated struggles or tries to forget them depends decisively on what its spiritual leaders—writers, journalists, artists, historians, priests, teachers—articulate. They, after all, are in the position that, by virtue of their profession, their words and silences constitute a public statement. It depends on them to decide if they will provide symbols of loyalty and models of endurance to be emulated. In Hungary, this stratum did not supply society with the instruments to enable it to remain loyal to its revolution while making peace with reality. Indeed, the selfsame intelli-gentsia evolved into the source and foundation of the consensus that insists that the cultivation of intellectual opposition is a 19th century romantic pose and inappropriate to *Realpolitik*. This belief is false and its success did not follow from the defeat of the resistance. But its popular success is another story and belongs in another essay.

---

99 See letters of Ferenc Donáth to Miklós Molnár and those of Imre Nagy to Ferenc Donáth, in Beszélő 2, 1982.

Bibliography

[n.a.] *A magyar forradalom és szabadságharc a hazai rádióadások tükrében*, [The Hungarian revolution and war of independence as reflected in radio broadcasts], 2nd ed., San Francisco, n.d.

[n.a.] *Ellenforradalmi események a gyulai járásban*, [Counter-revolutionary activities in the Gyula district], Gyula, 1958.

Az *Irószövetség december 28-i taggyüléséröl készült jegyzökönyv*, [The minutes of the Writers' Union meeting of December 28, 1956], Budapest, AB International Publishing House, 1983.

Bauer, Tamás, *Tervgazdaság, beruházás, ciklusok*, [Planned economy, investment, cycles], Vol. I, Budapest, 1984.

Berecz, János, *Ellenforradalom Tollal és Fegyverrel*, [Counter-revolution by pen and arms], Budapest, 1981.

Berend, Iván T., *Gazdasági útkeresés*, [The search for new roads in the economy], Budapest, 1983.

Bibó, István, "Tervezet a magyar kérdés kompromisszumos megoldására," [Draft Plan for a Compromise Solution to the Hungarian Question], in *Bibó István összegyüjtött Munkái* [The Collected Works of István Bibó], (Berne, 1983), Vol. 3, pp. 881–884.

Bozsik, Valéria, *A nógrádi kommunisták harca az ellenforradalom ellen*, [The Communists of Nógrád in their fight against the counter-revolution], Budapest, 1957.

Déri, Ernö, and Pataki, László, *Az ellenforradalom Miskolcon*, [The Counter-Revolution at Miskolc], Budapest, 1957.

Geréb, Sándor & Hajdú, Pál, *Az ellenforradalomn utóvédharca*, [Rearguard Actions by the Counterrevolution], (Budapest, 1983), pp. 183ff.

Hajdú, József, "A budapesti munkásörség történetéhez," [On the history of the Budapest workers' guard] in (eds.) György Fukász, Mihály Ruff and József Vági, *Utban a szocializmus felé*, *[En route towards Socialism]*, Budapest, 1985.

Halas, Lajos, *Az R gárdától a Munkásörségig*, *[From the R Guard to the Workers' Guard]*, Budapest, 1986.

HSWP, Educational Directorate of the Budapest Party Committee, *Válagatott dokumentumok és források a budapesti pártmozgalom történetéröl, 1956 november-1957 június*, [Selected Documents and Sources on the History of the Party Movement in Budapest, November 1956-Junius 1957], (Budapest, 1982).

HSWP, *MSZMP országos értekezletének jegyzökönyve*, [Minutes of the HSWP National Conference], Budapest, 1957.

Khrushchev Remembers, (London, 1971).

KMT, *Felhivás valamennyi üzemi, kerületi és megyei munkástanácshoz*, [Appeal to All Factory, District and County Workers' Councils], Budapest, November 27, 1956.

KMT, *Tájekoztatója*, [CWC Bulletin], No. 3, December 5, 1956.

Kovács, István, (ed.) "The Bibó Plan," *Facts about Hungary*, (New York, 1958), pp. 100–116.

Marosán, György, "Az élet újra indul," [Life Begins Again], interview with László Rapcsányi, *Jel-Kép*, No. 1, 1982, p. 90.

Micunovic, Veljko, *Moscow Diary*, London, 1980.

Molnár, János, *A Nagy-Budapesti Központi Munkástanács* [The Greater Budapest Central Workers' Council], (Budapest, 1969), pp. 93ff.

Molnár, Miklós, *Victoire d'une défaite: Budapest 1956*, Paris, 1968, pp. 269ff.

Petö, Iván and Szakács, Sándor, *A hazai gazdaság négy évtizedének története*, [The History of Four Decades of the Hungarian Economy] Vol. I, Budapest, 1985.

Radványi, J. *Hungary and the Superpowers*, Stanford, CA, 1972, pp. 11ff.

Sebestyén, Miklós, "A Nagy-Budapesti Központi Munkástanácsról" [Concerning the Greater Budapest Workers' Council], *Szemle* (Brussels), No. 3, 1961, p. 54.

Szabó, Arpád, *A magyar forradalmi honvéd karhatalom - November 1956–June 1957* [The Revolutionary armed forces of the Hungarian National Defense, November 1956 to June 1957], (Budapest, 1977), p. 51.

Szenes, István, *A kommuninista párt újjászervezése Magyarországon 1956–1957* [The Reorganization of the Communist Party in Hungary 1956–1957], (Budapest, 12976), p. 54.

Töke, Ferenc, "A Nagy-Budapesti Központi Munkástanácsról," *Szemle* (Brussels), No. 3, 1961, p. 60.

Toranska, Teresa, *Oni: Stalin's Polish Puppets*, London, 1987.

The Present Crisis and its Origins

The Present Crisis and its Origins[1]

I.

The present crisis was preceded by an unusually long period of tranquility. At first we should examine the roots of this exceptional political stability which lasted more than a quarter of a century. We must start by stating a historical fact. In 1956–57 Hungarian society suffered a total defeat: It was unable to salvage any of its independent organizations formed in October-November and was left without recognized leaders and spokesmen.[2] When five years later those in power embarked upon the path of gradual consolidation they did so not under societal pressure, but rather for the sake of convenience. The defeated society had no political groups capable of criticizing the nature of consolidation, determined from above, and countering it with a proposal of reconciliation, coming from below.

This initial trauma in itself, however, cannot serve as an explanation for the whole story. The regime had to be able to offer something to the

1 This article was written in December 1987 as an answer to a questionnaire sent out to 26 intellectuals by *Századvég,* a Budapest student review. The questions concerned: 1) the present crisis in Hungary; 2) the evaluation of the reform programs originating from independent sources; and 3) the authors' own reform proposals.
2 See "The 1956–57 Restoration in a Thirty-Years' Perspective" in this volume.

87

populace. I think that what the consolidation era yielded can be summarized in two slogans. The first was "the fundamental achievements of socialism."[3] This category includes the guarantees of existential security: full employment, stable prices, pensions with enduring purchasing power, prime consumer necessities cheaper than their costs, free education and health care, rents and utilities affordable to everyone. The other slogan was "socialist national unity"[4] which was expressed in the biblical phrase "he who is not against us is with us."[5] It is more difficult to define the content of this category with a list. Its essence was that the leadership was consciously trying to keep intrasocietal conflicts at a low level. The direct mobilization campaigns of the populace were discontinued, and the people were allowed to use their free time to tend to their private lives. The leadership was trying to make it possible that working men would be able to increase their disposable income through extra efforts and ensure that they could spend those proceeds as well. A process by which ideology would be excised step by step from culture and science was tolerated. And finally, the people were allowed to cautiously feel out the holes and cracks in the wall of official regulations, so by finding them they could improve their lot, or at least compensate for their losses.

The policy of consolidation, of course, did not supplant the policy of restoration overnight. It was a long process of learning and accommodation with ups and downs and blunders. Nevertheless, on the whole it gave rise to an unprecedented organic evolution, especially in three areas: In the development of the consumer market (in this regard the reforms of 1968 played a decisive role; while they left the labor and capital markets unaffected, they did liberate the market of consumer goods to a large extent), in the strengthening of the second economy (the 1968 reform gave a strong impetus to this area as well), and in the restoration of the internal norms of science and culture. All this was accompanied by a series of piecemeal concessions (e.g., the gradual expansion of travel opportunities)

---

3 This propaganda catchword was meant to denote those properties of the regime which distinguished it favorably from capitalism.
4 Toward the end of October 1956, Imre Nagy asked for a national unity around his government. After the Soviet invasion, Kádár declared that this was a capitulationist call because it implied the abandonment of the specific, socialist goals of the Communist Party. The correct slogan would be "socialist national unity," the unity of the nation around the party's socialist goals. At the time of the 1961–63 consolidation, however, this term got a new connotation, and it is this ulterior meaning which is described in the present article.
5 In a December 1961 speech, János Kádár made this biblical paraphrase alluding to a turnabout in official policy toward the public; Positive loyalty was not required anymore; it was sufficient to renounce active resistance.

which brought tangible improvement to people's lives without any substantial cost of the regime.

Solid existential security, gradual improvement of living conditions, and steady growth did indeed represent real achievements; thus, it is not surprising that the population—remembering the defeat of '56—did not want to risk these achievements in exchange for political struggles of uncertain outcome. The overwhelming majority of people lived under the illusion of healthy progress even when it was possible to realize that the entire system was built over a minefield. Let us recall the mood of the masses at the beginning of the '80s when in some Eastern European countries the economic catastrophe had already occurred: "We Hungarians are better, harder-working, more adroit; we are able to manage our affairs better, and our leaders are competent in running the country as well . . . " And we should not shy away from recalling the more sophisticated intellectual version of these platitudes: "In Eastern Europe two alternatives of creating civil society have been tested: the Polish and the Hungarian. The Polish path leads through political organization, and its objective is to limit and control the power of the regime. The Hungarian path represents the economic formation of civil society, albeit its main track is the expansion of the second economy. This transforms the state economy as well, yet does so without political conflicts, in a virtually unnoticeable manner. The Polish path, just as 1956 and 1968, by definition had to lead to catastrophe, while the evolution of Hungarian civil society moves ahead in an organic way . . . "

These sentiments were still prevalent in the early '80's, although by then the forced slowdown of economic growth was well underway[6] and foreign trade statistics provided crystal-clear evidence that Hungary, along with the entire COMECON, was slipping from the middle pack of world economy to the level of the third world's stagnating regions. Nonetheless, as long as it could, the regime continued the policy of avoiding conflicts even during the time of austerity. The hardships of belt-tightening were distributed in such a manner that they visibly aggravated the condition only of those marginal groups which were unable to express their discontent. Poverty became once again a widespread concern, but only for the traditionally poor strata, while those segments of the population which are critical to political stability were unaffected. For them only the maintenance of their earlier standard of living became more difficult: They gradually had to get accustomed to accelerating inflation, to the dismantling of state price subsidies, and to working harder to sustain their habitual level of

---

6 See "The End and the Beginning" in this volume.

consumption. The state, however, also expanded the sphere of additional work and income opportunites: Centrally-positioned strata received the chance to start private enterprises and to take part in the new, profitable form of overtime within the state sector, the so-called "economic workshop." Consequently, among those groups which determine the general public mood of society—the elite of the working class and the mid-level white collar workers—no psychological turnaround took place. Only some latent malaise started to spread as years went by and the slump did not let up, and the promised upswing failed to materialize.

The expiration of the consolidation era was first evidenced by the leaders', rather than the populace's, conduct. In 1985 the leadership, ignoring the economists' warnings, announced a new program of stimulating the economy: It promised more capital investment to industry and growing real wages to employees. The immediate consequence of this attempt was the alienation of the professional intelligentsia who concluded that the country's leaders had lost touch with reality and were helplessly drifting toward economic catastrophe. Its delayed consequences came into view at the end of 1986. By that time it became obvious even to the leadership that the attempt to accelerate growth had failed and that the attempt itself had led to imbalances in the economy which demanded immediate intervention. The leadership and its apparatuses suddenly lost their decisiveness and realized that they were not in control of the situation. At that point they were forced to demand unequivocal, severe sacrifices from those middle strata which until then had been more or less spared from such burdens—although it was not clear whether the collapse of the economy could be avoided even at the cost of such measures. The leadership could no longer conceal its confusion from the public. Those strata which had ensured the political stability of the regime were overcome by disappointment, frustration, and anger. And those prestigious independent intellectuals, who had earlier played such an important role in shaping public opinion favorable to the political leadership, were not at hand either. Thus, even before the worst consequences of the economic crisis become full-blown, we are in the very midst of a political crisis.

This crisis is the crisis of the consolidation course. It is the end result of that practice which kept Hungarian society in a state of tranquility. The Soviet-style socialist model of existential security and the minimalization of conflicts had to be realized within an economic system which was essentially unchanged since 1948. In this system the macro-economic processes have been regulated through administrative, hierarchical commands and not by market regulators. More precisely, the economy, in spite of the various reforms attempts, could not break out of its hierarchical structure, because the regime's stability was linked to the Soviet-style socialist formulas of existential security and to the avoidance of open conflicts. This dual bind, however, imposed limitations on the potentials of the consolidation course. Political stability could be preserved only as long as the GNP's growth was fast enough to simultaneously finance the insatiable capital-investment needs of industry, the prestige-expenditures of the apparatuses, the subsidies of consumer prices, the full employment of the population (which was engaged in non-productive work), and the continuous increase of income for those groups which were capable of expressing their discontent. Economies of predominantly hierarchical coordinating mechanisms, however, are capable of producing an acceptable rate of growth only as long as they have at their disposal an unlimited supply of cheap resources. When both labor and raw materials become scarce and expensive, such economies start to stagnate. This potential danger began to be a real menace for Hungary in the early '70s when the mobilization of rural labor reserves became virtually exhausted, and the heretofore ever-expanding rate of Soviet raw material and energy deliveries slowed down. The leadership did not respond to this challenge with a fundamental transformation of the economy's organization (at precisely this time it turned against even the fragmentary reform of 1968); instead, it chose the fatal policy of postponement. It took advantage of the abundant Western credit offers and financed an unchanged rate of growth with loans. This growing indebtedness made possible the preservation of political stability for another decade without giving up the course of consolidation. But at the same time this step led to the country's having to face not only the stagnation of economic growth but also its sudden decline, the collapse of the consumer market, grave shortages, and galloping inflation.

Once economic collapse takes place, it is very difficult to climb out of it. Not only because "the low-level disequalibrium trap" has a permanent pull-back effect but because it is not easy to find a policy of recovery. The leadership's resistance to reform ideas decreased in the '80s. In its indecision the leadership sooner or later tried to put to work almost any available idea, but without formulating a coordinated, comprehensive reform strategy. Consequently, on the surface everything is accomplished; in reality, no substantial change takes place. Our bankrupt economy bears a striking resemblance to market economies: We have commercial banks, corporations, insurance companies, a stock and securities exchange, and private enterprise. The only thing we do not have is a functioning market. Our political life is brimming over with corporativism; so many federations represent so many interests that our heads spin trying to keep track of them; there are independent movements and associations, real parliamentary debates, and probably even parliamentary caucuses. The only thing we do not have is functioning pluralism.

But the country's internal confusion will be overshadowed by its loss of external orientation. There will be no new hopes to strengthen our ties with the Soviet Union and other COMECON[7] countries; it is obvious that we cannot expect cures for our ills from that direction. But public opinion may easily lose its trust in the other direction as well. We should remember that no matter what the cause of the present economic crisis, the symptoms of the crisis are manifested by the country's monetary dependence of its Western creditors. In the population's perception the West may come to mean creditors' coercion: The package programs of the IMF to limit consumption, Neckerman department stores for those who have foreign currency accounts, empty grocery stores for those who do not; an astonishing increase in the traffic of smuggled goods; a currency black market with astronomical exchange rates; prosperity for the privileged few and destitution for the underprivileged many. In short, the West may come to mean the same thing that the United States means to the masses of Latin American countries. Let us imagine how this perception will affect the spirit of a society which never had the opportunity to digest fully the ethos of the market, of democracy and liberalism.

II.

Does it make any sense at all to ponder reforms in the face of such prospects? There is definitely no cause for excessive optimism. We should notice, however, that the crisis is not alone pregnant with dangers, it also creates new opportunities. The stability of the consolidation era forestalled fundamental changes. The end of stability opens the way for change.

On the one hand, the leadership and its apparatuses have never been so indecisive as to which elements of the regime are to be treated as untouchable and permanent and which can be subject to transformation. On the other hand—and I consider this the more important factor—the conservatism of those strata, which served as the pillar of consolidation, is shaken.

---

7 COMECON: Council for Mutual Economic Assistance, was a governmental organization of the Communist bloc to promote the coordination of economic policy and division of labor between bloc countries. After a period of extensive development which lasted from the early '60s through the mid-'70s, it entered a phase of stagnation and recession.

Nowadays official orators frequently complain that the populace is more dissatisfied than is justified by the actual worsening of its condition. Indeed, the *material conditions* of those strata which are capable of registering their dissatisfaction did not worsen as drastically as their grumbling intensified. Is this not a sign that there is much more at stake than the correlation of prices and wages? I believe it to be a well-founded assumption that this grumbling and anger is of a *moral nature* and is derived from the fact that the state relinquished its obligations as patron in exchange for which its subjects felt justified in accepting the role of clients. It is the very model of the state's and its subjects' coexistence that has been put into question. What the people lost was not a few banknotes but a way of life which was made possible by the existential conditions expressed and guaranteed in the slogans "the fundamental achievements of Socialism" and "Socialist national unity." It is certain that in the general disappointment and anger there is a lot of retrospective passion, the desire to restore the merry old times of consolidation. But since the past—no matter how it was—cannot be revived, it is possible that the politically-pivotal strata might become receptive to another model of social co-existence.

As for myself, I think that the primary task of comprehensive reform programs is to point out that an alternative model—for which it is worthwhile to accept the inevitable sacrifices—is possible.

First of all, it must be made clear that the type of economic system—a regulated, mixed-market economy—which may arrest the process by which the country is sliding to the level of the third world's stagnating regions, cannot be reconciled with the socio-political guarantees of the consolidation era. It simply is not possible simultaneously to meet the challenges of world economy and to provide the population with administrative guarantees of a life without losses and conflicts. Market economy—if it really functions— cannot be automatically safeguarded from, among other things, inflation or unemployment, and it does inevitably intensify social conflicts. Therefore, market economy has to be combined with a different kind of social protection network and political structure from the ones to which we became accustomed. The welfare problems of well-integrated strata have to be managed primarily through various market, insurance, and other arrangements, while the means of redistribution by the state must be retained for the poor and the unemployed who are unable to take care of themselves and their dependents. In the political sphere institutions are needed that are suitable for the regulated resolution of conflicts: trade unions, a functioning parliament, legally-defined freedom of the press, and effectively safeguarded civil rights. It must be demonstrated that such an econo-socio-political system would not be in conflict with the people's sense of justice: It would not leave the indigents to their fate; it would keep within acceptable limits of inequality of income and wealth; it would be able to deal with the problem of unemployment; and along with better economic performance, it would bring about a host of other advantages as well. It would take us closer to the ideal of citizens' equality; it would provide individuals and minorities with greater autonomy and legal protection vis-à-vis the state; it would widen the spectrum of available life alternatives.

This is not a blueprint for a new, superior social formation, superseding all others in world history. The task is not to outline the future for the world; it is to prevent the fatal deterioration of our country. If in the process we get closer to the solution of a historical dilemma, I would define this as bringing our country closer to the path of European evolution. The institutions and cultural examples which are to be emulated are well known, as are their advantages and disadvantages. We simply have to face them soberly.

With the same sobriety we must assess those conditions which constrain our first steps. We have to take into consideration a variety of givens such as traditions (aversion to certain liberal values), economic conditions (the state sector's domination cannot be eliminated overnight), and geopolitical factors (the post-Yalta status quo cannot be transformed in one stroke). Comprehensive reform programs have to demonstrate that a compromise is possible between the requirements of catching up with the world and the determinants which constrain our choices.

In my view these concerns adequately summarize the dominant intentions of the various existing reform programs. It is not certain that all reformers on record agree with this definition of the objective, but I believe that this summary accurately reflects the intentions of the program *Turnabout and Reform*[8] and is, of course, in harmony with the basic ideas of the Beszélő manifesto *Social Contract*.[9] I consider it noteworthy that even explicitly Communist reformers—among them the most significant is undoubtedly Mihály Bihari, the author of *Reformer and Democracy*[10]— focus their attention on the compromise between pluralization and the

8 "Turnabout and Reform" was a program of economic stabilization and recovery worked out by a group of independent experts in 1986.
9 "Social Contract" was a program for political transformation, written in 1987 by the editorial community of *Beszélő*, a *samizdat* political quarterly started in 1981. The author is an editor of this review.
10 "Reform and Democracy" was a proposal for change in the Communist reform discourse. Its author, Mihály Bihari, a political scientist, was expelled from the HSWP in 1988.

factors of initial limitations.

It is, of course, another question altogether what would be the concern of the various reformers within the political spectrum of a pluralist democracy (*Beszélő* would be somewhat to left of center). There are also differences as to which factors must be considered untouchable limitations in the short run and which ones are determinants with an enduring effect. There is also a lack of agreement concerning the ordering of priorities. These differences of opinion are inevitable and natural. But it is equally important that these positions do gravitate toward each other with regard to the fundamental issues.

III.

I do not think that this is an appropriate occasion to present additional reform proposals. I would rather use this opportunity to say something about the political problem of being a reformer:

At the beginning—in 1965–68 but even in the first half of the '80s—"reformer" meant a specialist who was included in the official decision-making process. Such a reformer worked in closed committees, and his notes to the decision makers were marked "confidential." Around the mid-'80s a radical group seceded from the body of official reformers. Its members wanted to address not only the leadership but the population at large. Since the acceleration of the crisis, a third form of reformism has been taking shape; its representatives would like to see the democratic renewal of the Party at the center of reform and address primarily those Communists who could be mobilized for this cause. Finally, there are those oppositional circles, like *Beszélő*, which want to address that segment of the population that places its hope neither in the reform of the apparatuses nor in the Party movement, but which could serve as the foundation for independent movements and organizations.

This differentiation is a positive phenomenon and may be the harbinger of a pluralistic political process which involves separate forces. Since within the constraints of our situation the resolution of the country's crisis is conceivable only in the form of a compromise, I believe that everyone should be happy to see that the reform camp is differentiated, with the exception of those who hope for a catastrophe (not that I know anyone who does).

Nevertheless, we have to notice that the political forces of reform are not yet on the scene. The leadership does not have a reform wing (at best it has a few individual reform politicians); the possibility of some real movement within the Party appears to be remote as well. The apparatuses' resistance to reform is probably weakened, but it does not turn into active reformism. And we may entertain only a very cautious hope that the massive social discontent will turn from grumbling into collective action. In reality, every reformer for the most part addresses the same intellectual audience which lacks organization but is engaged in an intense debate about the alternatives facing the country. It is possible that the surprising intellectual unity of the reformers is partially the consequence of this paradox: If the various programs were promoted by actual political forces—especially hetero-genous forces—the divergence of these programs would in all likelihood become greater. But right now I do not want to meditate about the modes of possible differentiation; they do not lend themselves to prophesizing anyway. I would like to call attention to a latent danger of the present, pre-political situation.

The weakened leadership is in need of some sort of authority external to it. It apparently cannot count on the public support of prominent intellectuals. In such a situation those in power can hope to strengthen their position only if they can claim that they *entered into a dialogue* with the dissenters. Such a dialogue legitimizes the leader, endows him with recognition without accepting any binding obligations. "He listened to every opinion, he did everything that could have been done in the given situation . . . "

I would not ask anybody to turn his back on dialogue. On the other hand, I am also aware that mere conversation might become negotiation only when the two sides are backed by political forces. Nevertheless, some immediate steps could be taken to ensure that the dialogue not become mere rhetoric which discredits and demoralizes those who enter into it. In my opinion, the most important thing in this regard is to insist that the dialogue receive publicity. No one is this country has anything to say to those in power that is not of equal concern to the entire population. We need free access to the media as a right, and not as a one-time privilege, but as a right, it has to belong to every Hungarian citizen, not only to those "dissenters" who are part of the dialogue. We need the right to public statement of collective views—which, along with the right to expression also includes the right to assembly and association. These rights can be won. The arbitrary, administrative control of the press, of assembly, and of association is under increasing pressure. If a breakthrough could be achieved on this point, it would significantly decrease the danger that reformers drift into a dubious role on the pretext of dialogue; the entire society would gain something that would probably enable it to organize itself into political forces.

From "Reform" to
"Continued Development"

From "Reform" to "Continued Development"

T he time when a sizable portion of the political public expected guidance from the Communist Party leadership passed long ago. Of course, it was also long ago when the leadership still meant to mobilize society with its guidelines. Nowadays if it makes an announcement it does so only to notify the apparatchiks of their required behavior. Nevertheless, if an outsider wants to know what sort of guidelines the bureaucracy will follow, he has to pay attention to the official announcements.

The April Resolutions of the Central Committee[1] complete a long period of preparation and formulate the direction of "continued development of economic policy." After 1978 when the leadership realized that production could not be expanded within the framework of the economic policies of the '70s without a catastrophic acceleration of foreign indebtedness, it quietly rehabilitated the reform of 1968[2] and decided to implement new changes in the spirit of 1968 as well. In the early '80s it called to existence one committee of experts after another and has been soliciting professional opinion from a host of think tanks. Part of the debate has even reached the public. Between 1980 and 1982 the freedom to discuss the necessity of reform, the advantages and disadvantages of the various proposals was even

---

1 Adopted on April 17, 1984.
2 The 1968 reform movement abolished mandatory planning and attempted to liberate the commodities markets. However, it left untouched the centralized framework of investments and the state's quasi-monopoly over the means of production.

greater than in 1965–66 when the principles of the new economic mechanism were drawn up. Consequently, we have the basis to make a comparison between the end result and the recommendations which preceded it.

1. The professional community of economists is divided concerning a number of important questions. With regard to some fundamental issues, however, a surprisingly broad-based consensus has emerged. As the public debates have shown, a large number of academic researchers, instructors and experts of the administration agree on the following:

- Hungarian industry's continued tendency to fall behind the world economy—which at best means lasting stagnation for the country—cannot be reversed without a comprehensive reform on the scale of the 1968 "new economic mechanism."

- It is not enough "to increase the companies' independence." Apart from well-defined exceptions, the hierarchical relationship between the state administration and the companies must be abolished. An organizational system must be created in which state agencies may influence the company managers' decisions only according to clearly-defined regulations, through market-adapted monetary and fiscal policies. The primary precondition of such a system would be that state agencies could no longer exercise ownership rights over the companies.

- Additional preconditions of dismantling the hierarchical structure are the radical curtailment of the government organs' participation in capital investment decisions; the establishment of competitive credit institutions separated from the central bank which currently functions as a government agency; and the formation of a capital market.

- In the area of regulators (taxes, prices, wages), it is not sufficient to simply make the system better organized and more rational. Government agencies must not have the power to directly influence a company through the manipulation of regulators. The general objective should be that the market regulates the price and wage structure, and any administrative correction of prices and wages follows strictly defined rules.

- Companies of unwieldy size should be dismantled. In all cases where the maintenance of huge monopolies is economically not justified, they should be broken up into several competing companies.

- The conflicts of interest—intensified by the economic crisis—should be resolved through a fundamental reform of society's self-protective system, and not through measures which are contrary to the reform's spirit and undermine the mechanism of market regulators.

The recommendations for the most part urged the renewal of the trade unions, and some authors even mentioned the need to modify the role of the National Assembly.

The minor differences of the various views need not be discussed here. There is, however, one fundamental issue which is present throughout the reform discussions. While most economists agree on the necessity of implementing all measures simultaneously and in concert, this consensus falls apart when it comes to the question of whether the reform program is to explicitly spell out this notion. Some believe it to be more effective to make it appear as if all these steps involve no more than marginal changes which, even in their totality, do not add up to a comprehensive reform of the economic system. The motivation behind this approach is obvious: this way would be easier to win over the political leadership; the apparatus' resistance would be less fierce; and the ideological suspicion of Hungary's allies would not be awakened. Others, however, argue that a new second reform, the "reform of reform" should be announced openly. The advocates of this position are the so-called radical reform-economists. They argue as follows: After 1972–74[3] the actors in the economy realized that even in the reformed system it was more advantageous to them to act according to the old pattern. Although the government does not break down its national economic plan into detailed directives which are binding on the companies, bargaining with the government agencies is still a more decisive factor in the companies' success than their market performance. The only difference is that the bargaining no longer is concerned with the target figures imposed by the plan but rather with the rate of taxation, prices, and credits. And similar vertical bargaining maneuvers dominate all other economic relationships all the way down to the factory workshops. If the reform program does not emphasize that something fundamentally new is about to begin, everyone will think that old reflexes will take them further than

3 During 1972–74 the 1968 reform movement was repudiated and brought to a halt.

learning new ones. However, not only this socio-psychological reason necessitates the open announcement of the second reform, but political considerations do as well. The preservation of the old economic system and of its concomitant behavioral patterns is motivated by the multifaceted interests of those in power. Consequently, the reform may become successful only if it is supported by a broad social movement on the popular side. Social support can be garnered for the reform if those involved fully understand that significant changes are at stake which make active participation worthwhile.

2. Official guidelines never go as far as the individual or collective recommendations of social scientists. The 1966 reform resolutions[4] of the Central Committee also contained quite a few elements which the participants of the preceding debates had considered too tentative. This time, however, the difference is more significant. We can positively state that *the April Resolutions are in direct opposition to the radical reform-economists and indirectly so even with the broader consensus of experts.*

The Resolutions not only leave the "reform of reform," the "second reform," unmentioned, they no longer even use the word "reform." In place of those expressions we find locutions like "the continued development of the economic system" and "the continuous, concerted improvement of the economy." This is a seemingly negligible difference, since the words "reform" and "continued development" are rather close synonyms: both mean a change which occurs without a shock and leaves essential features of the system intact. Nonetheless, in the political consciousness of the country the word "reform" evokes 1968, the year when more things were changed and in a more profound way than at any other time since 1956/57 restoration.[5] Someone who uses the word "reform" means changes of such dimension that the economy functions according to a "new mechanism."[6] Thus the consistent omission of the word "reform" suggests that changes of such dimension are not to be expected this time: the somnolent economic system of the post-1968 period is to be accepted as a given. The modifier "continued" also receives added meaning from its juxtaposition with the

---

4 The May 1966 resolutions of the Central Committee outlined the framework for the reforms introduced in 1968.
5 The crushing of the 1956 revolution was followed by a period of bloody reprisals and of re-establishment of the Soviet-type regime. See the essay "The 1956–57 Restoration in a Thirty-Years' Perspective" in this volume.
6 The reformed economic system was also called "New Economic Mechanism."

language of the reform: we are not to expect a package of more or less simultaneous measures, but separate actions spread over a period of time. The message is unmistakable. Nobody is to worry or to hope that changes of such magnitude as to upset the existing power structure and involve a profound modification of behavioral reflexes are about to take place.

3. Thus the Resolutions turn against the radical reform-economists who urged the open political proclamation of the reform. But the document also fails to satisfy the majority of moderate reformers who would have been content if comprehensive reform measures had been implemented in the disguise of foggy rhetoric. The document devotes only a third as much space to the most important institutional changes (the redistribution of company property, the decentralization of the banking system, and the creation of a capital market) as to the continued practice of those regulatory modifications which have ben in effect throughout the '70s. Consequently, it creates the impression that the leadership understands "continued development" only as an "improvement" of management techniques. In addition, the ideas of the Resolutions are frequently blurred to the point of being completely meaningless, and there are obvious contradictions between the interdependent areas of planned changes.

- On the regulatory system the Resolutions, for the most part, repeat the same old requirements. Concerning prices they state that "the dismantling of producer price subsidies is to be continued" and that similar steps are needed in the area of consumer prices as well. All this does not affect the mechanism of the pricing system. This policy reduces budgetary expenditures and makes the price system more rational, but it is still completely inexplicit as to whether the market or arbitrary bureaucratic measures should regulate prices. The Resolutions offer barely more in the area of wage formation. Although they state that the regulation of average wages has to be discontinued "in those areas where incentives to increase productivity are available," they also indicate that this is not a rule to be applied to the majority of companies, but a concession to be given on the basis of a one-by-one determination.

- The document is even more hesitant concerning the reduction of the average company size. Instead of clearly stating that between 1949 and 1979 excessive centralization took place and the breaking up of huge companies thus has become inevitable, it takes care of the whole issue in one neutral sentence: "The size of companies should follow the requirements of profitability and productivity."

- The institutional decentralization of the banking system is mentioned only as a distant possibility: "We should move toward a banking system within which the functions of the reserve board, of the national credit bank and of the commercial bank become separated." It is noteworthy that the published Announcement (as the Resolutions are called for popular consumption) does not contain even this cautious phrase, does not even allude to the separation of commercial banking from the central note bank.

4. The Resolutions answer with a somewhat tangible program only one issue, i.e., the organizational relationship between the government and the companies.

According to this program the state-owned companies would be divided into three categories. In the future only communal and public utility companies and "companies selected by the Council of Ministers for national interest considerations would operate in the existing form of management—that is, with appointed chief executive, board of directors, and supervisory committee." Medium-sized companies and some large companies would be managed by company councils. This body would exercise several of those "administrative and employer rights" which until now belong to the supervising government agency. Some of its members would be elected by the employees, others would be appointed by the company management, and *ex officio* members would be the secretaries of the Party, of the Communist Youth League[7] and of the trade union. Finally, at smaller companies it would be the employees' or their delegates' assembly which would exercise some of the administrative or employer rights; the directors and his assistants would be elected by this assembly.

It is too early to tell how these new company management forms will function in reality. Let us make it clear that both new forms move toward employee self-management and the fact that the leadership accepts this principle's validity is already a significant change, although in and by itself it is only an ideological one. The importance of this measure is made clear

---

7 CYL was the HSWP's youth organization, founded in 1957. In the 1960s and '70s membership was virtually obligatory for high school and university students. The organization's gradual demise began in the mid-'70s, and was accelerated by the emergence of FIDESZ (Union of Young Democrats) in March 1988. In 1989, CYL was federalized and renamed the Democratic Youth League.

by the fact that a large number of company directors and Party functionaries received its announcement with barely-concealed anxiety. Their fears, however, are not matched with optimistic expectation on the part of the employees; and, unfortunately, this indifference is not an accident. First of all, the Resolutions do not make clear enough what sort of rights the new company councils will have or by what procedural system they will function; also, they leave ill-defined how these councils will be elected and in what proportion the state companies will be divided between the three categories. Secondly, some of these things are rather predictable and not conducive to optimism:

- On the whole the apparatuses of the Party and of the various mass organizations will increase their influence. In the case of large companies it is definitely not going to decrease. In the case of small and medium-sized companies it will increase because the Party and its auxiliary forces hold in their hands all electoral procedures. At the medium-sized companies it will also increase for the added reason that the representatives of the Party will automatically participate in the company councils' meetings, where they may easily assume the role of arbiter.

- The state apparatus will retain some trump cards as well. While the Resolutions take away from the state agencies some of their authority over property disposition, they immediately give back that curtailed influence through measures which aim at increasing their "market supervisory" role (the Resolutions specifically state that "various ministries are to take part in this task"). As for the definition of "market supervision," it is rather similar to the responsibilities of the "branch" ministries[8] as they were defined in the '70s: "The ministries should ensure that foreign trade be in harmony with our econo-political objectives, that the legal norms of the economy be observed and that company conduct—deriving from monopoly status or other circumstances—which violates national economic interests be curtailed."

8 Hungarian government administration makes a distinction between "branch" ministries and "functional" ministries. The so-called branch ministries are specialized in the administration of a particular sector of the economy (e.g., Ministry of Industry, Ministry of Agriculture, etc.). "Functional" ministries carry out functions which are relevant to the overall regulation of the national economy (e.g., Ministry of Finance, State Planning Office).

Significantly, the scope of issues left untouched by this "well-advertised" "continued development" is considerable: the control of investment resources and credits remains in essence the authority of the government, as do many other things which determine the leverage of company management.

- It is likely that at most companies a quiet struggle will begin between the Party and mass organization hierarchies and the government hierarchies about who will have influence over the companies. But no matter in which direction the balance of power shifts, there is no reason for celebration. If the government comes out on top, everything will remain as it has been. If the Party and the so-called mass organizations gain the upper hand, a largely incompetent political bureaucracy will have the last word rather than the professional administration—which at least has expertise in economic management. This would neither cure the organic troubles of industry (it might even worsen them), nor contribute to the companies' democratization.

- In the case of smaller companies it might happen that election procedures slip out of the control of the supervisory organs, and the community of employees elects its own people to the leadership—or, at least, vetoes every candidate imposed upon it from above. In cooperatives such things are already happening. Thus it is not impossible that, at least as an exception, alongside the hierarchies of the Party and the mass organizations, a third force also will appear on the scene: the assembly of employees. It is another question whether this force would be able to sustain its independence in the long run. Knowing the other sides overwhelming superiority both in terms of organization and means of communication, the chances of this are very slim. Nevertheless, even a partially and temporarily increased openness in this struggle might bring valuable social experience.

If to this minimal achievement we add the measures already implemented between 1979 and 1983[9] and the various minor modifications which may be added in the coming years, plus the fact that even these hesitant changes provide new stimuli to the crumbling of official ideology, then we have said

---

9 Faced with the threat of an insolvency crisis, the HSWP leadership turned once again to reforms between 1983 and 1989, but did so late and too indecisively. This half-hearted reform allowed only a limited existence for small private enterprises.

everything that is to be said about the Resolutions' "continued development." The mountains have been in labor for five years . . .

5. Why have the results turned out to be so lean?

It is common knowledge that the risks involved in a comprehensive reform are much higher today than they were in 1965–68. At that time it was still possible to accumulate substantial reserves to meet increased demands and to absorb the shocks of transition; today we are faced with grave shortages. In those years the standard of living could rise parallel to the introduction of reform; today it is stagnating or falling. In those years the expansion of East-West trade had just begun and cheap Soviet raw materials and energy were flowing in amply supply; today Soviet resources are increasing in price and shrinking in quantity, and East-West trade is hampered by the foreign debts of the COMECON states. At that time the world stood at the threshold of a seemingly lasting global thaw; now we are riding on a rising wave of cold war. At that time there was one more country (Czechoslovakia) which was experimenting with economic reform similar to the Hungarian, and reform was also the issue of the day in the Soviet Union; now Hungary stands virtually alone. At that time the long-term intentions of the Soviet leaders appeared to be intelligible; now it is not even clear who will lead the Soviet Union over the next two to three years.

All this is true, but in itself it does not explain the Hungarian leadership's timid hesitancy in introducing reform, since the risks associated with postponing it are even graver, and this is common knowledge as well. For an accelerated growth we have at our disposal neither a surplus of labor, nor cheap and plentiful raw materials, nor advantageous credits, nor hospitable foreign markets. Stagnation could be overcome only by a more effective utilization of our resources. If the economy's performance does not improve, only import restrictions could ensure a healthy foreign trade balance. Such a measure would not only slow down growth, but would also accelerate the aging of production facilities and hold back technological progress. Consequently, the gap between the standard required for the world market and Hungarian industry's performance would widen, which would further worsen our export potential and become an additional cause of decreasing imports. This economic *circulus vitiosus* would set in motion a political one as well. The decline in the standard of living (or, at least, the growing gap between Western European and Hungarian consumption) would give birth to discontent, which would force the authorities to increasingly isolate the population from foreign information—to reduce the import of films and books, to curtail the admission of cultural and other trends. These measures enhance the discontent even further; the mushrooming expressions of malaise must be suppressed. And since the first expressions of this mood appear in the social sciences and journalism, restrictive measures become necessary against the intelligentsia as well. This, in turn, induces grumbling once again, and through various invisible channels leads to the further worsening of the economy's performance.

The question therefore is: Why is the leadership more afraid of the short-term risks of reform than of the risk that in the long run it may squander away everything that a combination of good fortune and prudence brought to existence in the last 25 years? At first glance the answer appears simple: every bureaucracy is conservative. Yet the leaders of the same bureaucracy showed considerably more daring between 1966 and 1968. True, at that time much less was at stake, and the risk of hesitation was considerably smaller as well. All in all, the 1968 Hungarian economic reform was the most profound institutional and ideological change ever implemented in a satellite country of the Soviet empire without revolutionary shock. Why is the current Hungarian leadership so much more conservative than its predecessor?

No matter how strange it may sound, the primary reason is the continuity linking the two leaderships, i.e., the fact that the 1968 leadership managed to survive the political defeat of the new economic mechanism. True, the reformers had to strike a bargain with the opponents of reform who—encouraged by the newly-emerging anti-reform mood in the wake of Czechoslovakia's occupation—after 1969 were demanding the return to planned economy more and more loudly. But the bargain turned out to be a bargain indeed and not a sharp turnaround. The still-pending measures of the reform were taken off the agenda, some features of the new economic mechanism were chopped away, foreign elements were attached to its other segments, but neither the 1966 Resolutions of the Central Committee nor the January 1968 measures were revoked as such. The continuity in leadership personnel was not interrupted either; a few people had to relinquish their posts, but they could do so without official reprimand. The partisans of "progress" and "regression" got used to each other and adapted to each other in the context of this compromise. They all learned that it was not a good idea to initiate programs which might divide the leadership, induce resistance in large segments of the apparatus, and mobilize a portion of the population at large. Such programs are not in the interest of individual leaders, since they might be held responsible; such programs are not in the leaders' collective interest either, because their introduction might result in admitting new players into the political arena who might turn to the public at large. And the neighboring smaller and bigger brothers might not look at such changes kindly. Thus, it is the most advantageous for all involved to moderate their conflicting views as a matter of course. At the end of 1978 the leadership set off on the new period with this shared conviction. Significant personnel changes were avoided once again; the responsibility of those advocating the 1972–74 turnaround was not made explicit, and the very fact that a turnaround had occurred at all was left unmentioned. Is it then a surprise that the return to the programs of 1968 is now made to appear as "continued development?"

In this context the leadership could even allow the economists who were assigned to prepare recommendations a free rein to their fantasy, since the consensus of the decision makers had already drawn the limits of possible reforms. That is what the leaders presumed, what their radical critics presumed, and, finally, that was what really happened.

6. In the meantime, however, a couple of things occurred. The crisis proved to be more profound than anybody (with the exception of a few economist-prophets) expected it to be, and the economic pressure pointing to reform also surpassed expectations. As the committee sessions and public debates began, it suddenly became apparent that the ideological ramparts of anti-reform resistance had become considerably more weakened in the preceding decade than had been believed. Therefore it became conceivable, especially in 1981–82, that economic pressure, coupled with sufficient pressure of ideas, might weaken the consensus within the leadership and open the way to a more radical reform.

That this was not to be became apparent when between October 1982 and April 1983 the radical reformers were censured. It was done, of course, Hungarian style, without anybody getting hurt. Although the public debate came to a halt, the participants of closed-committee meetings were still able to submit daring proposals (however, only about those issues which were presented to them, and without hope of influencing the final decision).

The series of censures had one notable result. Earlier the reform camp had retained its unity; there had been plenty of conflicting views, but political confrontations had not occurred. Now, however, juxtaposed to the radical reformers another new faction is emerging and has even entered into open polemics with the former group (see for example, the article of Iván T. Berend in the April 13, 1984 issue of *Élet és Irodalom*). The gist of their reasoning is identical to the phraseology advanced by the spokesmen of the apparatus: "science" is one thing and "politics" another. It is the task of "politics" (meaning the job of the leading bodies of the Party and its apparatus), having taken stock of the social and international situation, to make the first step, to give assignments to "science." And it is the job of "science" to fulfill these assignments and submit recommendations. After this, "politics," once again taking into account the broader situation, chooses from the various alternatives. If "politics" does not listen to the opinion of "science," the result is voluntarism reminiscent of the '50s, since politics lacks the expertise indispensable to the preparatory stages of decision-making. But nothing good happens if "science," with its impatient radicalism, tries to outdo "politics"—since "politics" alone knows what is, and what is not, possible in the given social and international situation. It is also "politics" which bears sole responsibility for the consequences of its decisions.

Let us now disregard the fact that this reasoning is circuitous, since the leadership is in possession of privileged knowledge only as long as it is able to bar others from its sources of information and bears sole responsibility for political decisions only as long as "politics" equals the actions of the authorities and their agencies. Let us focus instead on the thought hidden between the lines: "You radical reformers, it is your doing that the result is so garbled, because your provocative ideas induce resistance by the leadership's conservative elements, scare away forces sympathetic to change and even prompt the Soviet (Czech, East German) leaders to realize that it is time to intervene." We have to admit that this reasoning has its own rationale. Nevertheless, we cannot accept it, and not simply because it is not to our liking.

First of all, the leadership does not seem to be particularly eager to introduce the necessary reforms, even when it is not "spooked" by more outspoken economists. On the other hand, the suppression of delicate political questions deprives the advocates of reform of their only means to influence meaningfully the decision-making process, i.e., lining up social support behind their ideas. If they cannot mobilize the public, they have no influence on the leadership's decision as to what sort of tasks are assigned to them and how serious a consideration their recommendations receive.

Secondly, it is not self-evident that the preparation of reform, apart from "politics," is an exclusive concern of "science," of invited experts. If the public is excluded from the preparatory debates, then the bigger part of the professional community who did not get an invitation to the reform committees is also excluded. Is not their expert opinion "scientific" opinion? And what about the opinion of non-experts, of those social groups which would be affected by the reform in one way or another? How about those social interests and objectives which are contrary to the intentions of the selected game-players, or which, because of not having a voice, are left unnoticed?

It would not be auspicious if the issue of reform is decided only by the political decision-makers and their selected experts. It would not be auspicious either from the point of view of whether or not the reform is successful or from the point of view as to *what sort* of reform might be given a chance to become successful. Therefore, we do not find the debates too extensive but, on the contrary, too limited. We do not attribute the failure of the reform economists to the fact that they have gone too far but, on the contrary, that they did not go far enough. They were dreaming up a social reform movement but in reality they were busy ensuring a seat on the committees which were instituted from above. It is no wonder that their recommendations also contained many ambiguous elements. They were hinting at the idea that the economy must get out of the direct tutelage of the Party apparatus, but they did not think through what the institutional implications of such a change would be or how it could be reconciled with the sovereign authority of the Party within the state. They were hinting at the necessity of reforming the trade union; but while they implied that in the present situation they were not suggesting the pluralization of the trade union, they left obscure what sort of changes are necessary within the unified trade union. Some experts stood up for self-management but failed to face the fact that the elected bodies of self-management might easily fall into the hands of the Party and other mass organizations. Others wished to assign the company ownership rights to organizations which are endowed with capital ownership rights and which have an interest in the preservation and growth of the value of property, but failed to consider that the leaders of such organizations might easily revert to being middle-men between the government and the companies. Thus, the reform economists failed to appease the leadership, and also failed to win over the public at large.

The April Resolutions of the Central Committee have made it clear how far the leadership, the apparatus, is willing to go on its own. What has happened since then only underlines the fact that the text really means what it says: "continued development" of one kind or another is possible, but there is no chance for reform. The reform economists either resign themselves to this or change their tactics. But is a more consistent reform policy feasible?

The central corps of the 1979–84 reform movement came from the ranks of state experts who have an above-average dependence on bureaucratic institutions. It could not be expected that they would in large numbers step over the official limitations. It is, however, conceivable that such groups within the reform camp that have greater leverage would stand up more independently and forcefully. There are several opportunities to do this.

First of all, it is worth considering such examples as Tibor Liska,[10] an economist on the periphery of his profession. Liska has always been conspicuous for not staying in line with his colleagues. He has been trying to have his ideas implemented through propaganda, experimentation, mobilization, lobbying—not through traditional committee channels. Nobody can claim a greater success than can Liska. Secondly, the reform economists could attempt to enter into a dialogue with such members of the intelligentsia—sociologists, writers, journalists—who represent causes related to economic reform. The prerequisite for this approach is that the reformists think over the social consequences of their economic ideas more thoroughly: how would the new system affect employment, income distribution, social policies, the protection of popular interest, regional development, and the expansion of the infrastructure? Finally, they should attempt to form a widespread network of reform clubs and association which would provide legal, but non-official, forums for discussing the reform's problems.

The Resolutions of the Central Committee are not the last word. The pressure of the economic situation still necessitates fundamental reform, and ideological decay cannot be stopped with Party resolutions.

---

10 Tibor Liska was an economist famed for ingenious blueprints combining free market individual enterprise with state ownership of the means of production. His book *Econostat*, written in the early '60s, could not be published in Hungary before 1988.

On Our Limitations and Possibilities

On Our Limitations and Possibilities

S ince 1956 the Hungarian public has firmly believed that it is useless to think in terms of comprehensive alternatives to our predicament, for the Soviet state will do with this country whatever it pleases anyway.[1] Even the concessions received in small inconspicuous increments are surrounded by an air of contingency: the Soviets may have enough of them any time and may rescind them altogether. This feeling of uncertainty is enhanced by the fact that the Soviet leaders' expectations vis-à-vis the Hungarian leadership are not formulated publicly: they are a matter of speculation. Furthermore, it can only be guessed at which moment they may deem it necessary to express their displeasure, whom they can count on, and what methods are at their disposal to support their demands. The public, left to unverifiable hearsay, suspects categorical orders even in those cases where probably a relatively balanced bargaining is on going on; it fears intervention when even the intention of intervention is absent.

It appears to be certain, however, that the Soviet state does not tolerate a transformation of the system. And the reform ideas of the Hungarian intelligentsia have certainly reached the point at which the system's invariables are put in question. In part the experience of the post-1968 slow-down and reentrenchment, and in part the impact of the crisis which

---

1 1956 was the date of the Hungarian revolution (October 23–November 4). On the lasting effects of the bloody reprisals following the revolution see the essays in the first part of this volume.

began in the late '70s, have led to an ever-more-widespread recognition that the problems piled up by the country's Soviet-style evolution can be solved only by dismantling the monocentric, hierarchical system. Around 1968 many people still seemed to believe that it was possible to reconcile the primacy of market regulation with the existence of companies subordinated to the Party-state. At that time the promotion of increased societal participation in, and control of, public affairs within the hierarchical structure seemed sufficient to the political democratization of the country. Today only a very few still think this way. This conceptual step forward, however, is taken in a paradoxical way. The more bold the reform projects are, the more skeptical are their authors and the more ominous is the question: is it possible that in the periods of 1961–63[2] and 1981–83[3] Hungary reached the limits of development which is possible in a Soviet-style regime belonging to Soviet empire? If this is the case then we simply have to face the fact that we have come to a stalemate between progress and stagnation for an unpredictable period of time. We have to face the fact that the slow Balkanization of the country's economic, political, and moral conditions will inevitably continue.

I would like to submit a few thoughts in this debate. At first I shall argue that since 1956 the Soviet empire has undergone some rather important changes and the consequences of these changes have started to show: the leaders of the Soviet Union are less and less able to rule the dependent states of our region in the old way. Then, I would like to show that Hungary's recovery from the present crisis may take shape due to this increased leverage. I would like to emphasize both components of this location: I refer to a *recovery*, an evolutionary process, and not to the inducement of political collapse. And I refer to an evolution whose components would emerge from within the organic development of *Hungarian* society.

During the first decade after the 1948 Communist takeover, the lack of sufficient societal support, the atmosphere of terror, the cold war-related isolation from the West, the forced drive toward economic self-reliance placed the local leaders completely at the mercy of their Soviet bosses. Their fate was decided solely in Moscow; they were not dependent either on the people—which they terrorized to the limit during the period of forced industrialization and Sovietization—or on the hastily assembled

---

2 1963–63 were years of the regime's consolidation which closed the restoration period.
3 1981–83 were years of the last, and failed, reform attempt of the Kádár leadership. This attempt was a reaction to the stagnation forced on the Hungarian economy by its indebtedness crisis.

Party apparatus which was the tool and the target of their terror at the same time. From the mid-fifties on, however, the situation slowly started to change.

At first the lessening of terror modified the power structure. The apparatus which enjoyed increased security became more stable and emerged as a political factor. Its members could form cliques, factions, and alliances of interest. At moments of weakness within the leadership they even might attempt to seize power. The populace regained its independence at least to the extent of answering the most blatant wrongs with strikes, demonstrations, and public disturbances which all presented the danger of undermining the leadership's power. The intelligentsia was emancipated step by step from the tutelage and control exercised by official ideology, and developed a certain capacity to formulate alternative values, social goals, and practical ideas. Since by then those in power did become dependent on the loyalty of their own population and apparatus, they became less dependent on the will of the Soviet leadership: their role of governor-general was transformed into that of a subordinated middleman. The stability of their power depended on their ability to buy public peace with concessions which were acceptable both to their own apparatus and to the Soviet leaders. The Soviet leaders, of course, did not tolerate every concession, but they could not forbid all of them, either.

The other reason for the shift of power was that parallel to the lessening of mass terror the political isolation of the Soviet empire also decreased. This process produced the lasting results of the '60s and the '70s. These results included the settlement of the European status quo by which the Western powers recognized the finality of the borders drawn in the wake of World War II; accepted the de facto division of Germany and the legitimacy of governments in countries within the Soviet sphere of influence. (Implicitly they even agreed that the Soviet Union may use force if one of its satellite governments is in trouble.) In exchange the Soviet Union agreed that these governments would settle their relationships with West Germany, that the two German states would establish special relations, and that the Western powers would establish separate ties with the satellite states of the region. All this proved to be a durable change which even the new wave of cold war could not sweep away. More uncertain is what can be expected in the long run from the concession given in return, incorporating human rights guarantees into the international legal regulation of East-West relations.[4] In spite of bad experiences I do not

4 The allusion is to the Helsinki agreement signed in 1975.

consider this issue hopeless, but right now I will refrain from arguing this case.

I attribute, however, the most important role in loosening our dependence to a third factor: economic pressures. In the '80s COMECON[5] is no longer a regional economic organization capable of yielding an acceptable level of growth. The countries of the region might have been satisfied with the operation of COMECON as long as the Soviet Union provided a virtually unlimited supply of cheap raw materials and energy and in return purchased, also in unlimited quantities, those products—unsalable in other markets—which the Soviet-style industries of Eastern Europe manufactured using these resources in their wasteful manner. As time went by, however, this relationship became more and more lopsided. While the absorbing capacity of the Soviet market is still enormous and for Eastern European companies there is still nothing more convenient than procuring Soviet orders and cooperating with Soviet partners,[6] the Soviet Union's ability to provide raw materials and fuel since the mid-seventies has been growing at a slower rate than the uninterrupted growth of Eastern European economies requires. And in the last few years it has even shown a decline which does not appear to be a transitory disorder but a permanent tendency. The only way out of this situation is to transform the wasteful economic system and turn to markets which would link the region's countries to a circuit of faster technological progress. Without such a change Eastern Europe is facing the danger of joining the underdeveloped, stagnating regions of the globe exactly at a time when in the West another technological revolution is taking place which pulls along some parts of the third world. The Soviet Union has nothing to offer that could substitute for this change, and consequently it is unable to halt the disintegration of its empire.

Poland's history after August 1980 vividly exemplifies the present state of this process. *Solidarity* was born, outlawed and reorganized underground at a moment of historical stalemate when the Soviet state is still able to force the defeat of a huge social movement yet is unable to politically neutralize the defeated society. Imagine that in the Hungary of 1960 the underground Central Workers' Council published its national and local weekly newspapers, organized mass demonstrations in the larger cities on May Day, and operated educational institutions for the workers. Imagine that the autonomy and political resistance of most universities and academic

---

5 See note 7 of "The Present Crisis and its Origins" in this volume.
6 Even this has been changed dramatically in the second half of the 1980s.

institutions was intact and that the churches played the role of mediator between the authorities and the resistance. It is likely that this flight of fancy does not appeal to everybody since the preservation of pluralism in Poland depends on the momentary balance of power and has to be defended in relentless struggle. Many Poles, most probably, would gladly exchange their somber independence for the cheerful dependence of the Hungarian '60s. Personally I would prefer to join the ranks of the resistance. The issue, however, is not in whose shoes we would like to be. The Poles cannot arrive at a Hungarian-style consolidation and in our country there is no chance of repeating the experiment of *Solidarity*. It is the correct assessment of the general lessons of the Polish case that truly matters. We should notice not only the fact that the decision was made by force once again, but also that four years after the banning of the democratic mass movement the restoration of the old regime still could not be accomplished. If this is the case in the country the control of which is among the primary aims of Soviet regional policy, then in Hungary, which has lesser geopolitical importance for the Soviet Union, we ought to rethink the question: Is it possible to leave behind the path of the last twenty or so years (which turned out to be a dead end street as the overall crisis has besieged the region of the '80s)?

•   •   •

The post-1961 to 1963 development of Hungary has produced a particular version of the Soviet model. The Hungarian version did not change that feature of Soviet-style regimes that neither individuals nor organizations have clearly-defined, defendable and enforceable rights vis-à-vis the political authorities. Large areas of life—e.g., culture—are not regulated by laws at all, but rather by guidelines of leading Party organs and occasional pronouncements of apparatchiks. And the decisions of the Party—whose legal status is completely undefined—may override the law even in those cases where legal statutes do exist, as happened in the stormy nomination process of candidates in this year's elections.[7] Government agencies may invalidate statutes of the law with their decrees and orders as well: see the

---

7 On the 1985 parliamentary elections, see "The Fall Session of the National Assembly" in this volume.

press regulations which directly contradict paragraph 64 of the Constitution.[8] The provisions of the law frequently provide the state with loopholes or explicit authorization to enact arbitrary measures, as in the case of association or passport regulations.[9] The authorities may disregard a statute even if it happens to be unequivocal, since it cannot be enforced by the courts: a citizen is either unable to turn to the courts for redress (as in the case with the mandatory police measures which violate his interest) or may rest assured that the ruling is not going to follow the precepts of the law but rather the interests of the authorities.[10] This legal anarchy, strangely enough, is not always disadvantageous to the governed. In some favorable situations the government may quietly overlook or even encourage a series of minor progressive changes, knowing that it may intervene at any moment it deems necessary. Lack of clear rules makes life easier as well for those who are trying to find loopholes to their own advantage, since not only are citizens' rights not clearly formulated, but equally undefined is what is forbidden to them. In the last 20 to 25 years Hungary has been using this practice with unmatched success: among others, culture broke away from the yoke of official ideology and the parallel, illicit economy slowly blossomed in this manner.

This state of affairs, however, has its disadvantages. This is why every concession is considered a favor which entails gratitude and reciprocation and may be revoked at any time. This is why clear-cut bargains are so rare, and tenacious opportunism so common. This is why it has become so natural that custom and practice contradict the law. This is why corruption, bribery, and favoritism have become so widespread. This is why it is considered an act of bravery if a journalist winks at his readers in between the lines of standard lies, and a sign of bad manners if he bluntly states the truth. This is why shrewd maneuvering is valued so highly and the upholding of principles so little.

---

8 Paragraph 64 of the 1949 Constitution provides for freedom of the press. However, until the end of the '80s, the decrees and laws regulating publishing activities demanded that publishers get government permission before starting publication, and that the police had the power to punish press law infringement without any trial; No appeal to courts against such police decisions was allowed.

9 A 1981 decree on association, in effect until 1989, made organizing conditional on government permission. The authorities were free to decide whether to give or deny permission, and there was no appeal to a court against their decisions. The same discretionary power was conferred on passport authorities until 1988 when it was restricted although not eliminated completely.

10 Independence of the judiciary is not provided for in Hungary. Since the 1948 Communist takeover, judges are selected and supervised by the Ministry of Justice, and they are under constant pressure from the party apparatus.

Is this a high price to pay? Enormously high. This practice destroyed the public mores of political life and has started to eat away private morals as well. One of our very first tasks is to make it understood that only people who are conscious of their rights and ready to defend them may become citizens with self-respect.

But right now I do not want to talk about the moral and political price of a progress which circumvents legality. I would rather call attention to the fact that it is less and less possible to move ahead in this way. These well-tested tactics still may be carried on here and there, but they are considered less and less suitable in solving the country's increasingly urgent problems. The practice of traveling by roundabouts, through loopholes and side doors could have been the dominant strategy of a society which, having awakened from the shock of 1956,[11] tried to get along by forsaking the conquest of its institutions. The developments of the last 25 years produce the need to codify the results of this period.

This is necessary, in part, because organic growth has reached the limit beyond which it can go on with unbroken elan only in the presence of legal guarantees. The illicit economy has produced enterprises controlling such sizeable capital and work-force that they can stabilize their position and achieve further growth only within legality. The proliferation of small groups and informal circles which gather and dissolve under the temporary protection of private homes, an occasional club, and community centers is about to reach the point where the sheer temporary tolerance of the authorities is not sufficient anymore. Legal rights are also necessary for the further growth of the various nascent intellectual and cultural movements.

The transformation of institutions has been made necessary, in part, by the crisis which started in the late seventies: the progress which occurred within a Soviet-style framework, came to a halt and—without substantial institutional reforms—cannot proceed. The stagnation of the GNP has put to test the existing economic mechanism, has placed into a sharper focus the well-known but until now more bearable anomalies of earlier growth, and has made the conflicts between various interests increasingly clear. Legal rights are needed in order for the economic organizations to function as market enterprises and to enter into a relationship with the state as taxpayers and contractual partners. Legal rights are needed to find a mutually acceptable compromise for the increasingly sharp conflicts of interests. Legal rights are needed so the needy may call the state to account

---

11 On the shock caused by the crushing of the 1956 revolution, see the essays in the first part of this volume.

with regard to its socio-political obligations, ensuring at the same time that the redistribution of resources not take away arbitrarily either from other strata or from economic enterprises.

It is noteworthy that the shift towards demanding legal rights and codified guarantees has begun in the same areas where the loosening of rigid forms, the circumvention of regulations, and the bargaining and reciprocation of favors have led to the accumulation of tangible results. These demands do not aim at the heights of national politics, rather they are directed at certain areas of everyday life. It is no accident that at first they emerged in the non-official sector of the economy when the various forms of small enterprises became legalized.[12] It is no accident either that apart from the economy the primary target of these demands is the right to association and the realm of cultural and intellectual activities. Nevertheless, it is true that in order to solidify the legal achievements "below," changes are also necessary "above." Yet so far this ferment has affected the top only indirectly. For the time being the demands are open administration of public affairs and rule of law as indispensable preconditions for greater independence "below." At this moment the ill-feeling of the people concerning the fundamental institutions of the regime has not reached a point where the majority of people would not be satisfied with such guarantees if it sees tangible rights and tangible results "below."

As for the country's external situation, we must consider this state of affairs an advantage. If not for a potential compromise between those who govern and those who are governed the choice would be only between the regime's collapse and slow decadence. The latter is undesirable under any circumstances, and we would consider the former desirable only if we did not have to reckon with the repetition of the outcome of 1956, 1968, and 1981.[13] In the present state of the Soviet empire, however, it might be possible to defend a new compromise against external pressure. On the basis of recent experiences and ideas, I will try to summarize the structure of such a defensible compromise.

The crux of this concept is what is generally called separation of the state and civil society. In our case, however, this locution is probably not the most fortunate, since it does not draw the line along those points where it might

---

12 Private enterprises of up to twelve employees were recognized by law in January 1982. However, the legal framework for limited liability and shareholding was not created until 1988 when the upper limit on workers employed by a private firm was raised to 500.
13 Allusion is to the crushing of the Hungarian revolution, to the military intervention against the Czechoslovak reform movement, and to the *coup d'etat* which led to the outlawing of Solidarity.

be drawn in Hungary in the coming decade. For, on the one hand, it is not clear whether "the state" includes the Party, the trade union, the People's Patriotic Front,[14] and the Communist Youth League,[15] all of which are closely interwoven with public powers. I consider this question important since, in the short run, I do not see the possibility of realizing a formula which would simply abolish the public status of these organizations and their political monopolies. On the other hand, we usually do not include in the concept of "civil society" those companies and financial institutions which in spite of their separation from the Party-state hierarchy, do manage state property. This separation of publicly-owned companies, however, would be an essential element of reforming the economy (and, partially, social policy). For this reason, in the following description I prefer to make a somewhat different distinction of "public law" and "civil law" respectively. According to this concept those between the spheres regulated by institutions and organizations which are listed in the Constitution, or whose establishment and public privileges are legally regulated, belong to the sphere of "public law." At the other end of the spectrum we find the private realm of family, kinship, and informal relations. Now, the territory lying between the public and the strictly private is the province of what I would call "civil law."

At the present time the boundaries between the domains of public and civil law are blurred. For example, although the employer-employee relationship is a contractual private relation the employer nevertheless may invoke public law vis-à-vis the employee; and public authorities may intervene in the execution of rights based on the employment contract. The situation is similar in the case of associations, companies and a number of other organizations. This state of affairs must be changed. New conditions have to be created in which the state may interfere in the sphere of civil law only by the application or enforcement of existing laws or through economic incentives, the forms of which should be defined in fixed regulations. To achieve this, not only the chaotic state of legal provisions must be overcome, but also the independence of the judiciary must be increased and the courts given a larger role in regulating the relationship between the two spheres. Organizations belonging under the jurisdiction of civil law should be both formed and dissolved only though judicial action, and it must be guaranteed that any such organization or any citizen in case of dispute with any public institution can turn to the courts.

14 On PPF see note 6 of "Can 1956 Be Forgotten?"
15 On CYL see note 7 of 'From Reform to Continued Development."

The separation of the two spheres would not alter the political privileges of organizations and institutions formed under public law. But precisely for this reason considerably more independence should be allowed in the sphere of civil law than is now allowed. Along with the public companies, kept under government control and provided with economic privileges, a whole variety of companies could flourish—from various types of state-owned companies formed under civil law, to cooperatives and private enterprises. Alongside the National Bank of Hungary a multitude of competing financial institutions could be formed. Alongside the state social security system, private pension and medical insurance companies could come to life. Alongside the only trade union recognized under public law, professional associations could emerge under civil law. Alongside the publishing houses and newspapers, founded and supervised by organs existing under public law, groups belonging to the province of civil law also could launch publishing houses and newspapers. Of course, the latter organizations and their mass media forums would have more limited opportunities than their counterparts formed under public law. Thus, only the trade union recognized under public law would have veto power and the right to call strikes. Only the state social security system could impose additional levies on the employers and employees. Nevertheless even limited rights ensure a more independent way of life than unpredictable concessions without guarantees. And following this concept we would not have to renounce a flexible progress either. Every time the sphere of civil law is to be regulated with legislation it could always include a target date for the law to be reviewed and a decision made as to which of the original limitations could be lifted.

In the sphere of public law, changes of another kind would be necessary and conceivable. The content of the Party's so-called "leading role"—which right now is unclear—should be clarified: the relationship between the decisions of the Central Committee and the National Assembly should be codified; it should be made public which posts will be filled under the jurisdiction of the Party's personnel decisions; and the legal authority of regional Party organizations should be circumscribed. The practice of governing by decrees should be brought to an end and the primacy of legislative regulations should be restored. A modification of the election laws should ensure that the National Assembly always have at least a few independent representatives whose presence would guarantee that contested issues would be debated. The foundations of local self-government, especially in smaller communities, should be laid. The protective functions of the trade union have to be freed from functions aimed at promoting production. Through the modification of election procedures and some other measures, it should be ensured that the union representatives at the work place would answer primarily to the rank and file, and that they would represent its interests while their rights of intervention and veto power also receive clarification. Based on the differentiation of the social security system, it should be determined which of those basic benefits are state obligations, and those should become unequivocal rights of the citizenry.[16]

•   •   •

In this outline I was not trying to describe a finalized, self-perpetuating model, but only the direction of progress. For this reason its details are somewhat sketchy. Those changes which I mentioned for the sake of demonstration would not necessarily take place, nor in that sequence. The crux of the matter is the concept itself, the idea of dual mobility: in the sphere of public law towards constitutional state, and in the sphere of civil law towards pluralism.

I am fully aware that my thoughts raise more questions than they answer. The first question is whether those in power will be willing to accept significant innovation. The leaders who now are balancing at the very top[17] seem to be willing to accept a series of small changes only to the point that individuals or organizations do not gain unequivocal rights in any specific area. They have never given such rights, except to a tiny group of small entrepreneurs; when they drew the line on new reforms in the '80s, they made it clear that they were not willing to do so then either. The recently emerged pro-discipline-and-order faction[18] is unhappy even with this tentative process and tries, through advocating popular anti-market measures, to gain support for the conservation of the apparatus' traditional

---

16 At the time this paper was proposed for a discussion, even such modest changes were seen as inconceivable or extremely dangerous by the public. "Social Contract," a program for political transformation proposed by the editors of *Beszélő* (including the author) in 1987 went much further. And the landslide after the departure of Kádár in 1988 made even "Social Contract" obsolete. See "After Kádár" in this volume.

17 That is, János Kádár and his closest associates.

18 Represented, at the time this paper was written, mainly by Károly Grósz, then first secretary of the Borsod county HSWP committee (General Secretary of the party since May 1988) and János Berecz, then editor-in- chief of *Népszabadság* (People's Liberty), the party's daily (secretary of the Central Committee since 1985). Berecz lost his Politburo membership in personal infighting with Grósz in 1989.

power. The pro-reform faction on the other hand, is weak and lacks cohesion.[19] Might the balance of power be changed for the better by the pressures of the country's situation and by the approaching generational change in the leadership? Will those members of the leadership and the apparatus who recognize the necessity of renewing the compromise with the population have the chance to become influential players, or will only those interested exclusively in retaining their own power have it? If the partisans of reform gain strength, will it come too late? Will accumulated bitterness be too much, or political passions too overheated for a compromise to be struck? In what direction does the crisis move the passions of the people: closer to a growing need for democracy, or towards the growing hatred for other classes, races, and nations? Does a growing democratic sentiment have a chance at all when the domestic affairs of the Magyars have to be brought to order in the context of an external situation which makes us utterly helpless to do anything for the plight of Hungarian minorities abroad?

The answers to these questions will come not from theoretical musings, but from future events. But those events themselves depend, at least in part, on us. And thus, we cannot avoid asking these questions and trying, time and again, to answer them.

---

19 The reform wing of the party had no representatives in the Politburo.

"Troops of Weary Seekers . . . "

"Troops of Weary Seekers . . . "

Hungarian public opinion is increasingly dispirited. People have a growing sense that the country is in a crisis of economic origin and they believe less and less that the leadership is able to show the way out of this crisis. In the midst of general malaise only the propaganda sounds optimistic. In the spring of 1984 the government announced that we had passed the worst part of belt tightening, that import restrictions might soon be eased (i.e. in 1985), and that the seventh five-year plan,[1] beginning in 1986, would be once again a plan of economic upswing.

To get to the heart of the matter: the leadership's optimistic rhetoric is a sign not of strength but of weakness. It is not a reflection of the government's expanded *economic* leverage but rather of its reduced *political* leverage.

Why are they promising growth?

The results of the 1981-85 period did not provide the basis for a plan which could project even a modest upsurge: none of the objectives considered by

1 Central planning was made the basic institution of economic coordination in 1949. It followed a five-year plan. Five year plans determine the main targets of economic growth: its rate structure and direction. They are set in physical terms; the so-called financial plans are only translations of physical plans into monetary requirements of the national economy. Such plans are by their nature overtight and can never be met.

the government indispensable to enter a "new cycle of growth" was realized (even this expression went out of fashion). There was no significant decrease in per unit raw material and energy consumption; and there are indications that without radical redevelopment of energy-hungry industries and investments for modernization, it is impossible to achieve a break-through in this area (*Népszabadság*, October 16, 1985, p. 10). The average age of industrial products has grown even higher: the ratio of products introduced within the last three years fell from 17.2% in 1980 to 13.9% in 1983, while the average age of industrial products grew from 15.7 in 1980 to 16.4 in 1983 (*Statisztikai Szemle*, #11, 1984, p. 1073). The makeup of hard currency exports has become worse: by the end of the current five-year plan more than one-third of industrial exports to hard currency markets came from industries (steel, chemical, and construction materials) with extensive standing capital, energy, and raw material needs. This is a higher ratio than it was in 1982, while the already low share of the tool-producing industry decreased further and the bulk even of this reduced share was made up of traditional products (*Népszabadság*, November 27, 1985, p. 10). If the precondition of accelerated growth is that each point of growth would require a lower ratio of raw materials and energy purchased for dollars than earlier, and that the export of goods would cover the import cost of their manufacturing, the situation is no better today than it was at the beginning of the previous five-year plan.

In my opinion, government economic experts and cabinet members themselves are fully aware of these facts. When on May 16 of last year[2] Lajos Faluvégi, deputy prime minister, briefed regional leaders about the estimated figures of the new five-year plan, he virtually admitted this. For Faluvégi considered it necessary to tell his audience what the subsequently-published five-year plan bill already concealed, i.e., that the projected modest improvement can be hoped for only if productivity grows by 24 to 26% (an annual rate of 5%) and if tool-industry exports of hard currency markets increase by 30 to 40% (an annual rate of 6 to 8%)! (*Magyar Hírlap*, June 4, 1985, Supplement) As a comparison: in the years of 1982–84 and 1976–78 productivity grew at an annual rate of 2.7%, which is barely more than half of the growth projected for 1986–90 (*Népszabadság*, July 17, 1985, p. 10). The stagnation of the tool-producing industry has already been mentioned.

From where would the leap-like improvement included in the new plan come? Since the economy's performance between 1981 and 1985 did not

2 1985.

improve, there is only one source of hope: maybe the rise of the investment in itself will prompt the improvement of productivity. Well, the increasingly bad performance of the Hungarian economy is indeed, at least partially, connected to the fact that the forced cutbacks in capital investment have led to a faster-than-usual obsolescence of manufacturing facilities. Yet the experience gained from previous increases in capital accumulation are not very encouraging: the bulk of invested capital was not used for modernizing industry, but for the expansion of its backward branches. And the seventh five-year plan assures in advance that this would remain unchange: a significant portion of the increased investment is earmarked for contributions to projects in the Soviet Union (the Yamburg gas field, the Krivoj Rog ore refinery), for coal mining, for the electrical industry and for the dam on the Danube.[3] We are left to guess at the exact amounts involved, since the government did not honor its citizens by releasing the spending plan of the nation's income which the people themselves had produced. Nevertheless, according to objective estimates, there cannot be much capital left to develop the upcoming industries: the electronic industry for example, will receive a mere 100 billion forints, which is barely more than 8% of all planned investments (*Hirmondó*, #1, 1989, p. 4).[4]

But if the plan is so shaky, why is the leadership pushing it? Why does the government keep promising things when it must know that it will not be able to deliver them? Why does the leadership not stick to the econo-political rhetoric of the early '80s: "We must accept the 'realities' of our situation?"

In my opinion the reason is that the regime no longer has the strength to take on a consistent economic policy. That belt tightening is necessary may be asserted for one year, two, or probably three. If in the meantime it becomes uncertain whether the lean years will ever come to an end, it is increasingly difficult to repeat this line.

The population grumbles about inflation, demands that pensions and other benefits retain their buying power, and urges stable prices and decent salaries, ensuring an acceptable living. The people are increasingly impatient with the disruptions in the energy supply and with half-empty coal yards. Dissatisfaction is on the rise concerning the present state of schools, public health care, public transportation and telecommunications. Statistical data on declining life expectancy—particularly that the death rate per thousand continues to rise, especially among men between the ages of

---

3 See note 14 of "The End and the Beginning" in this volume.
4 *Hirmondó* (The Messenger) was one of the leading *samizdat* magazines of the mid-80s.

35 to 55—is a subject of increasing concern. The population wants to see effective measures and tangible results.

The leaders of the crisis-ridden industries—coal mining, railways, metallurgy and chemical products—plead for immediate help. They all say that the cutbacks in government investment have brought their industries to shambles. We have to admit that they might be right if we think about the causes of the recently-more-frequent mining disasters.

But even the leaders of successful industries demand the acceleration of investment, citing the increasingly obsolete manufacturing facilities and inevitable technological decline. This argument too, has the ring of truth. Restrictive economic policies proved to be a trap indeed: since the Hungarian economy lost its competitive edge in the world market, imports and domestic consumption had to be curbed; these curbs in turn led to the further worsening of the Hungarian economy's competitive position. This is the primary reason for the continued worsening of the trade balance and, at least partially, for inflation at home.

Technological research requires money as well: if the funds earmarked for research and development continue to be reduced, it will become impossible to catch up with world leaders and we will irrevocably miss out on the electronic and biotechnological revolution of the West.

The most neglected budgetary area, regional public administration, also requires money in order to meet at least its most elementary community functions. All in all, everybody expects the state to spend more generously than it did before.

The leadership did give in to the pressure coming from all sides when in 1984 at the time of the Central Committee's April session it decided that investment had to be increased and economic growth had to be accelerated.

What will be the result of this?

The alternatives

One of the possibilities is to give in only in words, while in reality continuing the restrictive economic policy. The point of departure of this approach is that the objectives of the five-year plan by definition are not going to be realized. After all, this would not be the first five-year plan which was not fulfilled (just look at the one that preceded it). To those economic leaders who consider it most important to maintain the economy in equilibrium in order to avoid insolvency, this solution seems to be the least unfortunate. This position is represented in the government by the leaders of the Central Planning Board and the Ministry of Finance; in the Party, by Ferenc Havasi, a secretary of the

Central Committee.[5] The trouble is that this position demoralizes the agencies and their specialists. It is virtually impossible to muster energetic support for a policy in which even its representatives do not believe. And the less anybody believes in it, the more difficult it becomes to postpone measures which would satisfy the ever more pressing needs.

The other possibility is to take this plan seriously, but to give a green light to investments and something of value to the population as well. The weakness of the Faluvégi-Hetényi-Havasi line lies in the fact that until the end of 1984 there were no spokesmen either in the Party leadership or in the government for lifting the restrictions on budgetary spending, today there are some in both. This position is represented most forcefully in the government by Imre Kapoli and in the Party leadership by Károly Grósz, the Budapest Party secretary. Kapolyi, the Minister of Industry,[6] acts as the advocate of big company interests; Grósz[7] is trying to forge an alliance between the Party apparatus tired of its unpopularity, and the population which pleads for stable prices, higher wages, and well-functioning public utilities. His vocabulary also contains such key words of anti-market ideology as "order," "discipline," "organization," and "execution of directives." If the Grósz-Kapolyi line succeeded, in the short run its accelerated spending and increased money supply would cheer up everybody. Unfortunately, its outcome is predictable: such an adventure in growth would lead to the same result as Gierek's[8] policies did in Poland of the '70s—to economic collapse.

5 The Minister of Finance was, at the time, István Hetényi. President of the State Planning Bureau was Lajos Faluv Égi. The first was relieved from office in December 1986; the second was dismissed in June 1987 in an attempt by Kádár to consolidate his power by sacrificing his aides, one after the other. At the same time, Havasi was demoted to first secretary of the Budapest party committee, a position he lost in 1988, after he had been voted out of the Central Committee by the extraordinary conference of the HSWP.
6 László Kapolyi had to relinquish his post as Minister of Industry in 1989.
7 Károly Grósz (1930–   ) has been a professional party functionary since the early 1950s. In the late '70s and the early '80s, he was first secretary of the Borsod county committee of the HSWP. Supported by Romanov, then secretary of the CPSU and chief rival of Gorbachev, he came to Budapest in December 1984 to become first secretary of the party committee of the capital. Through 1986 and 1987, as a leading spokesman of the party conservatives he attacked economic reform, pleaded for central command, discipline, and order, and defended the regime's performance in the years of Stalinism. He suddenly changed course, however, when he was nominated for Prime Minister in June 1987. In May 1988, he successfully ran for the office of General Secretary. In November of the same year, he relinquished his post of Prime Minister to Miklós Németh, a secretary of the Central Committee since 1987.
8 Edward Gierek (1913–   ), General Secretary of the Polish United Workers' Party between 1970 and 1980, was dismissed after the conclusion of the Gdansk agreement, following a vigorous strike movement in August 1980. Subsequently he was expelled from the party.

One of the alternatives is slow decline and perpetual demoralization; another is stirred-up hopes ending in catastrophe. Is there a third alternative? Is there another course of economic action apart from the one which the two factions within the leadership—the guardians of equilibrium, on the one hand, and the partisans of growth, on the other—try to impose on the country at each other's expense? There is such an alternative: that of announcing a fast-moving and decisive reform of the economic mechanism; of making clear that the Hungarian economy's primary objective is to catch up with the world market and that its dependence on COMECON[9] should be loosened. Appropriate measures should be enacted to ensure the organizational conditions for world-market cooperation. A real turnabout in economic policy is necessary, including the redevelopment of industries with great raw material and energy needs. Having done this, the necessary change in the export-import structure could take place more quickly, and the dangers associated with borrowing from foreign creditors could be reduced. Such a program could lay the foundation for a growth which could really take off in a few years, a growth involving structural transformation.

It is true that the execution of a program like this involves considerable political risks in the short run. For one, it would not make the Soviet leaders very happy. The bulk of the Party apparatus would, most likely, resist it, and influential industry leaders would also protest it. And since such a program would result in temporary unemployment and make it even more difficult to keep inflation in check, it would not be easy to win the support of that segment of the population which is employed in the manufacturing and service industries. It is certain that without political reforms—without a trade union controlled by the rank and file, without greater freedom of the press, without marked democratization of the representative bodies, without improvement of the individual's legal security—such economic reform cannot win societal support. The implementation of political reforms, however, would actually increase the political risks involved.

So it is no wonder that János Kádár,[10] known for his cautiousness, made it unmistakably clear in 1983-84 that there was not going to be a second reform, that he was not willing to set off on the path suggested by reform economists. In his traditional manner, however, he did not commit himself to the enemies of the reform nor did he take a stance in the struggle between those who represent the economic policy of equilibrium and those who stand for growth. Kádár continued his tactical maneuvering between currents and cliques, giving a little bit to everybody without taking away too much from anybody.

9 See note 7 in "The Present Crisis and its Origins" in this volume.
10 See note 3 in "The End and the Beginning" in this volume.

To the reformists, instead of the "reform of reform" he gave "continued gradual development" of the economic and political system; to the opponents of reform the demagoguery of anti-enterprise rhetoric. To court the favor of those who urge accelerated growth he announced a new period of capital accumulation and individual consumption, but was quick to add that this could come only if the economy's performance improved. He agreed that a positive trade balance was still a priority, but added that improving the standard of living was a priority as well.

The problem is that it has become increasingly difficult to reconcile all these conflicting priorities. It has become more and more difficult to give a little concession to one side without making the other side incensed. It has become increasingly difficult to create an appearance that the central power, which is maneuvering among the various groups who are wrangling with each other, represents a well-grounded, farsighted policy. The maneuvering more and more appears to be nothing else but vacillation. More and more people think that Kádár is unable to adapt himself to the new situation: that his time is up.

The measures and events are without direction:[11] on the one hand, tax laws discriminating against private enterprises are being enacted; on the other, the decentralization of the banking system is underway.[12] The economic police becomes more active,[13] while a bankruptcy law is under consideration.[14] Leaders of the Party's agit-prop department are attacking the media ("We need a media which informs the people about our achievements."), but there is no sign that the unusually critical voices are about to subside. The tentative reform measures only make the conflicts more visible, but are not suitable to cure them.

Thus the 1985 reform of company management, dismantling of mammoth companies, and making the tax system more uniform could not transform the companies into successfully competitive market entities without restricting the market supervisory functions of the government. Nevertheless, it was more than enough to make a large number of company directors and regional Party organs grumble nervously. Actually, in its wake only a small number of old

---

11 The statutes in question discriminate against state firms which enter into contractual relationships with private enterprises.

12 In 1987, four commercial banks were established outside of the framework of the Hungarian National Bank, with the aim of separating investment banking from macroeconomic monetary policies.

13 Economic police are a special section within the Ministry of the Interior, set up in the early '80s. Its campaign-like, arbitrary interventions into economic activities help create an atmosphere of insecurity around the private sector and the enterprising state firm managers.

14 The bankruptcy law was adopted in 1987. It was intended to provide a legal framework for selling out loss-producing companies.

directors were replaced (by November 30, 1985 only 17 out of 370; *Heti Világgazdaság*, November 30, 1985, p. 54). Still the introduction of elections for company directors has made their positions more insecure and has made it more difficult for the Party to exercise its right of investiture. On the other hand, in some cases the director-bashers also had to realize that while they had theoretically gotten voting rights, they could not really exercise them. (Although Róbert Burgent, the director of the Bábolna State Farm, had been voted down, he kept his post anyway; and his is not the only such case. The same thing happened in the wake of election reform for the National Assembly; *Beszélő*, #13–14, 1985). Discontent may be voiced with an increased frequency, but not in forms which would channelize and dampen it.

"Troops of Weary Seekers . . . "

There are numerous signs of growing exasperation. The stormy Party meetings before the Party congress were one such sign. The outburst of passions was such a surprise to the leadership that it found it advisable to suspend the "how-successful-we-are" propaganda which had been dominant since the spring of 1984 and to transform the congress into an orchestrated grievance day. Then came the elections for the National Assembly, the fights at the nominating meetings, and the unusually high number who voted against the candidates or expressed disapproval by not voting at all.[15] Next was the plebiscite, administered according to units of public administration, on a settlement-development tax.[16] More than 50% of Hungarian communities rejected the new tax. In Budapest only three of the twenty-two districts voted for it. The general secretary of the People's Patriotic Front[17] was correct in saying that the majority voted against it because it was "irritated" that "in many settlements the objectives of development were determined, not by the interests of the population, but

---

15 On the 1985 parliamentary elections, see "The Fall Session of the National Assembly" in this volume.

16 Settlement-development tax is an annual contribution by citizens to local community investments. Considered by the party leadership as a minor issue, it was proposed for popular vote with the hope of reinforcing the state's shrinking authority. However, the vote, arranged in 1986 in somewhat chaotic circumstances, turned out to be instead a vote of no confidence in the government. Attempts at fraud contributed to stirring up anti-state and anti-party sentiments.

17 Imre Pozsgay was General Secretary of PPF during 1983–88. Since 1988, he has been a member of the ruling Politburo and Minister of State. On PPF see note 6 of "Can 1956 be Forgotten?" in this volume.

by the logic of the apparatus" (*Figyelö*, November 28, 1985, p. 3). This year the preparations for the trade union congress continued this trend. The atmosphere of the meetings was dominated by the same impatient dissatisfaction which characterized the preparatory meetings of the Party congress a year before.

This spreading exasperation gives weight and importance to the emergence of the small but notable groups of intellectuals who try to initiate a broad social movement either by expanding or loosening the existing institutional framework, or by stepping beyond it. These groups sense correctly that the readiness of the public has grown considerably since the 60's and the 70's. They are also correct in their belief that the population trusts the government's word less than it did before the crisis. They sense correctly that there is a growing need to oversee the government's decisions and to have a say in matters of critical importance.

But they may sense something else as well: *The growing activity of the public is not fueled by hope and self-confidence, but rather by despair over the government's ineptitude and by fury over its arrogance.* The vast majority of the people no longer believe that there is a solution to the present crisis, a solution which they could reach on their own. Who can tell exactly how much of this gloom can be attributed to the long-run effects of the shock of 1956, to the reinforcement this effect received in August 1968 and December 1981, to the far-reaching psychological impact of the 1960–63 consolidation, to the paralyzing circumstances of the global political situation or to the lack of social imagination? The majority, in any case, does not think of political action. Millions are grumbling, but only 20 to 30 thousand people even take advantage of the election or Party and trade union meetings to express what is on their minds. Furthermore, there is no continuity between these occasions: each time everything starts from point zero.

And the number of those who are willing to go beyond the opportunities offered by such occasions, to try to put active pressure on the authorities with means of their own (e.g., signing petitions), is not more than a few thousand. That number decreases to a few hundred when it comes to systematic, target-oriented action. Moreover, this tiny nucleus is as pessimistic as the majority. The environmentalists[18] do not believe that they will succeed in preventing the construction of the Danube dam. The reform

---

18 The environmentalist movement lacked, at the time, formal structures. Its main center was the Danube Circle, a loose coalition of 20 to 50 people. See note 14 in "The End and the Beginning" in this volume.

economists[19] do not believe that they will succeed in convincing the government about the introduction of necessary reforms. The populists[20] do not believe that the Magyars of Romania can be saved. SZETA, the Foundation for Help to the Poor,[21] does not believe that it can force the leadership to implement a more human and effective social policy.

This is the dilemma of the activist minority. If it goes so far that larger groups of people cannot see the point of following it, the machinery of oppression may be set in motion: its groups become liquidated as in the case of "Dialógus,"[22] or isolated, as in the case of the Democratic Opposition gathering around *samizdats*.[23] If, on the other hand, the minority stays within those forms of action which are acceptable to larger groups of the population, then it, by definition, forsakes the means of putting effective pressure on the government. "Soft" resistance is of no concern to the authorities; on "hard" resistance they crack down.

This is why the feeling is so common: "Something has to be done; nothing can be done." This is why every activist group is experimenting with putting up a resistance "soft" enough not to provoke a crackdown but "hard" enough not to be ignored by the authorties. This is why every action has a built-in tendency to withdraw as soon as the power apparatus shows its fist.

19 A trend in opinion rather than a movement, economic reformism played a significant political role in the mid-'80s. See "From Reform to Continued Development" in this volume.

20 Populists are a group of Hungarian writers primarily preoccupied with what they call "issues of national destiny," like the loss of one-third of the ethnic Hungarian population to neighboring counties after the Versailles peace treaty concluding World War I, the decline in the birthrate within the borders of post-Versailles Hungary, and the cultural and social gap between Budapest and the countryside. Launched in the 1930s, the populist movement originally tried to link national questions to the cause of the landless agrarian population. In it, peasant radicalism combined with the hope that Hungary's particular history, belonging neither to the "East" nor to the "West," offered a third way between capitalism and socialism.

21 Foundation for the Help to the Poor (SZETA), was started in 1979–80 by people belonging to the Democratic Opposition with the aim of marshaling support for the rapidly-growing underclasses and focusing public attention on their lot. Its activities were constantly harassed by the police so that after 1982 it had to restrict its activities. It succeeded, however, in consolidating itself as an officially-recognized organization after the fall of Kádár, in 1989.

22 "Dialógus," an independent peace movement launched in 1982, primarily by students, was liquidated in 1983 by administrative measures. Some of its leaders then joined the official Peace Council, others retreated from public activity, while still others sought out surviving independent movements like the Danube Circle or the Democratic Opposition.

23 The Democratic Opposition, born in the mid-1970s, was a loose movement of intellectuals who gathered around various *samizdat* publications (*Beszélő, Hírmondó, Demokrata, Égtájak Között*). Its heritage is continued, under the conditions of an incipient multiparty system of the late '80s, by the Alliance of Free Democrats, a party on the liberal-to-social democratic end of the political spectrum.

In all probability only some sudden, horizon-opening event could cure this all-prevailing pessimism. For example, if the Soviet leadership entered upon a new course in its Eastern European policy, as it did in the spring of 1953 and in 1956;[24] or if in the domestic struggle for succession, a committed reform coalition emerged as the victor. It is no accident that a segment of the politically active public is so attentive to Gorbachev's moves and to the turn of fortune of those domestic leaders who are considered progressive. The people are waiting for a sign, for unmistakable proof that this time democratic movements will not end according to the old recipe.

But the longer we wait for that favorable sign, the more unfavorable the chances of economic and political recovery become. The price to be paid for it keeps rising and, alas, it is not even clear whether we will ever enjoy a recovery. Ought we not try instead, like Baron Müchausen in the fairy tale, to pull ourselves out of the swamp by our own hair? Ought we not try to bring about the necessary psychological change on our own? Let us imagine that the workers of a large factory are unwilling to remain without having their interests represented; they oust the union leaders—chosen in manipulated elections—and elect their own leadership; they call on the workers at other plants to follow their example and form horizontal contacts between the local trade union committees. Or let us imagine that influential representatives of the intelligentsia step in front of the state and the nation with an analysis of the situation and an action program.

The latter has a better chance of occurring since the intelligentsia has access to means of expression and communication and is also equipped with some political experience, while the Hungarian working class has been deprived of both since 1957.[25] But it is, of course, even easier to picture the country as a driverless wagon rolling unstoppably downhill, the vibration loosening nuts and bolts, as people and belongings fall left and right.

Hegel once wrote: "Every nation has a government it deserves." A part of this statement applies to us as well: by stating the government's responsibility, we cannot refuse to accept our own. The leadership and its agencies are the main culprits; but if society constantly points at the authorities instead of taking its fate into its own hands, it will also share the guilt for its predicament.

24 In March 1953 Stalin died. Following his death, a virtual general amnesty was declared and a new economic policy attempting to restore equilibrium between the investment sector and the consumption sector was initiated. At the 20th congress of the CPSU, in February 1956, the so-called personality cult was condemned; Khrushchev in a secret speech denounced the dictator's crimes.
25 It was in the fall of 1957 that the last remnants of the 1956 revolution, the industrial workers' councils, were liquidated.

Kádár Must Go

Kádár Must Go[1]

A turning point

Consensus has come to an end.[2] It has suddenly dawned on the country that those in power are not going to fulfill their promises. The consequences of economic decline[3] are already beginning to affect even the blue-collar elite and the middle stratum of intellectuals. The public no longer believes that there is any sense in making ever-newer sacrifices.

The leadership is wavering. It does not understand why it is unable to turn the worsening trends around. It has not the faintest idea what to do about the sudden tide of dissatisfaction. It has less and less control of its own actions and is increasingly unable to conceal its internal division.

1 Originally published as part of a program ("Social Contract. Conditions of Overcoming the Political Deadlock") proposed by the editorial board of *Beszélő* in the first half of 1987.
2 "Consensus" was the key work used by the Kádár leadership and its propaganda apparatus to describe the political atmosphere in the country from the early '60s through the late '80s.
3 In 1985, at the 13th congress of the HSWP, the leadership promised economic recovery starting in 1986. Instead of triggering a new growth process, however, its policies resulted only in doubling the country's gross foreign debts (from $8 billion at the end of 1984 to $16 billion towards the end of 1986). The imminent threat of an insolvency crisis forced the government to announce new austerity measures in the late fall of 1986. Until then, restrictions did not hit hard on the middle strata. The new price hikes, however, have cut deeply into the household budgets of both the blue-collar elite and the white-collar strata. It was this turn which suddenly convinced the public that the leadership was not in control of the situation.

The apparatuses are uneasy. They sense the mounting anger and find that their customary techniques are not always sufficient to keep the people in line. And they are missing their proven agents: prominent personalities outside the party are withdrawing their support of official policy, and the party's rank and file is becoming unmanagable.

The general dissatisfaction personifies its target. Just as earlier the country associated the successes of the consolidation period with János Kádár, now it is associating with him the failures at the end of that period. The general secretary's popularity is declining even faster than the value of the forint. There is just one thing on which everyone, from blue-collar worker to party cadre, is in agreement: Kádár must go.

New faces or new policy?

János Kádár has been the symbol of the golden middle road in Hungary. He, in contrast with Rákosi, has not attempted to force on the people grandiose programs for society's transformation. And unlike Imre Nagy, he has been unwilling to accept curbs on the Communist Party's rule. Holding a monopoly of power, he has avoided encroachment of his interests by any group capable of voicing discontent. And he has allowed everyone to find compensation for one's losses, wherever possible.

The country—tortured by Stalinism, disappointed in the irresistible force of the 1956 uprising, exsanguinated and worn weary during the years of reprisal—approved of Kádár's policy of consolidation, longing for a secure and peaceful life. In exchange, it accepted that the party ruled in the name of the people, and the apparatus ruled in the name of the party's rank and file. This was the so-called consensus.

But by now nobody believes that social conflicts can be avoided by deferring drastic decisions. Caution is seen as inability to act, secrecy as the concealment of failures, the monopoly of power as an obstacle to resolving the crisis.

Kádár bears personal responsibility for the leadership's inertia. He was the one who announced in 1983 that there would be no second reform. In 1984, he was the one who insisted on the seventh five-year plan's irresponsible program for reviving the economy. In 1985, he orchestrated the party congress that simultaneously promised more investment, more consumption, improvement of our balance of payments, and more moderate rates of inflation. He played a decisive role in concealing the magnitude of the problems from society, and barring the public from the debates on finding a way to resolve them. There will be no meaningful change when the Minister of Finance and the chairman of the State Planning Board rather than Kádár, are retired[4] or as long as "our policy" is sound, and there are mistakes only in its "implementation."

But Kádár's departure in itself would not solve anything. If his successors attempt to correct the "mistakes" of the past few years by reverting to the party's policy "proven over 30 years," then the crisis will run its course. We will be left to vegetate amidst ever-worse living conditions. And in the background there will be the specter of catastrophe: the state could become insolvent within a few years, and there may come a period of power cuts, endless queues, and plunging real incomes.

Actual collapse does not even have to occur: the constant threat of collapse is in itself sufficient to make the situation untenable.

We need a radical political change.

From a tacit consensus to an explicit social contract

There is no simple solution to the Hungarian economy's present problems. It is not enough to say, as it was said in 1953, that if the artificial forcing of investment in heavy industry were stopped, there would immediately be more for consumers. Abandonment of the spendthrift industrial policy would also adversely affect the population in the short term. Even the best program of consolidation and growth would produce temporary unemployment and a decline of the living standard, and would create tensions between social strata, industries, and districts.

What could the leadership do about these conflicts? One possible course of action would be to attempt to compensate the masses with social, national, or racial demagoguery. Launch order-restoration, mobilization, and centralization drives in combination with political hysteria: a sort of northwestern Romania. But we see where that leads.

Another course of action would be to enforce the requirements of a market economy and to suppress with an iron hand any manifestation of society's dissatisfaction: a police state in combination with free competition, a Hungarian version of South Korea. But Hungary is not in Southeast Asia. Here the very institutions for whose grip the market must be pried would harden back into dictatorship.

The third and final course is to proceed from the breakdown of the tacit consensus to open negotiations: a social contract instead of a mobilizing or

4 See note 5 of "Troops of Weary Seekers . . ." in this volume.

disarming dictatorship, working out of the compromises with the participation of those concerned.

There will be no national renewal without a social contract.

Don't just grumble, demand!

But a compromise requires partners. During the past 30 years, the HSWP has done everything possible to prevent any interest group or opinion-forming circle from becoming a partner. Now, in the hours of political uncertainty, the party does not have anybody to negotiate with, even if it wanted to. It cannot reach an agreement with the designated representatives of the strata concerned, because society would not honor such an agreement. Only those below can demonstrate that they regard their spokesmen as their leaders and heed them. But they must bestir themselves to do so.

The intellectuals already have a politically active core—economists, social scientists, journalists, and writers—that is pressing for a dialogue. On their own initiative, several groups of experts have come out with comprehensive reform proposals. They are not satisfied with merely placing their ideas at the leadership's disposal. Their writings are circulated freely and are debated in research institutes, professional societies, clubs, universities, and private homes.

However, the immediate audience and support of these experts are only the intellectuals, for the time being. There is merely growing dissatisfaction within wider circles of the population. They are not thinking in terms of alternatives and are not presenting demands.

Admittedly, the public mood is full of expectation. But the suspense cannot last. Unless it changes into initiative, it will be replaced sooner or later by resignation. And then there will remain only the worst possible course of action.

The key political question today is whether the termination of the tacit consensus will be followed by pressure of an explicit social contract?

It is not enough to grumble about the consequences of a bad policy. You have to demand another policy.

How?

There are many things dissuading people from starting to present demands including pessimism: the feeling that the economy's downward slide cannot be halted; reform has lost its credibility: everything is supposedly being reformed since 1979, yet nothing has changed except for living conditions becoming ever worse; and there is a sense of the power structure's resistance: regardless of what "we" consider good, "they" do what they like.

Pessimism can be overcome as long as hope is not extinguished. Dumping the old leadership might permit distinguishing between reform and mere tinkering with reform. But what can be done to overcome the power structure's resistance?

Indeed, the regime is designed to isolate, disarm, and punish any demand from below. But note that the system does not function the same way in a crisis as it does under normal conditions. The wavering and divided leadership and the uneasy apparatuses are unable to sweep aside every initiative.

Any forum will do where those below can have their say. The briefing sessions that deputies of the National Assembly or council members hold for their constituents are good for this purpose. Programs sponsored by the People's Patriotic Front[5] or the TIT [Society for the Dissemination of Scientific Knowledge],[6] as well as the clubs, political seminars, and open party meetings[7] are good. But best of all are the public forums at work: the production conference, the shop meeting, and the meetings of the trade-union and party locals. Invite the country's leaders to the factories and institutions. Bombard the headquarters of the political and interest organizations with resolutions put into writing. Respond to the announcements of the Central Committee,[8] the SZOT [National Council of Trade Unions],[9] and the government. Demand that the materials of the reform debates be made available. Invite the authors. Adopt standpoints on their

---

5 See note 22 of "Troops of Weary Seekers . . ." in this volume.
6 TIT, or Society for the Dissemination of Scientific Knowledge is an adult teaching institution created in 1949. Its original aim was to disseminate atheist and socialist propaganda. Since the 1960s, however, its militant anti-religious and anti-capitalist stance gradually faded into oblivion.
7 Open party meetings are meetings of local HSWP organizations which non-party people are free to attend.
8 Central Committee is the supreme deliberative body of HSWP with more than one hundred members. Between 1956 and 1983 it did not convene more than four times a year. Executive power lies with the Politburo and the Secretariat (The latter, however, was abolished as a separate body in 1988).
9 Between 1945 and 1948, trade union pluralism and autonomy was suppressed. Professional unions were consolidated into huge "branch" unions and these, in turn, were subjected to the command of a central body, the National Council of Trade Unions (SZOT). It was through this body that the Communist party managed to use the unions as transmission belts to its policies and as instruments for repressing working class militancy.

proposals. Elaborate concepts regarding the future of your workplace. And organize reform clubs at work.

We have our elected representatives, and it is their duty to represent us. If the trade-union secretary fails to stand up for the membership's interests, or if the party secretary comes into conflict with his constituents, he can be recalled. Let these elected officials feel that now they are more dependent on those below.

Note that the prospects of organizing cooperation have improved. People cannot be intimidated or dissuaded as readily as before. And if conquest of the official framework fails, it can be by-passed. The scope for civil disobedience has broadened in recent years. Consider such examples as the mass protest against paying the [settlement development contribution] or the shop-level strikes that ended in a negotiated settlement or the thousands who have demonstrated on March 15 every year in the 1980s.[10]

Publicize the initiatives from below. Instead of just submitting demands upward, send them also to the press and to the organizations at related workplaces. Invite outsiders to your meetings. Hold joint consultations with the representatives of others in the same situation. Try to publish an information bulletin, regularly, if possible, but at least occasionally.

Those in power will enter into a dialogue only if they find that intellectuals are not the only ones with whom they have to negotiate.

What to demand?

According to the present leadership, we consume more than what we produce. But would it not be closer to the truth to say that economic policy is sinking more into investment projects, which will never pay off, than what it has been able to take away from the consumers?

Until the leadership admits its responsibility for the evolved situation and eliminates the causes of wasteful capital formation, it will be in the workers' interest to attempt to wring higher wages and benefits from it. Until then

10 March 15 was the date of the 1848 democratic revolution. In 1971, 1972, and throughout the 1980's illegal student demonstrations commemorated that event. In the early '70s, many of the demonstrators were arrested and some were sentenced to prison terms of 1 to 2 years. Through the 1980's, brutal police interventions, preventive detentions, and beatings of demonstrators were still the rule. In about 1985, the March 15 demonstrations became identified with the Democratic Opposition. In 1989, March 15 was declared a national holiday, and the government recognized opposition organizations' right to demonstrate.

the only answer society will be able to give to appeals to economize will be: "They cannot squander what we have already eaten."

But we must realize that higher wages and benefits will not help us in the long run. There is a price to be paid for the crisis, regardless of who is responsible for it, but it is not irrelevant how we pay that price.

Either there will be a program to stabilize and reform the economy and society will assume temporary losses for the sake of restoring market equilibrium, or there will be no economic stabilization and reform, and we will have to bear the consequences of the decline.

Since we have to pay anyhow, it is in our national interest that we pay for the reform, rather than for having missed it. The reform would mean catching up with the world economy's developing regions. Missing the reform would mean sinking among the stagnating countries of the Third World.

What are the prerequisites for catching up?

- Equal rights for the various forms of ownership in the economy's market sphere. Legal assurances for establishing private businesses and for private capital investment. Uniform tax rules, credit conditions, and business and foreign trade opportunities for every type of business organization and every enterprise.

- Restriction of demand through monetary control rather than through the arbitrary administrative withdrawal of income.

- Curtailment of official tinkering with the price and wage mechanisms.

- Development of a money market and capital market, and substantial reduction of the proportion of central (nonmarket) investments.

- Dismantling of the proliferating monopolies, the breakup of enterprises of unwarranted large size, and the establishment of many enterprises of small and medium size.

- Instead of administrative compulsion to export and restriction of imports, a flexible price policy in the interest of balance-of-trade equilibrium.

- Abandonment of the program of COMECON[11] self-sufficiency, and an opening to the world economy. Within COMECON, the expansion of business relations between enterprises, and turning away from the economically disadvantageous cooperations brought about politically.

Can such a reform program find wide support in Hungary? In our opinion, it can. Considering its planks in themselves, very many people find most appealing.

But there are also numerous reservations. Resistance to reform is generated in part by interests (and not only the interests associated with power). It is not clear how much inflation, reduction of income, and unemployment the reform would bring at its start; certain industries, districts, trades, and plants would be especially hard hit. And in part resistance to reform is generated by principles (and not merely the ones professed by the power structure): by a kind of ideal of equality that does not tolerate additional income from entrepreneurship or profit from investment, and by a kind of ideal of economic security which cannot be reconciled with temporary unemployment or fluctuating real income.

However, such misgivings will weaken:

- if the population sees that the state, before restricting consumption, has suspended all nonessential or questionable investment projects (development of the Yamburg gas deposits, the Bös[Gabcikovo]-Nagymaros dams,[12] and defense spending);

- if the drive to economize includes also proportional cuts in the administrative apparatuses, beginning with the party apparatuses;

- if the private sector, once the legal guaranties for entrepreneurship are in place, becomes one of the principal employers of the labor force shed by state industry; and

- if, in addition to the compulsion to succeed in the marketplace, the interest-representing organizations also begin to exert pressure.

However, misgivings regarding economic reform cannot be dispelled entirely, because reform is not possible without consolidation that will involve painful restructuring.

---

11 On COMECON, see note 7 in "The Present Crisis and its Origins" in this volume.
12 On the Bös-Nagymaros project see note 14 of "The End and the Beginning" in this volume.

But even those who long to be back under the protection of the income-withdrawing and -redistributing state agree that political changes are desirable. It is unnecessary to convince anyone outside the power structure that:

- lies in the mass media must cease;

- the practice of adopting decisions without consulting the people, and then of making them pay for the wrong decisions, must cease;

- the trade unions must cease representing the state against employees; and

- the mockery of civil rights must cease.

By relying on this consensus, it is possible also to gain support for the cause of economic reform.

The program of economic reform must be based on a program of political change.

Outlines of a political program

Hungary last received a political program in 1956. We share the opinion that history has not made obsolete the basis demands of October 1956:

- Political pluralism and representative democracy in government;

- Self-management at the workplace and self-government; and

- National self-determination and neutrality in foreign policy.

However, these demands cannot be placed on the agenda in the country's present political situation, which will probably not change significantly for a long time to come. But the conditions have improved for similar compromise solutions that the remnants of the democratic parties and the workers' councils proposed in November 1956.[13]

13 On the compromise proposals of the November 1956 revolution see "The 1956–57 Restoration in a Thirty-Year Perspective" in this volume.

After all, what we have today is not a defeated revolution fighting its rear-guard action against a restorational regime that is settling in. The development since consolidation also counts: mass consumption has gained acceptance; the patterns of market behavior are more acceptable than before; several collectives of Western orientation have been formed in the social sciences; the official ideology has been relaxed, and specialized knowledge has gained in prestige; and the gap between the new generation of cadres and the professional elite has narrowed. External conditions have also improved: Hungary is more open to the West than 30 years ago; the possibility of Soviet intervention has declined; and the Soviet Union's leaders are more prone to toleration.

Starting out from these premises, we are considering ways to shape the growing dissatisfaction into goal-oriented political demands. We accept, must accept as given, one-party rule and certain executive prerogatives of the party. We are investigating how we could finally raise anew, within this framework, the basic political questions that have been deferred continually since the revolution's suppression.

For it is time to raise them anew.

We are proposing compromise solutions that fall far short of what we aspire to. But these compromises would produce changes perceptible now in the relationship between the power structure and society. And their implementation would permit further orderly progress toward a democratic, self-governing,and independent Hungary.

We propose the adoption of the following slogans:

- Constitutional checks on party rule, a sovereign National Assembly, and an accountable government

- Freedom of the press entrenched in laws

- Legal protection for employees, representation of interests, and freedom of association

- Social security and an equitable social welfare policy

- Civil rights

After the Fall Session of the National Assembly

After the Fall Session of the National Assembly

Since 1948[1] no session of the National Assembly was awaited with such anxious expectation as the fall session of 1987. Of course nobody thought that the government's fate would be decided in the Parliament. Nevertheless the suddenly accelerated political crisis noticeably expanded the representative's sphere of maneuvering.

The stakes were high as well. The country's leaders were set for the second time in ten years to avert the nightmare of state bankruptcy which they themselves had induced.[2] The government's program of stabilization submitted to the National Assembly anticipated higher inflation and forecast a decrease in real wages. The tax reform, also submitted for debate, proposed direct income reduction and reorganization of the income structure at the expense of large families, pensioners, and those employees forced to moonlight.

---

1 The so-called year of turn lasted from the fall of 1947 through the summer of 1948. It was during that time that the banks, factories, and commercial organizations still in private hands, as well as parochial schools, were nationalized; that the Social Democratic Party was forced to merge with the Hungarian Communist Party; that opposition parties were wiped out; and that Hungary signed a treaty of mutual assistance with the Soviet Union, laying the foundations of its formal dependence on Russia. After 1948 the National Assembly was only a ceremonial institution, and until 1986–87 it had no say in important political or economic questions.

2 The first meek attempt since the 1972–74 anti-reform turn to marketize the economy took place between 1979 and 1983. The only lasting innovation of this period was the legalization of small private enterprises of up to 12 employees.

Clearly, the National Assembly would decide questions of critical importance. But how did the National Assembly get to the point where something of consequence was expected from it after forty years of make-believe existence?

The beginning

No matter how minor a change the 1983 election law represented, it was enough to break a hole in the wall of state institutions.[3] Through this hole the growing dissatisfaction of the people gushed into the political arena. The 1985 elections provided the first opportunity for relatively large segments of the population to express their wishes and to try to bring under their control the state apparatus.

As a result of the election system's inconsistencies, massive election frauds and instances of intimidation, only two independent candidates managed, in the final count, to persevere all the way to the Parliament.[4] But there were a few even among the official candidates who learned their lesson from the electorate's surge of spirit. It was, then, these official candidates and one of the independents who formed a tiny avant-garde of representatives, who started to speak independently, first on not-explicitly political matters, and even cast an occasional independent vote. Their example encouraged a wider circle of representatives. Some were trying to speak their own voice at least at committee meetings and on a few occasions voted with the avant-garde in legislative matters. At the 1986 spring session the unimaginable did come to pass: in the debate on a law concerning excise taxes the majority voted for an amendment which had been rejected by the Minister of Finance. The substance of the amendment was insignificant politically; the precedent, however, was of extraordinary political significance: it demonstrated that the government can be voted down.

3 Law III of 1983 mandated multiple nominations for each seat in the National Assembly. As a result, in each district at least two candidates had to be named. People's Patriotic Front automatically nominated one candidate; inhabitants of the electoral district gained the right to nominate spontaneously one or more others (in case no spontaneously-presented candidate showed up, it was the task of PPF to nominate the second candidate also).

4 Zoltán Király, a journalist from Szeged, became a member of the National Assembly by defeating a retired local party boss. László Czoma, director of the Keszthely local museum, was elected against massive apparatus resistance, manipulation, and fraud. Note, however, that both representatives were party members. Király was once a member of the Communist Youth League's Csongrád county committee, while Czoma had previously worked in the central party apparatus.

That was already too much for the Party leadership. At the earliest opportunity they ordered a closed session and behind the public's back pushed through a change in the house rules.[5] For a moment it seemed that they did get the National Assembly under their control.

This turned out not to be the case. Before long the parliamentary debates spilled over to the discussion of important political issues.

The crisis widens

By the end of 1986 the government was forced to acknowledge that the budget deficit was twice as big as the original forecast and that the trade balance, instead of an anticipated surplus, showed a 400-million-dollar deficit. It became apparent that the program adopted at the 13th Party congress in 1985 and aimed at stimulating a growth in investment and production was leading to catastrophic results. In spite of this the leadership was still postponing any significant change. During the winter session of the National Assembly the Minister of Finance asked for the approval of a budget which contained the largest deficit to date. That was the moment when some representatives realized that the government was not in control of the worsening economic situation. Two representatives voted against the budget proposal and seven abstained.

In the summer of 1987, after discussion of the budget report, five members voted disapproval of it and the number of abstentions doubled as well. Everything that happened between December and June convinced the legislators that the leadership was helpless and, instead of solving the country's problems, was busy securing its own survival. A few days before the session's opening the Central Committee of the Party held a meeting. The public had expected the election of a new leadership which would at last introduce new policies. Instead, Kádár[6] solidified his position and the old guard simply played musical chairs. Before the budget debate a new

5 The primary aim of modifying the house rules was to reduce representatives' room for maneuvering. Three changes were introduced: 1) It was ordained that a motion to amend a bill under discussion could be introduced only prior to house debate, and the house committee in charge of the given area would first take a stand concerning the drafted amendment. 2) In addition to the existing form of interpellation a new category was introduced: the "question asked by a representative." In this case the Assembly listens to the answer of the cabinet minister but does not vote on it, and the representative does not have the right of rebuttal. 3) It was established that the National Assembly would discuss in two readings only bills pertaining to five-year plans and long-term planning.
6 See note 3 of "The End and the Beginning" in this volume.

price minister was installed. He, Károly Grósz,[7] did not deliver a keynote address and in an unprecedented manner—even by the standards of the last forty years—asked for a vote of confidence to be taken behind closed doors. The country was not to know if one or two representatives abstained or, God forbid, voted "nay."

It is no surprise that the circle of those representatives who felt that the National Assembly must take the initiative widened significantly. Zoltán Király, a representative from Csongrad, expressed the sentiments of this increasing minority when he proposed calling an extraordinary summer session to discuss the situation.[8] This emergency session was intended not only to discuss the government's economic program but also to authorize a special parliamentary committee to work out an alternative program. Subsequently, Dr. Erika Tomsits (Budapest), a medical doctor, took to the floor on a matter of procedure. She objected to the forced modifications of house rules made a year earlier and proposed an amendment for their reversal.

The chair, István Sarlós, in the absence of any better idea, ignored the requirements of valid house regulations and decided not to open the floor for the discussion of these two proposals.

The electorate, the representatives, and power

By that time the entire politically-active public was fully aware of the failure of the leadership's economic policy. The population might have realized the impact of the inevitable belt-tightening measures on the standard of living only some time later but for the planned tax reform. The propaganda campaign for the two new taxes,[9] however, made the otherwise hidden interrelation of the two issues clear. The pillars of political stability, the working class elite and the middle stratum of intellectuals who until now were more or less able to counterbalance their losses through extra work, suddenly realized that they would become absolute losers as well. These measures had not even been introduced when the latent malaise transformed itself into active hostility.

---

7 See note 7 of "Troops of Weary Seekers . . . " in this volume.
8 Király is the most energetic and popular figure of the National Assembly. In the spring of 1988, he was expelled from the Communist party. A year later that decision was cancelled but Király immediately announced that he did not want to be reintegrated into the party's ranks.
9 A personal income tax and a value-added tax were to be introduced.

The leadership reacted to the economic failure and the faltering political stability with increasing hesitation. In the vacuum between the grumbling population and weakened leadership, the political role of the National Assembly gained importance. The representatives were now able to speak more openly than ever before. To get the austerity measures accepted by society the leadership needed an assembly capable of convincing the public that it was staunchly defending the electorate's interests and that it would vote only for the most unavoidable of cuts in consumption.

As the representatives' freedom of speech increased so did the weight of their responsibility. For the public now did expect something from them: either the refusal to sanction additional sacrifices, or the procurement of tangible guarantees that, this time, the acceptance of sacrifices was not going to be in vain.

Let us now see how much the lawmakers managed to accomplish.

"My constituents are full of worry"

The most noticeable novelty of this new situation was that the voices expressing the country's actual mood started to reverberate within the walls of the Parliament. Not only one or two especially daring speakers raised the issue of the growing malaise. The expression of dissatisfaction became the *leitmotif* of the four-day session.

The September 18 issue of *Magyar Nemzet* paraphrases representative Andrásné Szarvas, a quality control manager in a clothing factory (Békés) this way: "She reports that the opinion of her constituents is divided about the government's stabilization program. According to her it is apparent that the people agree with the objectives, but at the same time there is also some mistrust concerning their realization. Some people do not see the guarantees of realizing these objectives and they fear that the transitional period will be prolonged and that this would lead to the reduction of the already-low wages and to a greater-than-anticipated decline in the standard of living." Whether the representative herself used this colorless agit-prop language or the editor-censor toned down the text with expressions like "some mistrust" and "some people" we do not know. In any case the position expressed by Tamás Szabó, division head in a sugar refinery (Fejér), in his interview with the press sounds more authentic: "My constituents from the nine villages of the Ercs district are full of worry, they fear that the inflationary tendencies of the economy may produce an inflation rate which will exceed the forecasted 14–15% inflation many times over. They see the nightmare of a ghastly inflation in Yugoslavia. The people say that they work hard and it is not their fault that the country's economy is in such condition." (*Heti Világgazdaság*, September 26).

But no matter what language Mrs. Andrásné Szarvas and many of her colleagues used, their message was unmistakably clear. Even the speakers representing the government had no choice but to indicate that they had received the message. Even representatives like Imre Szabó, head of the Hajdu-Bihar local government, who clung to the practices of the last thirty years, spoke this way: "Here and there the citizens' trust got worn a little bit, because the last fifteen years produced a larger-than-expected number of unrealized hopes. This is the source of doubt—in the majority of the people only doubt, not mistrust—as to whether there will be enough strength to consistently realize the objectives." (*Magyar Nemzet*, September 17). János Kádár himself spoke in the same defensive tone: "It was also said that public opinion is divided. I know that this is really true. But I also do know the opinion of many people, of workers, peasants who say: 'If we have to make sacrifices, let us make them; but let us bring order to our affairs.' This is also the opinion of the public at large." (*Népszabadság*, September 17) One of the sides was clearly on the defensive. Still the other side did not go on the offensive.

"The government program: a *fait accompli* without alternatives"

It is not the number of "nay" votes that I find too few, although they also fell short of expectations. The outrageous move of István Sarlós in declaring the unanimous approval of the government program without calling on those opposed, concealed no more than one or two negative votes and four or five abstentions. Neither the one "nay" and the five abstentions cast in the debate on value-added tax, nor the ten "nays" and twenty-one abstentions cast during the roll-call on personal income tax, express the atmosphere which dominated the discussions of the parliamentary committees and caucuses between June and September. The government made far fewer concessions than the number of supporting votes it won back. In addition, its most important concession proved to be nothing more than a simple bookkeeping trick: it accepted the increase in standard deductions for families with three or more children, but in order to maintain the same level of tax revenues it cut back those social programs which benefit the very same stratum of people. And this was not the worst of it. The increase in standard deductions benefits those large families whose income is over the minimum taxable, i.e. 48,000 forints a year. The reduction or abolishment of social programs, on the other hand, affects those families who make even less. Thus the government made a concession in the budget proposal at the expense of the most destitute people. The Minister of Finance did not make a secret that this was intentional: "We do not give concessions to the lumpen." (*Népszabadság*, September 28)

I am not saying that the National Assembly did not debate the essential issues. The representatives criticized in a variety of ways both the government's stabilization program and particular aspects of the tax reform. With regard to the government program the following issues were raised:

- a comprehensive economic reform is still not in sight; the tax reform, if separated from the package of wage, price, currency, and monetary reforms, will not bring the expected results;

- the plans for industrial development exceed the budget's capacity, while the rationale for a number of major investments is questionable;

- the state support for non-profitable companies, as well as the budgetary expenditures earmarked for the state apparatus, the military, and social organizations, must be reduced.

Concerning the tax reform several representatives raised such issues as these:

- the new system of taxation penalizes large families;

- the life of those in the middle-income bracket, who are forced to moonlight to maintain their modest standard of living, will become unfairly difficult;

- a senior citizen who has to complement his pension by working will be at an unfair disadvantage compared to a retiree whose pension provides an adequate income.

Finally the necessity of reforming the political system was also mentioned. The representatives spoke about:

- reform of public administration and the establishment of local self-governments;

- reform in government accountability;

- and, in great detail, necessary changes in the National Assembly.

The parliamentary debate left untouched almost none of the issues which were addressed in public discussions of the recent past. If we disregard the legal regulation of the Party's status—and the time is obviously not ripe to raise this issue in the National Assembly—there were only three important demands which were not mentioned at all:

- the issue of the dangers of unemployment; nobody urged the implementation of social and legal protection for those citizens who are sentenced to unemployment;

- the necessity of strengthening the individual's civil rights vis-à-vis the state;

- and the problem of free association and assembly.

I do miss the discussion of these issues, but it is not their absence which makes me deem the representatives' conduct vacillating. What troubles me is that *the majority of representatives who did criticize the government and did submit proposals did it without the conviction that they could link their "aye" votes to certain conditions and demands.* "The program is a *fait accompli* without alternatives; and the representatives debate only the timing, the forms and the applicable methods of its realization" said László Nagy, president of a collective farm in Borsod. (*Magyar Nemzet*, September 18)

It appears that the representatives gave up on the fight in advance.

But why?

István Avar[10] told in the radio program "168 hours" (September 19) that during the debate on the government's program he was agonizing until the very last moment and that only the closing address of the prime minister convinced him to say "aye."

It is certain that Károly Grósz made quite an impression on the representatives. He understood that one of the reasons for the bad political atmosphere was the ineptitude of the leadership. He managed to distinguish himself from his colleagues on the defensive. He presented himself as the man of change, who at last speaks openly, who is not the mouthpiece of the anonymous apparatus. Rather, he presented himself as

---

10 István Avar, a well-known actor, is a member of the HSWP.

an individual in his own right; who not only tolerates, but prefers, contrary opinions; who is open to dialogue and does not postpone uncomfortable decisions, does not shrink back from conflicts and, above all, acts without hesitation. His behavior made the representatives feel that when they cast a vote of confidence for the government, they said "yes" not to the old leadership but to change.

Let us take note, however, that while the prime minister carefully crafted the *style* of his public performance, the *content* of his policies remained obscure. He did not identify himself with that Károly Grósz who had entered the arena of national politics in 1984–1985 and also failed to clarify the difference between the old and the new Károly Grósz.

At the beginning Grósz appeared as the spokesman for continuity with the pre-1956 period, for order and discipline, for a centralized economy, for accelerated accumulation, and for the crusade against "profiteers and speculators." The remnants of his old rhetoric can be detected in certain phrases of his closing address: for example, in his interpretation of social tensions ("Many people live under very difficult circumstances while a small group leads good and ostentatious life which is disproportionate with its input." *Népszabadság*, September 17), or his commitment to the COMECON investment projects ("It would be a grave economic mistake to change our decisions in this matter. Instead we should choose the path of their accelerated realization." Ibid.).

On the whole, however, the prime minister's performance in the Parliament is characterized by his intention to move away from his earlier image and to appear as the advocate of reform, of opening Hungary to world economy, of promoting small enterprises—in short, as an advocate of openness and dialogue.

Concerning the privotal questions, however, he avoided taking a stance. He did not commit himself to the idea:

- that economic reform must be introduced not in small doses but as a package of comprehensive measures;

- that necessary restructuring of the economy must be achieved through market regulators and not centralized programs;

- that political tensions will become manageable only if the regime's institutions undergo fundamental change.

There may be various reasons for a politician to obscure his basic choices: It is possible that he may want to mislead the public intentionally; it is possible that the context of the given balance of power does not allow him to speak more openly; and it is also possible that at this point even he himself does not see clearly what he is going to choose. It would be premature to prophesy about the prime minister's future policies on the basis of his address. Nevertheless, I would like to call attention to the fact that what I did not learn from his address the representatives also were unable to learn. They did not get any guarantees that Károly Grósz would break away from the bad policies of the past fifteen years and lead the country back to the path which was barely undertaken in 1968.[11] *The National Assembly was satisfied to receive a new personality, and did not insist on receiving new policies.*

The predicament of the National Assembly

The National Assembly is not in the position to evaluate and influence the government's policies as an independent entity. Its subordination is the result of its legal status as a body and the procedure of selecting its members. It could become a sovereign power only after thoroughgoing institutional changes.

There was no other topic which was addressed by so many representatives as the dependent, and consequently helpless, status of the National Assembly. They objected to several aspects of their situation:

- they did not have the data necessary to make well-founded decisions;

- they learned about new legislative measures when they were virtually finalized;

- issues which required legislation were frequently settled through decrees circumventing the National Assembly;

11 The 1968 economic reform was the most promising reform attempt of the Kádár leadership. It represented the first experiment to break away from the model of a centrally-planned economy. Mandatory planning was abolished, central allocation of production resources was abandoned, and price controls were relaxed. No changes, however, were implemented in the sphere of investment and banking, and enterprise managers continued to be nominated by government bodies. As a combined result of the defeat of the "Prague spring," the strengthening Cold War attitudes of the Brezhnev leadership, the lack of determination to defend reform in Kádár circles, and the weakness of the forces of reform, by 1972–74 the experiment had run out of steam and ultimately failed.

- representatives were unable to ask for alternative proposals, thus they could not make real choices.

These circumstances apparently contributed to the representatives' hesitant conduct. The program proposal submitted to them, for example, did not contain the most basic data necessary to formulate a position. The prime minister mentioned in his opening address that in 1988 the government expected a 14 to 15% inflation rate. Then in his closing address he said that the government wanted to reduce inflation to 9% in 1989 and 6% in 1990. But the fact that, according to official calculations, inflation would result in a 5 to 6% decline in real wages he announced only afterwards, at his press conference.

Even if he had made all this known beforehand, the representatives could not have judged whether such a decline in the standard of living was inevitable or not; what the chances were that the government would keep its promise not to cut more deeply into households' real incomes; whether the actual decline would not significantly surpass the forecast; and whether such sacrifice would at least avert state bankruptcy. To form an opinion in these matters they would have needed a host of additional data. First of all, they should have known the country's obligations to foreign creditors. They should have been made aware of how much is needed to service our loans in 1988, 1989, and 1990. Furthermore, they should have been made aware of what portion of these obligations could be covered from currency reserves and from the collection of receivables, and what portion could be rolled over by taking new loans. In short, they should have known what portion of the GNP of the coming years needed to be taken away from domestic use for payment of foreign debt.

It could be estimated only after all this was known what the government could do to reduce domestic expenditures by curbing central capital investments, subsidies for companies, and financial support for state and social organizations, and what share of the sacrifice would be passed on to the population.

The government did not provide even a fraction of this data. But even if it had, it still would not have been enough. Some of the information is simply estimates which depend on the interests of those who make them. Look at the example of state subsidized companies: to what extent can the subsidies be reduced without inducing an unacceptable number of bankruptcies? It is probable that the Ministry of Industry, which is linked to the interests of big companies, would consider acceptable smaller reductions than would the Ministry of Finance which represents the interest of a balanced budget. Or, it is also probable, that the government as a whole would consider smaller reductions than independent experts or the grass-root organizations of the population. This is one of the reasons why the representatives could pass sovereign judgment on the government's proposals only if they could compare them with alternative ideas.

There is another reason as well. Both the prime minister and the Minister of Finance, when submitting the proposal of the new tax laws, suggested to the representatives that if they voted against it, they would, in effect, vote for the continued inertia and stagnation of the previous years. And in the absence of an alternative program the representatives themselves felt that, in spite of all their doubts and worries, there was no third alternative: they had to choose between the conservation of what had proved itself bad and the chance of change.

The National Assembly, in order to make responsible decisions in similarly critical situations in the future, will have to gain a host of rights and privileges.

But just this would not be enough.

The composition of the National Assembly

In democracies the Parliaments consist of professional politicians. The career of the representative/politician is independent from the hierarchy of state apparatus and is completely different from the career of civil servants. In Hungary the largest block of representatives is made up of civil servant/politicians; the remaining representatives also are not given their mandate independently from the state hierarchy. Representatives are selected by those in power in order to insure that through their social affiliation they represent those strata of the population which are important to the state. Such representatives are not politicians and are not fit to politically represent the will of their constituents.

Their vast majority even lacks the ability to form a comprehensive understanding of the issues, an indispensable skill for any politician. From the speeches of the representatives it is clear that the speakers very seldom take into consideration the necessary preconditions and consequences of their proposals. Some of them urged that the non-taxable income base should be 10,000 forints higher, but left unmentioned whether the resulting loss of state revenue should be replaced in some other way and, if so, from what source. Most speakers reveal a rather narrow horizon: even if they discuss various issues, their discussion does not go beyond one specific area. For example, a speaker whose main topic is the impact of personal income tax on large families may bring up the social consequences of the same tax, but barely mention the overextended capital investments of the state or the issue of local self-governments. And the more areas the speaker touches upon the more likely it is that his position is going to be inconsistent. For example, at first he may urge that norms of public morality should be enforced to the strictest extent of the law, then move to recommend the introduction of a wage system based on self-interest. Altogether there were only two or three legislators who had a full command of the possible objections to the government program and who were able to take a consistent position on all questions raised.

We may be able to refine our observations if we do not treat the representatives as a homogenous body. On the basis of their social affiliation the speakers of the fall session fall into the following categories:

1. Members of the political leadership: the General Secretary of the Party, the members of the cabinet, one regional Party secretary, heads of local governments, leaders of the trade union, retired Party members.
2. Economic leaders from a chief executive to a company department head.
3. Leading intellectuals: a prestigious artist and scholar, a cultural administrator, a high-standing technological expert, a head of a medical institution.
4. Workers and foremen.
5. Intellectuals without rank or title.

Although the rhetoric of the political leadership's spokesmen does deserve attention, we will not deal with it, since this group unfailingly represents the various versions of the official line. I did not include the representatives of the churches in any of our categories, since their role is still limited to token representation. Finally, I could not fit Rezső Nysers,[12]—whose path is highly idiosyncratic—into any of our categories although he delivered one of the most important speeches of the session.

The expectations were met most completely by the group of foremen and workers. They were the ones who dealt most extensively with the social consequences of tax reform. Their speeches focused on the plight of large

12 Rezső Nyers was a social democrat until 1948 when his party was forced to merge with the Communists, and was secretary of the Central Committee between 1966 and 1974 when his name became linked with the case of economic reform. After a period of exclusion he was reintegrated into the Politburo in May 1988. He has been Minister of State since November 1988.

families, of middle-income people who are forced to moonlight, and of pensioners. But they proved to be the most narrow-minded as well: the scope of their interest did not exceed the social consequences of personal income tax. They did not say anything meaningful about the questions of economic stability and reform and did not mention the necessity of changing the political institutions. Their speeches also showed a conspicuous inability to think about the economic implications of the causes they represented.

The leading intellectuals brought some surprise. True, their keen preoccupation with the impact of tax reform did not surprise observers. It was also to be expected that they would represent divergent interests. Some of them embraced the cause of the underprivileged while the majority asked for a less progressive tax rate for the most privileged. It was also to be expected that the intellectuals' attention was not going to focus on one particular area but would encompass a wider circle of issues. The real surprise turned out to be the shoddiness of their positions. They ignored the economic implications of their proposals; they had nothing meaningful to say about the fundamental questions of the government program; as for questions of political reform, only the upgrading of the National Assembly's role was mentioned by one of them, and even he did so only in vague generalities. None of their speeches was based on a distinct political plan.

Even less predictable were the speeches of the economic leaders. This is, unfortunately, no surprise at all: the members of this category are rather insensitive to social problems, and the higher we climb in their hierarchy the more true this is. Their main concern is the environment necessary for economic stabilization. It is noteworthy that this is the only group within which there was a sharp division of conflicting views. The representatives of the crisis-ridden metallurigcal and energy-producing sectors greeted the government program with enthusiasm, but in exchange for their devotion they immediately asked for government support of their respective industries. Several other speakers, on the other hand, urged the radical dismantling of central redistribution of profit between companies and wanted a stable, uniform regulatory system. Others mentioned that tax reform in itself is not enough; it must be coupled with wage and price reforms. A few representatives spoke of the necessity of legislating company taxation. This demand already had political overtones, and one of the economic leaders openly stated that without change in the political institutions the economic reform would not have a chance of success.

Thus among the economic leaders there is a circle of reformists who have well-articulated positions, consistent views, and a relatively broad horizon.

This circle could have entered an alliance with the central corps of reformists in the National Assembly if such a thing had existed. All by itself, however, it cannot become the central force of reform.

A group which has no answer to the country's worsening social problems cannot become the leading force of some wider reformist alliance. Furthermore, the decisive word about political reform could be proclaimed only by those who do not approach it from the perspective of economic recovery. It is true that the reform of political institutions is needed to foster economic reform as well. But by now the primary motivation for political reform is something else: the quarter-of-a-century-old "social contract" fell apart, and within the old system can no longer be restored. Finally, the central corps of reformists could emerge only from a circle which has enough freedom of maneuvering to withstand various smaller and larger conflicts with the Party leadership and the government. And state company managers do not constitute such a group.

Thus the keynote addresses of the fall session were delivered neither by leading intellectuals nor by economic leaders. It was Rezsö Nyers who turned out to be one of the principal voices of the session. He did not touch upon all the important issues, but at least concerning one of them—the National Assembly's mandate and rights—he came forth with such a well-defined proposal package that it amounted to a keynote address. The two other leading speakers turned out to be two intellectuals without high rank and title: Erika Tomsits, a medical doctor, and Zoltán Király, a journalist. Only these two (especially the latter) were able to discuss soberly and systematically all the possible significant objections to the government program.

In sum, the representatives with direct involvement in production and the workers, just like the leading intellectuals, were not able to form a judgment about the implications of the government program. As for the social consequences of the tax-reform proposals, they did have a decisive opinion, but they were unequipped to challenge the arguments of officialdom and equally unable to comprehend what would happen if the tax proposals were simply voted down. The reformist economic leaders were in a better position to take a decisive stance on any of these questions, but, as we have seen, they were not in the position to become the flagbearers. Under such circumstances Király and Tomsits, who have marginal position within the representative body, could not have hoped for a broader following of their ideas. Instead, they had to adjust their position to the general atmosphere.

So what was missing? A few dozen Zoltán Királys. *For a force to emerge in the National Assembly which has the necessary political vision, a host of*

*such politically-able legislators who have not yet been elevated into the
official hierarchy of positions, ranks, and titles, is needed.*

The short-term prospects for the National Assembly

The representatives gave thousands of signals of their desire to become
emancipated, to act with responsibility, and to become the social organ
which oversees the government. They are clearly dissatisfied with a
situation where it is left to the government's whim to supply the National
Assembly with information, and to include the National Assembly in the
decision-making process of arbitrarily-selected issues. It obviously further
increased their dissatisfaction that during the September session they were
proven powerless vis-à-vis the government. Therefore it is to be expected
that the issue of the National Assembly's mandate and rights will remain on
the agenda. A routine occasion providing the legislators with the
opportunity of fighting for the Parliament's upgrading is approaching: in the
near future the National Assembly will debate a proposed bill concerning
the legislative process, and address the modification of the House Rules.

The advancement of the National Assembly's rights and privileges will
undoubtedly contribute to the gradual transfer of our public affairs from
dusky offices to the public arena. A breakthrough in the public role of the
National Assembly, however, cannot be expected as long as the composition
of this political body is unchanged.

Democracy is needed not only for the assertion of the citizens' will but
also to foster the emergence of a political group which can find its way in
complex political matters and be able to represent its constituency.

Such a group is in the process of formation in Hungary. It includes
journalists, jurists, economists, sociologists, political scientists, writers,
teachers, and cultural administrators. It is not an accident that the single
most influential representative/politician of this parliamentary cycle, Zoltán
Király—the only true representative/politician or politician/representative
in forty years—belongs to this group. But neither is in an accident that he
was elected to the National Assembly as an *independent* candidate. People
with similar backgrounds may become official candidates only if they have
already started to climb the ladder of hierarchy. And as the current session
has shown, the chances are very slim that any such person will have the
ability to represent an independent position with a broad horizon.

The National Assembly was brought into motion by the 1985 elections.
To challenge the National Assembly's way of operation, imposed on it in
1949, it was enough that two independent candidates managed to break

through the wall of officialdom. But for the National Assembly to regain its confiscated sovereignty we need new elections with a considerably greater number of independent candidates. If everything goes well, in 1990 fifty Zoltán Királys might make their way into the House of Representatives. If this is the case, Rezsö Nyers' statement will take on real meaning: "... sooner or later representatives of similar dispositions and views may form ad hoc alliances ..." (*Heti Világgazdaság*, September 26) This is the optimistic lesson of this legislative session.

The pessimistic lesson is that until that time one cannot expect much more from the National Assembly than it was able to deliver this time.

And the events which will decide the country's fate will take place before the 1990 elections.

The short-term prospects for the nation

Since the most important data of the country's foreign financial obligations are kept secret, we cannot judge whether there is still a chance to keep the country solvent. But even without this, it is clear that the danger of a catastrophe is as great as it was before.

Although the leadership did break with the adventurous policies of 1985–86 to stimulate the economy, the 1979–84 economic policies of administrative controls are virtually in place.

The architects of the 1979–84 economic policies turned to administrative methods of demand control not because they did not know that monetary restrictions would be more effective. They did so to avoid political conflicts with two important interest groups: the large companies and a significant bloc of wage earners. As a result of this, they were forced to maintain the chaotic system of subsidies even under those restrictive circumstances; the money supply could not be tightened and the activities of economic institutions had to be regulated through administrative measures. This method, however, conserved the outdated structure of production; and, while in words it still claimed a market-oriented reform, in reality the constant meddling confused market relationships more than ever since 1968.

There is a real danger that in the present, more critical, situation the same approach will be continued:

- The program of the Grósz government contains several elements which imply the threat of continued overspending, such as the commitment to large capital investments and the philosophy which expects the transformation of industry structure from centralized development programs.

- When the government announces centralized programs, it always provides a chance to those companies affected by these programs to obtain additional concessions. But there are other signals too, such as the fixed price and wage system, which indicate that the system of subsidies and bargaining is not going to be curbed.

- Continuation of subsidies and backing away from the structural transformation of the economy may be the result also of the government's unwillingness to formulate a well-defined policy of unemployment. If so then the government can tolerate only a tiny group of unemployed; and it will not be able to accept necessary company liquidations or necessary scaling back in production.

- The fact that the government failed to present a well-articulated, binding stabilization program to the National Assembly and that tax regulations for companies were not enacted makes it easier to break the rules and continue the old overspending budgetary policies.

In short: there are no guarantees that the government is going to be able to curb those interests which are in conflict with stabilizing the economy. This, however, does not mean that the relatively conflict-free atmosphere of the 1970–84 period will continue. One of the causes of the growing social tensions is accelerated inflation which is the price of the 1985–86 adventure. The other, more important, cause is tax reform, which will lead to significant income redistribution and will force much of the social strata to break away from their established patterns of social conduct.

Two elements of tax reform may bring about unforeseeable consequences: One is that in determining the personal income tax only the gross income earned in the person's primary job will be adjusted in such a manner that his net income will remain unchanged. It is probable that in response to this many people will give up self-exploitation or seek additional income in the illegal underground economy. The impact on the performance of Hungarian industry and on income structure of such a withdrawal from the labor market cannot be fathomed.

The other consequence will be brought about by the adjustment of gross income itself. It is already clear that not all companies will have sufficient funds to fully refund all the losses of every employee. The struggle is on: who gets more and who gets less? Such disputes will become exacerbated by the fact that there cannot be unequivocal rules of equitable distribution. In order to maintain the same real wage level an employee earning 4000 forints[13] will have to receive a refund of 150 forints; an employee earning 8000 forints will have to receive 600; an employee earning 15,000 forints, 4000. How will it be decided who will give up how much so that nobody will be put at an unfair disadvantage? In the case of those workers whose salary is based on performance it is already being debated which portion of the pay will serve as the basis for adjusted gross income. This does not even consider the various bonuses, benefits, and other monetary supplements, all of which can serve as a source of conflict.

So we suppose with good reason that the classical collective struggle of interest—which was successfully eliminated for twenty-five years by the consolidation—will return to the economy.

We know that the leadership and its agencies are also considering such eventualities. This induces them to contemplate some political concessions which, in more peaceful times, they had refused even to consider. But they not only prepare themselves for the eventuality of inevitable radical reforms; they also put on alert their arsenal of repression.

It is likely, however, that at first they will turn neither to political reform nor to the use of force, but to their old tactics. If the input of additional labor decreases, if there are confrontations about the size of adjusted gross income, if they are forced to lay off large number of people, then the government will give in to the pressure of managers and will simply ease its fiscal rigor. In this way they will be able to avoid real social polarization, the Polish-style reawakening of class struggle. On the other hand, such a course of action will surely lead the country into the Yugoslav-style dead-end street of decline: local strikes without the formation of a political workers' movement, accelerating inflation, disruptions in production and supply, unmanageable budget deficits, and forced rescheduling of foreign debts. And in the background we will see the disintegration of social solidarity, the faster decline in work ethics, the ever-more vicious rivalry of interdependent social strata, and ethnic, minority, and national hatred.

It would have been a miracle if in this crisis situation the National Assembly could have played the role of mediator between the leadership and the population, if it could have articulated the preconditions and guarantees of stabilization, and if it could have started those political processes leading to the orderly settlement of the sharpening conflicts.

---

13 4,000 forints=about 67 dollars.

However, miracles do not exist. The National Assembly disappointed the public, especially that part of which only lately became sensitive to political issues. Many people simply wave their hands as if saying: "It was a charade and nothing else." I disagree. If this parliamentary debate took place in 1979 at the beginning of the first attempt at stabilizing the economy, one would have said: "It is only the beginning, there is still time." At the present moment the trouble is that there is no time left; therefore, the majority's opinion is vindicated indirectly. No matter how important is the ferment in the regime's institutions, the change—if it is still possible at all—cannot come from that side alone. Pressure coming from outside the official institutions—from independent social initiatives and independent social movements and organizations—is sorely needed.

What Should We Fear?

What Should We Fear?

N ineteen eighty-eight has begun with the expectation that this time
around something really must happen. Some people with anguish,
some with apathetic resignation, some with expectation of a sign,
some with mere curiosity, but all without fail have been expecting that
protests, demonstrations, strikes, and clashes between the masses and the
police will return to Hungarian politics.

And these expectations are not groundless.

The situation has become wide-open

If people look around in the Eastern European region of the Soviet empire
they see the signs of decay everywhere. In Romania despair has reached the
point where even perpetual terror is no longer able to force it underground.
In Czechoslovakia the clique which has been ruling for exactly twenty years
has slowly started to disintegrate. In Poland the post-coup regime has failed
to drive the organized workers' movement and the intellectuals' opposition
out of politics. Even the seemingly stable East German regime is forced to
reckon with a strengthening of resistance.

The acceleration of local crises is undoubtedly connected to ferment
within the Soviet Union, and the eventuality of Gorbachev's downfall or
retreat would not bring it to a halt. The long-term cause of the crisis is that
the Soviet Union is no longer able to ensure a rate of economic growth for
Eastern Europe that would keep social conflicts on a manageable level.

The Hungarian public follows with anxious attention the growing turmoil
and disorientation in the region, the diminution of Soviet leverage, and the

shrinkage of the power basis of local authorities. It senses that for the first time since the period of 1953–56 not just one Eastern European country is in crisis, but the whole region.

Only a few years ago, however, the same perception would have strengthened the public's belief that Hungary is an island of tranquility and relative prosperity. At that time there was an almost unanimous belief that we would be able to withstand the decline of the neighboring countries without a political trauma.

This belief started to crumble almost unnoticeably in the first half of the decade, and then in 1987 it suddenly collapsed. The sense of self-confident superiority with regard to our neighbors was displaced by a fear of economic disaster, the trust in the leadership's competence by a sense of outrage of being duped. Once again a yawning gulf—which had been filled with the steadfast work of consolidation—separates the political leadership and society at large. The representatives of the Party-state no longer enjoy moral credit, and the term "Communist" which for decades they alone have used to describe themselves is now being applied to them by the public with passionate hostility.

People see a decaying and demoralized political power. The leadership is divided by barely-concealed personal strife. The old guard, accustomed to a cautious balancing, appears to be helpless; but the heirs-apparent, who carry their decisiveness on their foreheads, also do not create the impression of knowing how to lead the country out of its crisis. The infighting and vacillation confuse the apparatus; the apparatchiks have the feeling that they are caught in the crossfire and that nobody tells them what they have to do, what they are allowed to do.

The impression that political authority is falling apart is not altered by the rumors that the police forces are being mobilized. On the contrary, such rumors feed the people's expectations: "See, those in power indeed fear that the people will not put up with it any longer."

That those in power are afraid is not surprising. We should give some thought, however, to the fact that fear is spreading not only at the top. "Catastrophe" is the key-word even in those circles where the independent social forces organize themselves: in clubs, societies, and associations which are mushrooming—that is, in those forums of public openness which are independent or are on their way to becoming independent. And even those who are hopeful do not really believe that the mass movement, if it takes off, has a chance. Rather, they hope that it is not going to take off, that disillusionment and fatalism will prove stronger than anger and despair, and that social apathy will leave a margin for maneuvering for a successful implementation of economic and political reforms.

That may prove to be the case. It is possible that looking back from the '90s we will understand that we believed that something had to happen because we were still not used to the idea that calm and order might endure even in an atmosphere of hatred toward the rulers. But it is also possible that it will not be the case, and that the expected trauma will take place. I do not intend to prophesy. What I would like to say is that the partisans of democracy and national recovery should place their hopes not in overall despair, but rather in the eventuality that society will take action. Democracy cannot be received as a gift; it has to be earned through struggles of the *demos*. I consider the biggest danger, even from the point of view of overcoming the economic crisis, to be that nothing happens.

The greater evil

Poland and Romania have fallen into the abyss. Hungary has been inching toward it for ten years. At this moment there are still no lines-around-the-block in front of the bakeries, we do not have extended blackouts, and gasoline is not rationed. But the performance of our economy is irresistibly sliding to that of the third world's stagnating regions, and the country's foreign debts are growing ever larger. Therefore, no solution to any of our social problems seems possible: the decline of health care and education continues, scientific research and development is falling behind, the chances to get an apartment are getting worse, birth rate decreases while mortality is on the rise, culture is becoming improverished and poverty is increasing dramatically.

Neither the restrictive measures nor the attempts to continue the reform brought a turnaround, and under present political conditions, further restrictions and reform measures are not going to bring one either. The decline of the Hungarian economy could be stopped only if the government had the courage to entrust the restoration of equilibrium to market forces. The market would pass a merciless verdict on the economic development of the last forty years: obsolete branches of industry would be sentenced to swift redevelopment; imports would become more expensive and domestic labor would become devaluated. Only a leadership which does not have to be afraid of the population can assume the responsibility for such a trauma.

In democracies turnarounds on such a grand scale are usually preceded by a change of government. When the majority of the electorate realizes that state expenditures and subsidization of non-profitable factories costs more than fiscal rigor, a new party comes to power and receives a mandate to restore equilibrium. But how could the only existing party—which is inseparable from the state, and which in the eyes of the population is the cause of all the troubles—receive a mandate for a drastic reduction in the standard of living and for the forced increase in temporary unemployment?

The leadership and its apparatuses have every reason to fear the wrath of the people. And in a state of fear the liberalization of the market cannot be undertaken. Who knows? In another ten years the *structure* of Hungarian economy might resemble more closely that of market economies than the structure of Soviet-style planned economies. We will have privately-owned companies, cooperatives, corporations, competing insurance companies, and commercial banks; we will have a stock exchange and a flexible exchange-rate policy, but the decisive means of *regulation* will nonetheless remain administrative intervention aimed at avoiding economic shocks which could cause political turmoil.

If this is the case, we will not be able to avoid the slow slide to the bottom of the pit; and from there—see Poland, see Yugoslavia—there is no way in the foreseeable future to climb out.

A new policy of national unity?

Even some of the Communist politicians are aware of the danger. Although in a minority and forced to the periphery of power, they nonetheless are proposing to the Party a new policy.[1] They are trying to persuade it to make real concessions and to introduce comprehensive political reform, thus obtaining the social approval necessary to put the economy in order.

These politicians are not initiating a changeover to a multi-party parliamentary system. The time for such a demand has not yet come, even outside the Party, and to bring up such an idea in the groves of power would be a straight-out absurdity. The Communist reform politicians are urging the renewal of the tradition of the Popular Front of the '30s and '40s.[2] "I am for the complete rethinking of the Popular Front policy" said, for example, Rezsö Nyers. "We should return to the Popular Front policy

1 See note 19 of "On Our Limitations and Possibilities" in this volume.
2 Popular Front was originally the name of a left-wing coalition in France which frustrated an attempted Fascist coup in 1934 and brought the socialist Léon Blum into the government. From 1935 through 1939 (with the signing of the Soviet-German non-aggression and friendship pacts) the Komintern demanded that Communists establish broad anti-Fascist popular fronts of the French type. The idea was revived in the 1945–48 interlude. It entailed a tactical retreat from the goal of the "dictatorship of the proletariat" without, however, an unqualified acceptance of competitive, multi-party democracy.

practiced during the anti-Fascist resistance and the post-liberation period. And this Popular Front would continue that tradition and function in an updated fashion according to our present altered situation. Its task would be to unify the various progressive movements in Hungary; further, as an ally of the Party it could play the role of a policy-forming force, thus broadening the organized camp of socialist reform policy." (*Magyar Ifjúság*, December 18, 1987) In essence this position proposes that the Party move into the axis of a broad united national front, that it line up the support of circles which command the respect of public opinion, and that they submit to the people—as part of a more comprehensive reform program—the program of economic stabilization as a program of national unity.

The idea is undoubtedly daring. Such a policy is meant to win over not only those people who only grumble but those who do voice political demands in clubs, associations and alliances, i.e., those forces which fight for forums of public openness. Nonetheless, anybody who is familiar with this social milieu knows that within these circles, which are in a state of growth and ferment, there are many people who yearn for something like an *entente* with the power wielders. It is doubtful, however, whether the reform wing of the leadership will be able to gather enough strength to make a serious offer of conciliation and afterwards keep its own word. It has to overcome formidable opposition within the groves of power—the opposition of those who are held responsible for the public for the grave condition of the country; the opposition of those who can think only in terms of administrative-police solutions; and the opposition of the local Mafias of the apparatus who fear for their power. But this is only one side of the difficulty. The real question is whether a reformist unity front, should it emerge, could secure social approval for economic austerity measures.

Five to ten years ago approval could perhaps have been secured. Between 1979 and 1984 when the first attempt was made to stabilize the Hungarian economy, general suspicion toward the leadership and anti-Communist sentiments were not yet dominant. And at that time the liberalization of the market required considerably less sacrifice. But now it is a disillusioned and irate society whose consent must be obtained for a drastic curtailment of the standard of living, for temporary unemployment, for accelerated inflation, and for the rearrangement of income distribution.

The Party is unable to place a broad enough front of intellectuals between itself and the society at large to convince *factory workers* that it is justified and worthwhile for them to accept such a trauma. The workers would accept the burdens of economic recovery only if *their own leaders* struck a bargain with the government.

As long as the transfer of power is out of the question in the foreseeable future, those in power should at least enter into a *social contract* with the populace concerning the burdens and guarantees of overcoming the crisis.

The problem is that there is no one with whom they could make a pact; those strata which are pivotal to political calm are unorganized.

We are paying now for the advantages of the post-1961–63 consolidation.[3] It is no wonder that at that time the beaten and viscerated society felt that to yield politics to the power holders was not too high a price to pay for quiet evolution, since society was paralyzed anyway. In addition, consolidation promised not only that the status quo would become more comfortable, but also that the regime would be slowly transformed. De-Stalinization began anew, and the idea of economic reform, which in 1957 had been labeled revisionist, was revived. Nonetheless, after 1963–72 it could not help but be noticed that progress was faltering and that all that remained was the prolongation of the status quo. And it was exactly at that time that the myth sprang up in Hungary that we had found the best imaginable path of potential progress in the shadow of the Soviet Union. The myth of the specific Hungarian path was not dispelled even by the fact that by the end of the decade the leadership had to acknowledge that prosperity was based on foreign borrowing and could no longer be sustained.

By the time society realized what was going on and started to organize itself, it was already too late. Those circles which are trying to form political communities, which want to keep in check and influence the actions of those in power, for the most part still do not reach beyond the intelligentsia.

If this remains the case, if the factory workers do not start to organize themselves, even the grandest of political reforms will be in vain. The conflicts are not going to become more manageable, and we will see an exact replay of what has been going on in the economy for years: the nominal authority of self-government widening, the legal status of citizens becoming more secure on paper, the National Assembly getting closer to the ideal of popular representation, but the decisive means of regulating the political process nevertheless remaining administrative intervention.

But what would happen if the industrial centers of the country took action? It is certain that the conflict between those in power and society would become more intense. And since society's organization is very weak and those in power have no experience in seeking conciliatory solutions, the risks involved undoubtedly would be very high.

---

3 On consolidation, see "The End and the Beginning" in this volume.

Nevertheless, it is one thing to seriously consider the risks of the situation, and yet another to accept as a point of departure that a mass movement, by definition, would end in a catastrophe.

Dangers and possibilities

We have to weigh the possibility of two kinds of political catastrophies. The first one: an isolated demonstration takes place; the police use water cannons, tear gas, and rubber bullets to restore order; a few dozen people are swiftly sent to jail; the decisive action of the coercive apparatuses strengthens the faction of discipline and order within the leadership, which uses the general alarm as a pretext to initiate a grand campaign against "social anarchy."

The scenario becomes most likely if the main force of mass action comes from the lowest stratum of workers who are the most defenseless. The probability of an order-faction takeover would be enhanced if discontent breaks out in street disorder (and there are very good chances for that if the bulk of the participants comes from marginal groups of society). In such an event official propaganda will have no trouble presenting the events as the action of "criminal and lumpen elements." It would be the duty of the democratically-inclined intelligentsia to do everything in its power to unmask this propaganda, but it should be taken into consideration that the official inducement of sentiments is not going to be ineffective, and it might win over significant portions of the middle stratum to its policy of law and order. The chances of an effective discipline-and-order propaganda campaign are less if the bulk of the dispersed crowd comes from well-adjusted strata. In the case of such an eventuality it may happen that the confrontation and the subsequent reprisal will serve as the starting point of some sort of social self-defense organization. Organized resistance may gradually undermine the strength of the order faction, it may force a new realignment with the leadership and open the way for some compromise solution.

The other kind of political catastrophe takes place if the authorities do not crush the mass movement at its birth and the movement itself sweeps away the regime which will be subsequently restored either through external aggression or some kind of internal showdown like the introduction of a state of emergency. This scenario becomes most likely if the movement starts within well-integrated strata of society and quickly spreads to the larger centers of the country.

Something like this happened in 1956, and those who warn about the dangers of a political catastrophe refer to this memory when they admonish the public against excessive radicalism. In our opinion, however, it is time to rethink the lessons of the revolution. It is not self-evident at all that November 4 had to be the conclusion to October 23.[4] And it is even less self-evident that the Soviet Union might turn to military solution as easily as it did at that time.

We should not delude ourselves: if the regime collapses from one day to the next, and the disintegration of the Warsaw Pact becomes a real danger, the leaders of the Soviet state would surely choose military solution all over again. Still, it is worthwhile to contemplate seriously that such an intervention would cost the Soviet Union much more dearly today than it did in either 1956, 1968, or 1981 and not only because it would set back its foreign policy offensive. The price tag would be extremely high especially because intervention would further deepen the crisis of the region instead of bringing it to an end. This crisis originates in long-term economic problems to which the Soviet Union is unable to offer any solution. Soviet leaders either accept that the dependent countries adopt far-reaching economic reforms, open themselves to the world market and to the outside world, and seek such political institutions for themselves as would make the hitherto-irrepressible social conflicts manageable, or they risk that Eastern Europe, from the Bug to the Elbe, from the Baltic Sea to the Black Sea, becomes ungovernable.

Consequently, we have good reason to hope that ultimately the leaders of the Soviet Union will accept a more gradual and orderly transformation. The political catastrophe would become inevitable only if the mass movement becomes radical to the point of inducing the fall of the regime. Why should it be this way? Because the self-perpetuating dynamics of mass movements leads to that inevitable fate? This is not true, and particularly is not true concerning the kind of mass action which is most probable in our time: strike movements. A strike is a form of collective action which has a great deal of built-in self-disciplinary force. A strike makes its participants understand that they are players in a game which demands nerves and patience and has a limited stake. A strike requires organization, and, even in the absence of historical traditions, it readily offers effective organiza-tional solutions. A strike offers as its great fundamental experience an education in social solidarity, the recognition of strength born of unity, and

---

4 October 23, 1956 was the day the revolution began. November 4 was the day of the all-out Soviet military attack against revolutionary Hungary.

the insight that results can be achieved only through negotiations. Strikers learn quickly that they have to face the conflict, and that they need self-moderation and an ability to make concessions in exchange for gains.

The argument that even if the movement entered into a compromise it could agree upon nothing with the authorities appears to be more serious. The government cannot meet any economic demand without risking state bankruptcy. If this is indeed true, then action of the factories would only provide a last push to the declining Hungarian economy, the push which sends it into the abyss.

Well, the realm of compromise is indeed very narrow, but not so much that it would be completely impossible to strike a bargain. Parts of the demands would not burden the state budget and could even mean some saving: Demands would definitely include a radical curtailment of the Party apparatus, the abolishment of state support to the Communist Youth League, the reduction of military expenditures, the dismantling of the workers' militia, the cancellation or substantial modification of the agreement concerning the construction of the Danube dam, and the review of our participation in the large capital investments of COMECON.

The sums which could be saved this way are, of course, only crumbs compared to the annual debt-servicing expenses of the budget deficit. Nonetheless, it would not be without moral significance if society saw that those in power share the inevitable sacrifices and that they themselves give up every penny before asking the populace to tighten its own belt.

The remaining economic demands could be divided into two categories. It would be indispensable that the government give some immediate concessions. It would be advisable to yield in an area where a concession would not be unequivocally disadvantageous to the economy. (For example, the increase in the standard deduction for income earned in addition to the base pay would decrease state revenues, but at the same time enhance the workers' willingness to take upon themselves additional tasks.) As for the unresolved questions, the decision could be postponed to a mutually-agreed-upon later date. This interval should be utilized by representatives of the government and of the workers to find an agreement concerning a national unity program of renewal.

In order to reach such an agreement not only would the movement have to learn to accept conflicts in a self-limiting manner, but also the Party-state would have to learn to accept the curtailment of its power in order to avoid catastrophe. It is not an easy task because—let us remember the Polish example—the temptation is rather great for the Party-state to try to demobilize the masses with unlimited economic concessions, in order that it not be forced to acknowledge their independent self-representation. If those of power yield only because they are forced into a corner, they will always be on the lookout for when they could trash the agreements; and this would further enhance society's suspicion and hostile sentiments. A long-term, renewable contract can be made only with a regime that is able to perceive *as progress* the fact that independent, organized social groups enter the public arena, that there is a force with whom it can strike an agreement concerning the burdens of economic renewal.

Although *Beszélő* does not see its own future within the Popular Front urged by the reform-Communists, it considers it important that such a front be formed. But it is equally important that the advocates of such a front be aware that the political consensus necessary to its formation cannot be worked out *among themselves alone.* Such a consensus can be born, if at all, only as a result of a social contract made with independent mass movements, which are separate from the Party-state.

Let us not fear the emergence of such a movement, but the events to come if it is not formed.

After Kádár

After Kádár

I t was exactly a year ago that our paper—echoing the ever-louder political public opinion of the country—stated: "Kádár must go."[1] In his last year in office the increasingly-isolated General Secretary of the Party was only delaying the inevitable. His political past weighed heavily on his political present. He was unable to face the crisis which crowned his three-decade-long reign. In this situation, incomprehensible to him, even his famed tactical sense deserted him. The man who always knew how to balance between leadership cliques and political currents became in the end the captive of the weakest faction: the impotent gerontocracy. He antagonized absolutely everyone from the aboriginal Kádárist circle who still stood for something: they either looked for new allies or became isolated. Having realized that Kádár had no future even the discipline-and-order elements of the Party failed to side with him. His myth started to dissipate abroad as well. The Moscow leadership quietly cut him loose, and the Western financial and government circles that make credit decisions revoked their good will.

Kádár, however, did not want to acknowledge that his political career had reached its end. Even in the last few weeks of his tenure he was still duping himself with the illusion that at the price of sacrificing a few people he would be able to stay in power. He submitted his resignation just before the opening of the Party conference, two days after the Central Committee had

---

1 See "Kádár Must Go" in this volume.

returned its mandate.[2] Kádár with his long, desperate rearguard battle influenced the outcome of the Party's crisis more than anyone else, although not according to his own wishes. His rearguard battle was instrumental in bringing about the growing social discontent leading to division even within the ranks of the Party apparatus, the grumbling of public opinion spilling over into the Party membership, and an alliance emerging between Party members desiring renewal and the apparatuses interested in arresting social ferment. Everyone had enough of him and of the Kádárist old guard.

Without this general atmosphere dominating the Party conference, it would not have been possible to expel the entire Kádár clique from the Central Committee. Manipulations would have been futile if 30 to 40% of the delegates had not on their own initiative crossed out the old guard from the ballot. The great spread in the vote count for the defeated candidates is evidence of spontaneous emotions as well: Sándor Gáspár[3] received barely a quarter of the votes; Ferenc Havasi[4] missed the necessary 50% by only a few votes. But it was absolutely necessary that the general atmosphere of the conference receive help from a well-organized voting machine. It was able to deliver the necessary 20 to 25% of "nay" votes and explain why, in spite of the great differences in vote distribution, of all candidates only those five who had left the Politburo *involuntarily* did not receive the necessary 50%. Probably we will never learn the whole truth about the behind-the-scenes maneuvering of the balloting. But no matter exactly how it did happen one thing is sure: the old guard came to an ignominious end and its fall is an event of historical importance. The fall concluded the post-1956 era and did so with the disgraceful defeat of the victors of '56–'57. Although Kádár was turned out of office not by society at large, it was nonetheless the first time in 32 years that reorganization

2 In order that the Party conference scheduled for May 1988 would not dismiss him and his associates, Kádár tried to restrict re-election voting to one-third of the Central Committee membership. As a reaction to this move, however, members of the Central Committee, one after the other, offered their resignations until the Central Committee as a body resigned, making inevitable its complete re-election. Only at this moment did Kádár recognize defeat and enter into negotiations about his retirement.
3 Sándor Gáspár, a member of the ruling Politburo since 1957, was for decades the head of the Hungarian trade unions. He was considered the leading hardliner within the Old Guard.
4 Ferenc Havasi was until 1979 first secretary of the Komárom county party committee. In 1979 he was co-opted into the Secretariat of the Central Committee and put in charge of economic affairs. In this capacity, he supported moderate reforms. In 1987 he was demoted and transferred to the Budapest party committee as its first secretary. At the May 1988 party conference he was voted out of the Central Committee and, as a consequence, also lost his office in Budapest.

within the groves of political leadership did not remain the internal affair of those in power, and that the ferment of public opinion and the restlessness within the Party did play a demonstrable role in a leadership group's removal from office.

From now on the important question is: what will be the relationship between the pressure exerted by society and the manipulation of power by the leadership in the new era? The alliance of interests which was based on a generational conflict no longer exists. This fact was already noticeable at the Party conference. The major themes of the speeches and the distribution of applause gave the impression that the delegates were more easily won over by some loosely formulated outline of democratization than by the slogan of discipline and order. Instead of tangible results, however, they received only two new Politburo members: Rezso" Nyers[5] and Imre Pozsgay.[6] The adopted Resolution does not contain any of the more significant amendments put forth by the delegates; it is a non-binding, dead text, just as its earlier versions were. As far as the "strong men" of the new Politburo are concerned, Grósz[7] and Berecz[8] did not conceal what they considered their primary objective: the restoration of so-called Party unity and authority. And the third strong figure of the new leadership, János Lukács,[9] the secretary of the Central Committee in charge of Party organization (it was probably he who oversaw behind the scenes the machinery of the Party conference), in all likelihood will also represent the apparatus' interest to restore order.

Will there be any force which could counterbalance the efforts to discipline society? It appears, if there will be one, that such a force is not going to gather around the Party membership. The spectacular fall of Kádár & Co. cannot conceal the dispiriting fact of the Party conference's weakness vis-à-vis the leadership's manipulations. The conference could not even achieve a one-by-one vote on the amendments. When the demand to this end is put forth on the last day, the presiding Csaba Hámori becomes confused, does not know what to do. Voices from the hall: "Let us vote one by one." At that moment János Kádár rises from his seat, pushes Hámori

---

5 See note 12 of "After the Fall Session of the National Assembly" in this volume.
6 See note 17 of "Troops of Weary Seekers . . . " in this volume.
7 See note 7 of "Troops of Weary Seekers . . . " in this volume.
8 See note 18 of "On Our Limitations and Possibilities" in this volume.
9 János Lukács was first secretary of the Baranya county party committee in the mid-'80s. Since 1987 he has been secretary of the Central Committee in charge of nomenclature matters. He was elected to the Politburo at the May 1988 extraordinary party conference, but gave up both his Politburo membership and his post in the Secretariat in April 1989. Since then he has been head of the Central Control Commission of the HSWP.

aside and tells the gathering: "There is no need for separate votes." And the reprimanded delgates meekly raise their hands and, with a mere four votes of opposition, authorize the drafting committee to do with the text of the Resolution whatever it pleases. Thus, the already-defeated Kádár managed with a single interjection to rebuke the entire assembly.

The Party conference, of course, is not the Party membership at large; the delegates, as is well-known, were selected from above. But did the grumbling membership have enough strength to force a delegate selection from below? Was there any attempt to organize the advocates of renewal horizontally? The anger was real as was the confusion of the apparatuses; but if not for the confusion, the discontent most likely could not have broken through. Why would the apparatuses not defuse discontent after having reorganized their ranks?

Really, why *not*? Because such a move no longer depends solely on the power balance within the Party. The Party leadership's generational crisis is over, but the overall political crisis is unresolved. Let us see the difficulties the new leadership will have to face in the near future:

First, the state of public opinion is not favorable to introducing discipline and order. Fundamental personnel changes, of course, may calm the mood for a few months. A spark of hope may be struck from within the populace or, at least, a wait-and-see position adopted. The waiting period, however, cannot last longer than a few months. For a decade the gap has steadily been growing between the promises of those in power and the actual experiences of society. The time for reforms, development programs, and promises of renewal covered by warranty is becoming shorter and shorter. If the new leadership cannot convince the public that this time around—not as in 1978, 1982, 1984, 1985, at the end of 1986 and again in the summer and early fall of 1987—a decisive change did indeed take place, the crisis of confidence will begin anew.

And the Grósz leadership sowed the seeds of renewed crisis at the very moment of its formation:

- The streamlining of the Resolution sanctioned by the Party conference was too successful. The Resolution does not convince anyone that anything happened besides personnel changes.

- The fact that the newly-appointed General Secretary did not relinquish the post of prime minister caused general consternation. The bad mood could be dispelled only by the immediate transfer of this post.

But the appointment of a government technocrat would not suffice. Public opinion could be calmed only by the installation of a prime minister known to be strong enough—as was Grósz in Kádár's last year—to make the government an independent political factor in its own right.

- Many people were disappointed that the case of those Party members who were expelled from the Party in the spring was not re-examined by the Party conference. The explanation given—that such issues can be dealt with only by the Party congress—is not taken seriously by anyone. After all, Party rules also authorize only the Party congress to re-elect the Central Committee, and this action did not have to wait till 1990.

Second, the state of the economy does not grant a lengthy grace period to the new leadership. The sweeping personnel changes may temporarily return the confidence of Western financial circles; so Hungary may be able to get additional loans. Apparently, the Grósz leadership plans to take advantage of this opportunity. This way it might definitely gain some time. But if the government does not use the new loans to create more favorable conditions for the inevitable economic and political transformation, it only brings closer the onset of a debt avalanche. The economic and political transformation, on the other hand, would make the leadership face grave political decisions.

- The leadership should significantly reduce subsidies of loss-producing industries, thus facing up to the resistance of strong industrial interest groups and to society's trauma, caused by the jump in unemployment.

- Hungary should withdraw from some capital-intensive COMECON investments, and that would involve some foreign policy frictions.

- The state financing of the government, of the Party, of the so-called social organizations, and of the military should be drastically reduced. These measures would stir up the apparatuses and make inevitable some hardball negotiations with the leaders of the Soviet Union.

- Political restrictions concerning prices and wages, capital flow, and foreign trade should be lifted; this would lead to the intensification of already-growing social tensions.

If these steps are not taken, economic decline will continue, the spectre of a catastrophe will not go away, and political erosion will inescapably start anew. If, on the other hand, the leadership does take these steps, political liberalization also becomes inevitable; otherwise, those in power will not have enough strength to withstand the conflicts concomitant to the transformation.

Third, political liberalization can no longer involve less than the recognition of pluralism, i.e., the existence of independent organizations and opinion-forming forums. It no longer suffices to talk about dialogue, the continued development of the institutional structure, and tolerance toward dissent. It no longer suffices to tacitly acknowledge the existence of those movements, circles, and publications which are kept out of offical public awareness.

- The greatest challenge to the leadership is presented by the existence of the Alliance of Young Democrats and the Democratic Trade Union of Scientific Workers. The rhetoric of political reform will be measured against the leadership's conduct in their regard: whether the Party leadership will continue to refuse to settle the former's status and continue to push the latter to the periphery.

- The Hungarian Democratic Forum and the Network of Free Initiatives provide the growing social movements with a more permanent, widespread structure which is rising to the level of national politics. The present ambiguity of official conduct toward them can be sustained no longer. The leadership must decide whether or not to recognize the legitimacy of new political movements.

- The press is in a turbulent state from *samizdat* to university publications, and from the traditional cultural periodicals to mass media. Using the old arsenal of agit-prop methods it cannot be kept under control, but more forceful attempts at regulation do not promise success anyway and would also undermine the credibility of official *glasnost* rhetoric.

- A number of laws are being prepared which would codify the relationship between the Party-state and emerging pluralism. In the present situation the leadership would no longer get away with the game it played in 1986 when, under the pretext of press reform, the

National Assembly was made to pass press-law statutes which actually
undermined the right to free expression.

Fourth, the Party leadership has to deal with economic decline and political
decay in the midst of a grave ideological crisis. It is forced to acknowledge
that market economy with mixed ownership is more effective than planned
economy based on state ownership; it has no answer to the criticism leveled
against it that a constitutional multi-party system has legitimacy, while
one-party rule free of legal restrictions does not.

At the time when it still seemed that the one-party system established in
1947–48 could offer an acceptable future to Hungarian society, it was
sufficient to turn to the pronouncement: "It historically turned out this
way." Today, however, historical reality cannot serve as an argument. The
conviction that the present crisis is the crisis of the system itself is becoming
increasingly widespread; even the Communist reform-intelligentsia is
groping toward transitional forms which lead to economic and political
pluralism. And in the meantime the past is becoming the subject of an
overall revision. The Party leadership no longer has the strength to prevent
open public inquiry concerning the role that Communist manipulation,
terror, and show trials played in the fact that "it historically turned out this
way." The public re-evaluation of the 1947–48 turnaround is inevitable and
the end of the Kádár era will pave the way to a re-evaluation of the 1956–57
turning point as well.

What the Party is able to counterpose to the projected image of a future
pluralist Hungary and to the concomitant re-evaluation of the past is no
longer enough to give legitimacy to its hegemony even in the eyes of its own
membership and apparatus.

•　　•　　•

Those who believe that the resolution of the leadership's generational crisis
also brought an end to the country's political crisis will be bitterly
disappointed. Another question altogether is what the outcome of the crisis
will be: Will the general decay and disintegration continue; or will those in
power try to put the house in order by using force and after the
law-and-order attempt's failure will the process of the decay continue; or
will the leadership try to recruit a camp around itself by playing on those

prejudices and passions which divide society; or will it embark on a path which leads to a conciliatory process of recovery, to constitutional democracy, and mixed-market economy. We cannot predict. One thing, however, we know for sure: a recovery based on consensus will be possible only if those in power have a partner with whom they can find reconciliation. Therefore, it is indispensable that the discontent concerning present conditions not remain an amorphous general malaise.

Society's political organization does have some points of crystalization. Although the Party membership's restlessness in the first round was not decisive enough, we should not give up hope that it may start again and grow into a real movement. At the present moment, however, movements outside the Party represent the real force. They are still far from being a deciding word in the political process, either as negotiating partners or as an expression of public pressure. Nevertheless, the crisis' outcome largely depends on the question of whether these forces succeed in solidifying and expanding their influence; or whether, through intimidation, manipulation, promises, and cajolery the authorities manage to divide and disarm them.

The state-Party can change into a *governing* party only if it has a resolute, independent opposition.

Hungarian Society
and Hungarian
Minorities Abroad

Hungarian Society
and Hungarian
Minorities Abroad

In addition to the uncertain economic and international political situation, at the beginning of the '80s Hungarian society's suppurated national wounds started to burst. We cannot draw a meaningful comparison with other countries, although there are some limited parallels. National traditions are cracking the veneer of Marxist-Leninist ideology in other countries as well. And in other countries of the region, the recreation of a national cultural continuity goes hand in hand with the revival in territorial, political, economic, and cultural grievances caused by, or attributed to, other nations and states. What is different is that the subject of these grievances is usually the nation living within its own borders. To my knowledge there are no other state-forming people in Eastern Europe apart from the Hungarians who are so passionately preoccupied with the plight of their minority groups trapped outside of the national state. I do not think that the Hungarian minorities' growing trials in and of themselves explain this, since the oppression of nationalities is too customary a phenomenon in this part of the world. What is unusual is the ratio of Hungarian minorities in relation to the motherland's population. Hungarians who live abroad represent not a small fraction of the population as is the case with Poles in Czechoslovakia and in the Soviet Union or Serbs in Hungary or in Romania; rather, they are about one fourth to one third of the Hungarian population living in the basin of the Carpathians.[1] Comparable demographic proportions can be found only in the Balkans, and a more absurd ratio exists only between the population of Albania and Kosovo. Whatever happens to Hungarian minorities, a significant portion of Hungarian citizens learns about it and react to it as an important national issue.

This is why the worsening in the situation of the two largest Hungarian minorities, in Romania and Czechoslovakia, reverberates in Hungary with such force. And, indeed, there is a reason to worry. In both of those countries the Hungarian school system has been declining for decades; consequently, Hungarians living there have gradually been losing their high culture and have been squeezed out of respected professions. The ethnic homogeneity of Hungarian territories has been upset by intentionally-designed industrial development and administrative relocation of people. Hungarian cultural and special interest organizations have been abolished or restricted in their rights. The use of the Hungarian language is frequently forbidden at the office and the workplace. In Slovakian internal propaganda forums, in Romanian mass media, incitement against the Hungarian ethnic group is widespread: it is accused of collective national crimes and Irredentism.

Do they really believe in their accusations? The accuracy of the facts is apparently of no concern to them; their fear, however, is real: they do not feel secure themselves within the borders they received from the victorious powers of two World Wars.[2] They would like to create a *fait accompli* so that the the arrangement of the Trianon and Paris treaties could never be disputed again. They want a Hungarian-free Romania and Slovakia even at the price of forced assimilation of hundreds of thousands or millions of minority Hungarians.

---

1 In the wake of World War I, the Versailles peace treaty (June 4, 1920) reduced Hungary's territory to one-third its former size. The victorious powers divided the remaining two-thirds of Hungary's territory among neighboring states which for the most part came into existence following the fall of the Austro-Hungarian Monarchy, that is: Romania, Czechoslovakia, and Yugoslavia. As a result, every third ethnic Hungarian was placed under the jurisdiction of a foreign state. On the eve of World War II some of these territories were briefly reannexed, following the two "Vienna decisions" presided over by Hitler, but the 1947 Paris peace treaty re-established the Versailles borders. According to conservative estimates, 2.2 million Hungarians live in Romania, 700,000 in Czechoslovakia, 450,000 in Yugoslavia, 200,000 in the Soviet Union, and 50,000 in Austria. (The population of the motherland is less than 10.5 million.)

2 Hungary signed the peace treaties after both World War I and World War II as a defeated country.

It is not easy to think with a sober and cool head about this tragedy which is taking place in front of our eyes. It is not easy to harness the passions; to separate the outrage over the assaults against the minorities from day-dreams associated with Trianon;[3] to separate rejection of the incitement for hatred against Hungarians from hatred towards Romanians and Slovaks; to separate the condemnation of the neighboring countries' policies from the illusion that the Soviet Union will bring order to the situation. It is no wonder that in Hungarian public consciousness all these elements swirl around together, for there seems to be no hope for a fair solution. But understanding does not equal approval, and I think that anybody who takes a position on the minority question is also obliged to take a position concerning the contradictions of the domestic public opinion. Let me begin by stating my own position.

My point of departure is simple. I see people in front of us who speak Hungarian as we do and belong to the Hungarian cultural community as we do; but what is natural for us is the source of social discrimination and daily humiliation for them. If of their own free will, choosing from comparable alternatives open to them, they decided to abandon their nationality, I would take notice of the shrinkage of the Magyars with sorrow but without outrage. What is outrageous, however, is the flagrant violation of the minority Hungarians' human rights. What I want is respect for their human rights and their rights as a community, and the institutional protection of both. I speak of human rights, that is, rights which belong to every human being—Hungarian or non-Hungarian—and not about special treatment for Hungarians because of their history or cultural eminence. Of course I am particularly concerned if the victims of human rights violations happen to be Hungarians, that is, people who could be in my place and me in theirs if in 1920 the superpowers' arbitrariness had drawn the borders in some other way. But I am also particularly concerned if Hungarians violate the rights of other ethnic communities; this is why I am more preoccupied with the situation of the gypsies in Hungary than in Poland.

For me the question of minorities is put this way: how can the peoples of the region coexist in their human dignity as equal citizens, freely using their own language, freely cultivating their own culture, or freely choosing another—not their native—language and culture? Men and women who do not believe in the existence of superior and inferior peoples accept this demand without any difficulty when it is formulated in the abstract. To accept its consequences, however, is not always that easy. Let us face the difficulties.

---

3 The 1920 Versailles treaty was signed by Palais Trianon.

Everybody knows that the desperate situation of minority Hungarians is not caused solely by official oppression but by the endless humiliations of everyday life as well: on any bus someone may turn up who yells at them that they are to speak the language of the state whose bread they eat; in any store service may be denied them if they address the salesperson in Hungarian; their children may be mocked by their schoolteacher and their friends may be insulted on the street. These people, whose dignity is being violated daily, would need the meekness of Christ to see clearly at every instance: not entire peoples are their enemies, only the states' chauvinistic policies. Nonetheless, one should always bear in mind that such widespread and aggressive hatred, which is directed at minority Hungarians, never appears without systematic propaganda and organized incitement. No matter how difficult it is, we have to be able to recognize the victim in the Romanian and Slovak common man who may be full of hatred for Hungarians. We must know that those who incite him against the Magyars do this in order to avert his attention for his own human misery. We have to realize that the minority's special deprivation of civil rights is inseparable from the overall disregard for human rights of every citizen. What happened to Géza Szöcs[4] and the other editors of *Counterpoints*, a Hungarian *samizdat* review in Transylvania, had happened earlier to Romanian members of the free trade union movement. At the time of Miklós Duray's trial[5] dozens of Czech activists of Charter '77 were already in jail.[6] The Hungarian question cannot be solved without the full realization of human rights in general, and the state-forming nationality cannot expect respect for its rights until the minority rights of Hungarian and non-Hungarian nationalities are fully restored.

---

4 Géza Szöcs (1953-   ), Hungarian poet, was born in Transylvania, Romania. He was one of the editors of *Ellenpontok* (Counterpoints), a Hungarian language *samizdat* publication which was launched in 1981 and managed to bring out eight issues. Szöcs and two of the other editors, Attila Ara-Kovács and Károly Tóth, were arrested and severely beaten in 1983. Since 1986, Szöcs has lived in Switzerland. Ara-Kovács now lives in Hungary, and Károly Tóth in Sweden.
5 Miklós Duray (1944-   ) is a geologist, writer, and founding member of the Hungarian Minority Rights Defense Committee in Czechoslovakia. The committee was set up in 1978 as a response to the Slovakian authorities' plan for the gradual liquidation of Hungarian schools. Duray was arrested for the first time in 1982 when he was kept in detention without trial for six months, and again in 1984 when he spent one year in prison without sentence. Charta '77, which Duray joined in 1983, protested his case on the latter occasion.
6 Among them were the playwright Václav Hável and the engineer Petr Uhl, both convicted in 1979 for their participation in activities of VONS, the Committee for the Defense of the Unjustly Persecuted.

How can this be achieved? The Hungarian minorities are in no position to fight for their own rights: at the smallest sign of organizing, the machinery of police and court oppression is set into motion; the most active participants get arrested, vilified, and put on trial, and the people around them subjected to intimidation. The means available to the Hungarian state and its citizens appear to be weak as well. There is only one strong power in the region which could bring pressure to achieve a better treatment of minority Hungarians, and this power is the Soviet Union. Especially in relation to Romania there has been some hope in the public opinion of Hungary that the Soviet state eventually will intervene in this matter. A segment of the Hungarian population has been waiting since 1968 for a possible occupation of Romania. In my opinion, this hope is dangerous, and not only because it is without any foundation. Let us suppose that the Soviet Union is willing to take sides in the dispute of its two allies. What would happen in such a case in the long run? As soon as the other side recovers, it would fervently try to win back the Soviet Union's favor. We would be entangled in a fatal rivalry: which one of us could offer larger benefits, more valuable compensations to the Soviet power? In this rivalry Hungary as a small state would lose its relative freedom of maneuvering. And what is the most disturbing of all: we would not get in return a lasting solution to the nationality question. A lasting solution can only be based on reconciliation between the different peoples, on mutual respect for each other's rights, and not on a superpower dictate.

Finally the greatest temptation of all: linkage of the minority problem and border questions. We cannot say what proportion of the Hungarian public believes that the trials of the Hungarian minorities provide an additional justification to revise the unjust Trianon and Paris treaties. It is my impression, however, that many people do accept this reasoning; and, indeed, it sounds convincing. Nevertheless, we have to state that such reasoning does not take into account existing reality. The issue is not simply that the superpowers, who guarantee the existing borders, have absolutely no intention of risking a third world war just to provide historical justice and to do this on account of Eastern Europe for the third time.[7] The above-cited reasoning disregards a painful fact which is hard to accept: the chauvinistic minority policies of the neighboring countries essentially did achieve their objective. Along the Hungarian border, both in Slovakia and Romania, there are barely

---

7 The immediate cause of World War I was the assassination of Archduke Francis Ferdinand, heir apparent to the Austro-Hungarian throne, by a Serbian nationalist on June 28, 1914. One month later (July 28, 1914) the Austro-Hungarian Monarchy declared war on Serbia. On September 1, 1939 Germany invaded Poland and World War II began.

any contiguous territories left which are populated by Hungarians. One could still demand insignificant border corrections on the basis of the majority principle. It remains a question, however, whether a few square miles are worth the unleashing of the passions which would threaten the minority masses remaining on the other side of the new border. Larger territories, on the other hand, could be re-annexed by Hungary only if huge non-Hungarian populations would be attached to Hungary. In this case there would be only two alternatives left. One is massive deportation. We are already familiar with this approach. We know how much suffering befell the Hungarians in Slovakia during the 1945-47 relocation campaign.[8] In addition, we also know what little chance there is of successfully executing such campaigns. We know the obverse version as well, which took place under the Austro-Hungarian Empire: Slovak and Romanian separatist movements, Hungarian fear of the annexed nationalities' revisionism, and an attempt at forced accelerated assimilation. If we seriously believe that no people has special privileges over others, if we are unwilling to treat other ethnic entities in a manner which we condemn when Hungarian minorities are its victims, then the revision of the Trianon borders must be excluded from the possible solutions of the Hungarian question. We know that it requires an extraordinary detachment by every people to realize that the historical moment has passed when the injustice which befell it could have been corrected in full. Unfortunately, a people's future may depend on its ability to reach this realization. Think of the fate of the Palestinians.

What we need to do, without violating peoples' equality or their freedom and dignity, is to search for possible ways of reconciliation which are not contingent on a superpower dictate, to search for possible ways to restore minority rights without border revisions. I consider desirable a situation in which every Hungarian family has the opportunity to send its children to Hungarian kindergarten, to elementary, secondary, and trade school, to Hungarian university; a situation in which a Hungarian diploma is worth exactly as much as a non-Hungarian one; where a minority Hungarian may learn about his past and his present condition and may cultivate his own special culture. I consider desirable a situation in which Hungarian education

---

8 According to the 1944 Slovak Government Program (the so-called Kosice Program) every Hungarian living in Czechoslovak territory shared a collective responsibility for unspecified war crimes, unless he was an active participant in the resistance movement. This charge of collective guilt served as a pretext for depriving all ethnic Hungarians of Czechoslovak citizenship and for attempting to expel all of them to Hungary. By 1948, 70,000 to 80,000 Slovaks left Hungary and an estimated 150,000 to 200,000 Hungarians were forced to leave Slovakia. In 1948, this forced population relocation was stopped as a result of the Sovietization of both countries.

and the cultivation of Hungarian culture is placed in the hands of autonomous ethnic organizations; in which the relocation of people, necessitated by industry development, is administered by proportionately elected bodies of local government. I consider desirable a situation in which, barring the use of minority languages, incitement against ethnic minorities and degrading treatment of such groups would be punished; a situation in which the Hungarian minority would have free, unlimited access to the press and culture of its motherland, where it could freely move between its homeland and its motherland. I consider desirable a situation in which a member of the Hungarian minority could in his motherland attend school and university, could seek employment, and would be allowed to repatriate. In short, I consider desirable a situation such as that demanded by the Transylvanian *Counterpoints* for the Hungarians of Romania and by the Hungarian Minority Rights Defense Committee for the Hungarians of Czechoslovakia.

But if we do not count on Soviet intervention, if we are fully aware of the defenselessness of the Hungarian minorities in Romania and Czechoslovakia and know that the Hungarian state and its citizens have very limited means to influence the situation, can we then go beyond the expression of respectable but ineffective principles? We cannot entertain high hopes, that is true. Nonetheless, there is room for initiatives and we can take more assertive steps in fostering a gradual improvement of the situation.

First of all, there are things to be done to place the minority problem on the agenda. A leading intellectual (or several of them at the same time) might send a private letter to his Romanian or Slovak colleague—poet to poet, historian to historian, physicist to physicist—and express his worries concerning the situation of the Hungarian minority. The members of professional or cultural organizations might turn collectively to their sister organizations. If everything goes well, the letter might lead to correspondence, the correspondence might be followed by a meeting and an exchange of ideas. If it is necessary, a public statement or announcement might be issued. The state, of course, might make considerably more effective gestures; although, at the same time, the diplomatic relations of the region impose upon it more restrictions as well. It is clear that the state, especially publicly, cannot be as straightforward in presenting the grievances as can private persons. Notwithstanding this, it has the opportunity to express its position in such a way that neighboring states, no matter how ill-intentioned, cannot accuse it of interfering in their internal affairs. For example, the National Assembly would make up for an old omission if it passed a nationality law about the rights of minorities living in Hungary. The law itself could spell out, or there could be a separate offer, that the appropriate parliamentary committees of the countries involved monitor and from time to time review how the statutes of the law had been executed. It could be made clear that the Hungarian state would not object if its minority citizens turn with their grievances to these committees, and that the Hungarian side would be willing to investigate every grievance in cooperation with them. I also consider it conceivable that the HSWP leadership or the government could issue a declaration about the principles for handling minority problems, could initiate the discussion of this question by the Warsaw Pact's political council, and could pass a resolution about this matter. Furthermore, legislation could be enacted about the existence of universal Hungarian culture and about the Hungarian state's obligations—within its authority—for fostering this culture. Such public actions would somewhat increase the pressure on the neighboring states and as a result create more favorable conditions for the successful discussion of the essential issues in closed sessions.

There is also plenty to do to provide moral support to those members of the minority who wish to remain Hungarians. The private citizens' opportunities in this regard are so obvious that it is needless to talk about them in detail. It is worthwhile, however, to say a few words about the opportunities of the state. The state could reserve places for minority Hungarians in our schools, dormitories, universities; it could establish fellowships to cover their living expenses. It could support with subscriptions the minority periodicals published abroad; through private donations it could organize a book fund for the Hungarian libraries abroad. It could launch a special periodical to provide a comprehensive view of Hungarian minority culture. It could intentionally develop its television and radio transmitters to reach the largest possible territory along our borders. Although the minority question cannot be solved with repatriation, it would be an appropriate starting point that the Hungarian state receive anybody who wishes to repatriate. The state should simplify the procedure of immigration, should institute a fund for the temporary support of immigrants, and establish an agency which would assist immigrants in solving their problems of adaptation. Finally, while new custom and transit regulations are being legislated, careful consideration should be given to whether all those regulations are hospitable to the type of human and material transit which is necessary to maintain normal human contacts.

Much more could be done to inform the Hungarian public about the minority situation and to familiarize it with the principles of an equitable solution. Until now—in part, to avoid diplomatic complications, in part for fear of creating an overheated atmosphere around the question of nationalities in the country—the official information policy has been to treat this problem as the strictest of taboos. However, it is not clear whether this silence has the desired effect. It is true that the more said about the minorities' plight the greater the chance for diplomatic collision. It remains a question, however, of what would happen if meticulously precise, objective, and dispassionate information and principled announcements based on respect for the rights and dignity of the neighboring peoples were provided to the public. It is not at all certain that the diplomatic response would be so vehement that it would not be worthwhile to risk the advantages of straight-forward talk—among them the advantage of maintaining the pressure on the neighboring states by keeping the issue on the agenda. As far as the internal effects of mass information are concerned: it is an illusion to think that silence cannot nurture ill feelings. If the present situation of the minorities cannot be touched upon, the need to speak about it will spring up in other ways: through the repeated mention of the historical characteristics of the Hungarian Highlands[9] and Transylvania[10] through the dissection of the circumstances of the Trianon treaty. Since nothing else can be mentioned, the Hungarian public consciousness addresses all this in two simple phrases: "Transylvania is Hungarian"; "We reject Trianon." The sober presentation of the truth must be better than this.

We mention the most difficult task last: to break down the wall of hostility between Hungarian and Slovaks, between Hungarian and Romanians. In this area the state cannot do more than lay the foundations of this task: it can urge the opening of the borders, it can promote freer movement in both directions between our countries, it can advance the abolition of restrictions which make normal contacts difficult or impossible. The job of the building on this foundation belongs to its citizens: to the intellectuals who can easily establish professional and cultural contacts, to the young people who frequently travel and make friends easily. Finally, those who form public opinion have a lot to do to insure that society not receive with ill feeling those Eastern Europeans who do their shopping in Hungary; that our public understand that the Slovaks do not cause market shortages in Hungary; and that the Magyars also benefit if their neighbors consider it advantageous to visit Hungary.

---

9 Hungarian Highlands or Felvidék, the southeastern part of present-day Czechoslovakia, is located on the Hungarian border.
10 Transylvania, the western part of present-day Romania, belonged to the Hungarian Kingdom for almost 1000 years. In the 16th and 17th centuries it was an independent Hungarian principality, then fell under Austrian rule, together with other parts of Hungary. Since 1920, except for a short period between 1940 and 1944 when its northern part was re-annexed to Hungary, it has belonged to Romania.

A Program of Action in Favor of Hungarian Minorities Abroad

A Program of Action
in Favor of Hungarian
Minorities Abroad

I t is first of all our moral obligation to face the critical situation of the
Hungarian minorities beyond our borders. The part of a nation living
within the jurisdiction of the Hungarian state is responsible for its other
parts that have been forced into minority status beyond its borders. We
must assume deliberately the burdens stemming form this responsibility,
having clarified in public debate what we regard as an acceptable solution
of the minority issue and what we can do to achieve such a solution.

But there are also political arguments in favor of carefully considering the
minority issue publicly:

- Helping the minorities requires a common national strategy which
  cannot be devised surreptitiously.

- How the minority issue is handled will basically influence Hungary's
  relations with neighboring countries.

- Suppression of the minority problem clouds our national self-
  perception, could change our justifiable concern to blind fury, and
  could easily lead to a situation where compassion degenerates into
  collective hysteria that lends itself readily to manipulation.

Regarding the state's attitude to the minority issue, those in power bear a heavy burden of blame.

When the Sovietization of Eastern Europe was completed in 1948, the minority issue became a taboo. The government of each country received a free hand over the minorities on its territory. For Rákosi and his associates, Hungarian minorities living beyond our borders did not exist.

After 1956, Kádár and his associates accepted a shameful role in the campaign against the Hungarian minorities to the neighboring countries by loudly spreading the accusation that the revolution had raised territorial claims and by openly approving the campaign that Romania launched against Hungarian intellectuals of Romanian citizenship charged with irredentism.

In the early 1970s, the leadership strove to suppress the efforts to recognize Hungarian culture in the neighboring countries as a part of universal Hungarian culture. From the mid-1970s on, it stubbornly resisted the pressure to place on the agenda the worsening situation of the Hungarian minorities.

Only in the 1980s did the leadership yield to the mounting pressure of public opinion and begin to take at least occasional steps to halt the deterioration. And only recently has it reached the point of adopting a public standpoint.

At the (Helsinki) review conferences in Ottawa and Vienna, the Hungarian delegation cosponsored a proposal that the rights of national minorities be included in the human rights enjoying international protection. In one or two statements, responsible political leaders mentioned the grievances of the Hungarian minorities (particularly those in Romania). A Research Institute of Hungarology has been established in Budapest to coordinate the study of East European history and culture, including the history and culture of the entire Hungarian people. After lengthy procrastination, the monograph "Erdely Tortenete" [History of Transylvania] has finally been published.

These steps are welcome, but only as the first steps. A turnaround is needed also in the policy on the Hungarian minorities beyond our borders. We need clear basic principles, a carefully thought out strategy and established procedures, not campaigns.

Our principles

The principles that must be the basis of our policy on protecting national minorities are as follows:

- Every national minority is entitled to collective rights: to jointly foster their language, culture, and traditions, and to maintain contact with the mother nation. The rights of national minorities stem from the human rights of the individual: members of national minorities cannot be equal citizens of their country if they do not have collective rights.

- Respect for the rights of national minorities is not each country's internal affair. As human rights of a particular kind, minority rights belong under the protection of the community of nations. Every country has the right and obligation to protest against the disfranchisement of minorities in any country with which it maintains relations.

- It is the mother nation's specific duty to monitor closely the situation of its scattered co-national minorities, and to do everything possible in their interest that can be done within the framework of the international protection of human rights.

- In view of the ethnic composition of the population in our region, the minority problem cannot be solved through a fair redrawing of borders. What we must demand is not territory but the same individual and collective rights for minorities in every country.

- Freedom to emigrate must be protected. But emigration cannot help the situation of minorities collectively. The members of minorities who wish to remain must be given rights so their eventual emigration would be voluntary departure, rather than flight.

- Where the majority's human rights are being violated, there can be no hope of respect for the rights of a minority. Where the national majorities have been isolated and set against each other, there can be no hope of freely maintaining relations between the mother nations and their scattered co-national minorities in other countries. Settlement of the minority issue requires democracy, broader regional integration, and closer reconciliation between nations.

A mature long-term strategy is needed

The state's long-term minority policy must strive to bring the actual situation closer to the basic principles, and the state will have to declare its intention of doing so.

A declaration of the state's standpoint will be necessary for the following reasons:

- It will help to end speculation and dispel suspicion.

- It will serve as a compass for short-term measures and provide protection for voluntary public initiatives that are in accord with the basic principles.

- It will lend moral support to the humiliated and demoralized minorities.

The declaration will have to disclose the relationship between the Hungarian state and the universal Hungarian nation. The national declaration could be made by the government in the National Assembly, or it could be passed as a resolution of the Assembly itself.

- The declaration will have to start out by defining the Hungarian nation as a group of people who are characterized by community of language, culture, and historical traditions, but are not confined to the citizens of the Hungarian state.

- The declaration will have to state that Hungary does not claim sovereignty over Hungarians who are citizens of other countries, but recognizes a duty to help such Hungarians preserve their national identity.

- Such help may consist in part of initiatives that the Hungarian state is able to take on its own territory, without interfering in the internal affairs of other countries (the offering of scholarships, the establishment of places in schools, universities, and student dormitories, etc.).

- In part there may be actions taken abroad, on the basis of international agreements. (For example, bringing before international forums the minority grievances that constitute human rights violations).

- Finally, the state will have to undertake efforts to conclude bilateral agreements that can improve the situation of the minorities (for example, agreements on the free exchange of educational and recreational goods or on the lifting of travel restrictions between countries).

A National Minority Law will have to be enacted

It is important that the National Minority Law be enacted before, or at the same time as, the national declaration is issued.

- The law will have to guarantee for every national minority in Hungary (including the Gypsy minority) all the rights we are demanding for the Hungarian minorities living beyond our borders.

- It will have to make clear that every national minority in Hungary is free to maintain relations with its mother nation and with the latter's scattered co-nationals in other countries.

- It will have to recognize the national minorities' right to present their grievances either to the state of their mother nation or before competent international forums. Hungary will have to offer its cooperation in investigating and remedying the complaints.

A standpoint must be adopted on the desirable development of the order within the region

It will be the task of the government to issue its regional standpoint and commit itself to directions of development such as the following:

- A changeover to a market economy;

- Free circulation of ideas and cultural products across the borders;

- Freedom to travel, settle, and work anywhere within the region;

- Direct relations between cultural and scientific institutions, independent of agreements between countries;

- Encouragement of reconciliation between nations, and the withdrawal of the states from the international debates of the scientific and cultural communities.

The consistent short-term measurers that must be implemented are as follows:

- Efforts must be undertaken that will help to make borders more open. Tourism must be encouraged. Customs and foreign-exchange policies must be brought in line with the objective of continual expansion in passenger traffic.

- We must see to it that domestic books and periodicals get to the areas where the Hungarian-speaking population is concentrated. (In the case of Czechoslovakia, for example, the principal export destination should be Bratislava, rather than Prague.)

- The publishing of minority books and periodicals must be supported through orders, subscriptions, and agreements on swaps. We need a periodical appearing in Hungary, and perhaps also a publishing house for books, to publish the work of minority literatures and cultures.

- Minority scholarship must be supported, in part with research commissions, in part with joint research programs, and in part by providing scholarships and supplying research tools.

- The most dangerous trend in Romania and Czechoslovakia during the past 15 to 20 years has been the arbitrary curtailment of instruction for Hungarians in their native language. Efforts must be made to conclude agreements with the respective governments for halting this process and reversing it if possible. We must help to provide replacements for the shrinking pool of teachers.

- Hungarians are fleeing from Romania in increasing numbers. It is a shame that the Hungarian government is hampering their immigration by raising numerous administrative difficulties and, for political reasons, is not admitting persons who have been persecuted and vilified. Immigration permits should be issued quickly, automatically, and indiscriminately. Upon their arrival in Hungary, resettlers should be granted Hungarian citizenship if they apply for it. A separate office should be set up to help resettlers adjust.

In shaping short-term policy, we must strive to base the protection of minorities on reciprocity and good relations with other countries. If we act with determination, this could now bear fruit in Hungary's relations with Yugoslavia, and perhaps also with Czechoslovakia. The opportunities in relations with the Soviet Union have not been tested at all. The really hard case is that of Romania.

We will hardly be able to come to an agreement with the present Romanian government. An open dispute will be unavoidable if Hungary does not wish to lend a helping hand in the vilification and ruining of the Hungarians in Romania. It is more important, therefore, that the objectives and principles of the government's actions be made unambiguously clear.

In the short term we cannot hope to achieve much more than to let the Hungarians in Romania know that they have not been abandoned. Thinking in longer terms, however, we believe it is reasonable to expect that the power structure in Romania will undergo a deep crisis after Ceausescu disappears from the scene, if not before. In that situation it will be significant what stand the Hungarian government took in the preceding years:

- was it firm in protecting the Hungarian minority's rights, but not blindly anti-Romanian in areas where Hungary has no interest or perhaps has common interests with Romania;

- or did it mask its weakness by engaging in noisy polemics over grievances and by pursuing a shortsighted anti-Romanian foreign policy?

If the Hungarian government follows the latter course, then it will be merely a helpless spectator also in the coming Romanian crisis. But if it follows the former course, then it could act as mediator between a Romanian state striving for consolidation on the one hand, and the Hungarian minority on the other.

There must be openness on the minority issue

The Hungarian public is being informed intermittently and one-sidely. Usually the Hungarian press dwells on the issue of the Hungarian minorities only when a historical or literary polemic erupts (as a rule, between a Romanian and a Hungarian author).

- The government's spokesmen and information office must withdraw from cultural and scientific polemics. It is up to the cultural and scientific communities to defend themselves.

- Press control of the debate on the national (minority) issue outside the mass media must cease. Only free debate can help the emergence of a healthy national public opinion.

- Detailed and objective information is necessary on how the situation of the minorities is developing. The official information agencies must also assume a role in this, but without monopolizing the right to provide information.

The releasing of information must be a part of Hungary's strategy on protecting the rights of the minorities. But this is also necessary to give domestic public opinion a clear overview of the situation. The suppression of facts would give free rein to nationalist fantasies. Letting history dominate the polemics to the exclusion of everything else would inevitably make two questions the decisive issues: Who came first to Transylvania? And which pre-1945 regime served Nazi Germany better? Whereas the question of primary importance must be: to what rights are the 2 to 2.5 million Hungarians now living in Romania entitled?

It is necessary to support the voluntary public initiatives

Instead of supporting independent initiatives to aid the minorities, the state is hampering such initiatives every way possible. Until this practice is changed, it will be impossible to take seriously the official statements made on behalf of the Hungarian minorities living beyond our borders.

Groups of resourceful citizens are able to reach areas and people that state agencies cannot, to gather information that cannot be obtained through official channels, and to give the kind of help that the state is unable to provide. And it is also easier to tap society's generosity from below than through official drives.

- There must not be any recurrence of the unseemly fuss that preceded the licensing of the Gabor Bethlen Foundation. Private foundations and other groups must not be cut off from the public, as has happened since the Gabor Bethlen Foundation's licensing. Indeed, it is necessary to support them (with state subsidies, with tax exemption of donations, etc.).

- The state must recognize that the connections of the churches and religious communities are one of the most effective ways of delivering aid and must abandon its attempts to control and restrict these connections.

- The fact of our belonging to the same alliance cannot justify the collusion between Hungarian border guards and the neighboring countries' authorities. To prevent the export of Hungarian-language productions is contrary to the obligations assumed in the Helsinki Declaration and violates Hungary's national interests. The state has a duty to protect its citizens from the harassment to which the authorities of the neighboring countries—primarily Romania—subject them. It must stand up in defense of citizens' rights and dignity.

The opportunities for international reconciliation must be sought

The state itself can do much to promote international reconciliation:

- by persistently urging a solution of the minority issue on the basis of reciprocity and cooperation;

- by not confusing protection of the rights of the minorities with a policy directed against the neighboring countries' interests;

- by supporting and proposing measures to make borders more open; and

- by not getting involved in attempts to turn public opinion against the neighboring nations.

However, the lion's share of the task falls on the citizens who come up with independent initiatives. International reconciliation is possible only between nations, not between states.

Spokesmen for the cause of the Hungarian minorities beyond our borders must make unambiguously clear that the minorities in every country are equally entitled to minority rights, including the minorities living on Hungary's territory. We have to advocate tolerance of ethnic, cultural, and religious variety.

We must dispel the suspicion that, under the pretext of the minority issue, we actually want to achieve a redrawing of borders. When speaking of the injustices of the Treaties of Trianon and Paris, we must always bear in mind the defensive reflexes of the successor states' citizens.

In the historical polemics we must not fall into an escalation of accusations. We have to emphasize consistently that the issues of the historical disputes must be kept separate from those of the present political disputes, even when the other side is unwilling to accept their separation.

We must seek a dialogue with neighboring countries' democratic-minded circles. They are the ones who could be our collaborators and allies in the slow, gradual process of reconciliation. They must perceive that we are linked to them by commitment to the common cause of democracy, by real solidarity, and not merely by tactical interests.

Once More on Mandatory Labor

Once More on
Mandatory Labor

Mandatory labor law has been updated in Hungary. Our reader, however, should not lose sleep over it; he is not threatened by the 19th decree (1984) of the Presidential Council.[1] Social parasites who are to be made accustomed to regular work by the state through the assignment of mandatory residence and forced corrective labor,[2] do not read *Beszélő*. They spend their time on the streets and at watering holes. They are the ones who make well-established citizens fear for the safety of their property and their physical well-being. So, our reader should not lose sleep over it—unless his sense of justice, his social and political sensibilities prevent him from sleeping.

What does our sense of justice command?

A loafer, by not working, has not harmed anybody's physical well-being or property. He seems to be more likely to commit crimes causing personal injury

---

1 Presidential Council is a body established in 1949 to substitute for the parliament when it is not is session. The Presidential Council has the power to issue decrees with the force of law and to amend or to repeal laws passed by parliament. The National Assembly itself convenes four times a year for a few days only. The Presidential Council has 19 members. Its lawmaking powers were abolished in 1988.
2 The new institution, called restrictive forced corrective labor, has the specific provision that under such a sentence a person must work at a specified place, for a specified time (for low wages), and is not allowed to leave his assigned place of residence.

or property damage than if he had permanent employment. But according to current Hungarian law, he can be classified as a social parasite[3] even if he does not actually commit the crime which he has a greater-than-average chance to commit. Anybody who cannot prove that he supports himself by working—in case he lacks any other legitimate source of income—commits the crime of social parasitism. The Penal Code clearly states that such a lifestyle falls under the jurisdiction of criminal law, solely because of its *potential danger*: "From the point of view of criminal law, a person who is capable of working, but does not engage in employment, in spite of the fact that he does not possess means to insure his livelihood, is a social parasite." (Penal Code § 266., Brief of the Justice Department, 2nd point) Clearly, then, the decree on mandatory labor introduces a *preventive* sanction; it punishes an act which has not been committed, but which might be committed by the accused in the future. This is, in and by itself, unjust. It is a fundamental principle of criminal justice that a person can be held responsible only for acts which he actually committed against the life, physical well-being, human dignity, or property of others. If this principle is violated, then the distinction between guilty and innocent, based on the concept of personal responsibility, becomes blurred, and the court does not dispense justice any longer; it simply engages in institutionalized violence.

Is it really true that lifestyle-without-work endangers public safety? The explanation given in the mandatory labor decree for the necessity of the new and more severe punishment is that the number of social parasites has increased. The statistics, however, refute this statement: between 1970 and 1983 social parasitism has remained on the same level (*Heti Világgazdaság* December 6, 1984). Yet, during the same period the crime rate has shown a dramatic increase. According to the *1983 Yearbook of Statistics*, in that year the number of reported crimes was 25% higher than in the years between 1970 and 1975. This shows that there is no demonstrable connection between the increase in the crime-rate and social parasitism in the last fifteen years. "Social parasitism" is not a public danger. Then why is it punished, and with an ever-increasing severity at that?

Because the lawmakers and those who instruct them *believe it to be* a public danger. Why do they not consider it necessary to confront their belief with statistical data and dare to brand and punish thousands of people without checking whether their presumption is correct or not? This is precisely the

---

3 Under the criminal code adopted in 1979, anyone who remains without employment for a period longer than three months is considered a "social parasite." Lack of employment is punishable by fine, forced corrective labor, or imprisonment.

question. We find the answer to it in the legal terminology describing lifestyle-without-work. The Penal Code took the word "social parasite" from the vernacular, together with its inherent moral judgment. This is an unusual step. The law, as a rule, strives for neutral usage of the language in order to prevent legal definitions of observed phenomena from becoming inseparably intertwined with everyday moral judgments. In the case of lifestyle-without-work, however, the lawmakers demonstratively deviated from this tradition. It is a telling gesture, indeed. It reveals that their moral judgment is nothing more than *prejudice*. We speak of a person's being prejudiced when a certain way of life is so repulsive to him that he is even unwilling to examine whether it really leads to the consequences he attributes to it. In the case of "social parasitism" this is exactly what happened.

In 1983 drunk drivers caused the death of 130 people, and the statistics report 215 murders in the same year. Unfortunately, the yearbook does not specify in how many causes the murderer was a social parasite. But since the total number of crimes committed by social parasites was 1105, if we suppose that every tenth loafer killed a man—which is a gross exaggeration—then social parasitism is still responsible for fewer deaths than drunken driving. In spite of this, there is no evidence that lawmakers are contemplating that drunken driving should get the same punishment as social parasitism: 1 to 3 years of correctional labor after the first, or second positive breath test. But of course, a drunk driver, although he acts carelessly, otherwise is a decent man; he lives just like you and me, while the lifestyle of a social parasite is totally opposed to accepted social norms.

But is a lifestyle punishable solely for not meeting dominant social mores? Without violating the principle of citizens' equality before the law, lifestyles cannot be punished at all. People of different denominations, of different cultures and party affiliations are not treated as equals by the law if they can be punished when the lawmakers (even if in concert with the majority judgment) disapprove of their religious ethos, cultural customs or political views. Likewise, people leading different lifestyles cannot be punished on grounds of moral disapproval without violating their equal status as subjects of the state.

Since the early '60s two tendencies have been wrestling with each other in Hungarian lawmaking. One of them strives towards the rule of law and a constitutional state: some changes in the Penal Code such as the modernization of the statute on homosexuality; new elements regulating criminal procedure, such as a defense lawyer's increased sphere of authority during the investigation; some changes in the area of state, civil, and economic law—all belong to this tendency. The other tendency is preoccupied with maintaining the law as an instrument of arbitrary rule and oppression. The increase of policy authority due to the establishment of additional mandatory penalties;

the referral of the violations of press regulations to the jurisdiction of the police; the expansion of the patrol police's mandate, and several other measures belong to this second tendency. In the last ten years the mandatory labor law is the most brutal of the measures conceived in this spirit, and not only because of the preventive and moralizing nature of the punishment. The concept of "social parasitism" has always bee notorious for its extremely vague definition. It does not contain one single word about the criterion of how long a person has to be without work in order for his lifestyle to become a public danger, and what sort of (monthly, annual) income he must have so that, in the case of lasting unemployment, he would avoid classification as a social parasite. The Presidential Council did not seize the opportunity to at least define the concept of social parasitism in more precise terms, while brutally increasing its penalties. On the other hand, it wasted no time in eliminating the distinction between social parasitism as a misdemeanor and as a felony. In the past, only the lifestyle of second offenders was considered a felony; now a person who is caught by the authorities for the first time for not working is a felon as well. If there is any punishment which can be given only in an arbitrary manner, the correctional work imposed on social parasitism most definitely belongs to this category. Anybody who wishes to live in a constitutional state must reject it.

What does our social sensibility demand?

In the case of persecuting homosexuality or adultery, the law commits only legal, not social, injustice, since there is no reason to assume that at the bottom of the social hierarchy there are more people of the same sex who are attracted to each other or more of those who prefer a variety of relationships than in the higher brackets. The persecution of lifestyle-without-work, however, punishes those people who are at the very bottom. If this law is unjust, it is doubly so for the vast majority of "social parasites" is made up of unskilled, uneducated people who have a rather dismal chance on the labor market. For these people to achieve social integration would take an incomparably larger effort than for most other members of society. And what does society offer them if they struggle their way to an orderly, acceptable lifestyle? Unskilled labor at construction sites or in the factory yard and a bed in some workers' dorm. Let us give serious thought before we are willing to approve the law's pronouncing guilty and punishing those who are not tempted by these prospects.

But is not such reasoning barren sentimentality? People want order and peace; and the more jeopardized public safety appears, the more important it is for them to have law and order. It is possible that the increase of the crime rate is not related to social parasitism, nevertheless lifestyle-without-work invariably induces criminal behavior. We may pity those who find themselves in this situation; we may understand its causes; nevertheless, we have to be aware that they have become the enemies of social order. First society has to protect itself against them; only afterwards can it deal with the improvement of their social status. How can we answer this extremely popular argument?

First of all, we can repeat what has already been said: the law must protect citizens both from attacks on their well-being and property, and from the excesses of the authorities. If public safety becomes somewhat better, but legal safeguards are considerably reduced, the price is violation of the right of a social minority to equal protection by law; this is unacceptable. A slight (or even a greater) improvement in the condition of those above does not justify the violation of the rights of those below, and not because they are below, but because the state must respect their rights as those of every citizen. Secondly, the dangers—which, in our view, are exaggerated—inherent in lifestyle-without-work can be reduced in ways other than mandated labor. In the welfare states to the west of us, society provides the basic necessities of livelihood for those who cannot or do not wish to be permanently employed. This is, of course, a simple solution and certainly not free of cost. But is the persecution of social parasitism without a price tag? Finally, it is not certain at all that by classifying and punishing lifestyle-without-work we reduce the crime rate. If the customary lifestyle of a person is pronounced criminal, he is either forced to give it up or to learn how to evade the laws hostile to him. Since we know the social causes of "social parasitism," we should realize that the latter one is the more likely. The concept of social parasitism brands a social group that is continuously being perpetuated. Those people whose natural environment is this group becoming increasingly convinced that the state is their enemy; that the state not only unjustly deprives them of the benefits available to others, but in addition to this also sends after them its policemen, prosecutors, and judges. And with this we have arrived at our last question:

What does our political sensibility suggest?

The Minister of Justice, in this interview to *Népszabadság*, stated that the government satisfied the urging of society when it introduced the statute on correctional labor. This seems to be an exaggeration. Apart from the minister's statement, there is virtually no sign that public opinion had urged this additional mandatory measure. But the danger is real. Recession is in its seventh year in Hungary; real wages have been on the decline; investments in public services and welfare have been postponed; chances of finding employment have worsened. Everybody has to work more and more beyond official working hours in the second, third, and God-knows-how many-eth economy in order to maintain his standard of living. Anybody who cannot increase his own self-exploitation inevitably slips downward. The majority of people believes less and less that a competent government—which knows how to overcome the crisis—is handling the country's affairs. But the people do not trust themselves either. They think that to join forces, to express their demands, and to put pressure on the government collectively is pointless. In this increasingly frustrating situation the competition between individuals and social groups has become more fierce, and people have become noticeably more irritable towards each other. So it is quite possible that, as the situation does not show any sign of improvement, an actual agreement may emerge between the government and a substantial segment of the population, at the expense of the most destitute people the very bottom. (The other potential scapegoat is the new entrepreneurial stratum which moves upwards, away from the average.) The increasing social tensions are pushing the government towards the more-frequent use of intimidation and reprisals than has been customary in the last 20 to 25 years. A large part of society might support growing police oppression if they are frightened of the spectre of punks and social parasites.

For even progressive intellectuals easily forget constitutional principles when the life of marginal groups foreign to them is at stake. Unfortunately, we have learned this from experience. We did not receive as much angry scolding for any other article in *Beszélö* as for "Incitement" (published in our 10th issue), which reported the political trial of two punk groups. "Too much is too much," we heard from one of our esteemed readers, "After all, 'Mosoj' was engaged in primitive incitement against neighboring countries, while the members of 'CPg' tore into pieces a live chicken at one of their concerts! What do we have in common with people like this?"[4]

In spite of all our reservations, we apparently have more sympathy and compassion toward these very young people who have already been kicked around quite a bit than do those of our readers who indignantly protested our article. But this is a secondary issue. The crux of the matter is whether a person

---

4 "Mosoj" and "CPg" are punk-rock bands (CPg means Come On Punk Group). Members of the first have gotten sentences with suspension, while the second's leader, Zoltán Benkó, was sentenced to two years in prison for "anti-state agitation" and "incitement of hatred against people with socialist convictions."

whose views or conduct we reject is entitled to the same protection by law as we are? Anybody who cannot distinguish between these two issues takes an unjust and shortsighted position.

Yes, such a position is not only unjust, it is shortsighted as well. We started our article reassuring our reader that he can sleep without worrying; the decree on mandatory labor was passed not against him. The law on incitement, however, can be used against him as well. Right at this moment it is not being used against intellectuals, only against workers, boarding school kids, and punk musicians. But it can be applied at any time to the author of a short story in *Kortárs*[5] or an article in *Valóság*.[6] It is in our common interest that incitement cases not be manufactured without attracting public attention and that the repeal of the scandalous statute on incitement should remain permanently on the public agenda. Furthermore, it is also in the common interest that unlawful mandatory measures which almost exclusively strike down uneducated, poor people of peripheral social status not be multiplied. Not solely because in a society where exceptional injustice afflicts those at the very bottom the general atmosphere inevitably becomes poisoned. There are other reasons as well: between 1965 and 1968, at the time economic reforms were introduced, official tolerance towards cultural differences was on the rise and legal conditions improved (for example, it was at that time that the measure limiting freedom of choice in employment was repealed). In the first half of the seventies the rescinding of reform was accompanied by purges in the academic institutes of philosophy and sociology; official attacks dispersed the artistic avant-garde; the persecution of white collar crimes showed a sudden surge and a series of restrictive legal decrees were passed (e.g., the restriction of the right to abortion, the statute about the mandatory reporting of employment). The new wave of reforms beginning in 1979 brought along some improvement in other areas as well. And now when the reform has run out of steam, laws and decrees befitting a police state are being passed one after the other. Arbitrary solutions to conflicts between the government and the intelligentsia have become more frequent, and the police are being used more and more visibly against the activists of the independent, *samizdat* press. When the legal status of those struggling at the very bottom of society becomes worse, so does that of everybody else who demands economic, cultural, and political pluralism. It is in the interest of all of us that the fundamental principles of a constitutional state should not be violated even in the case of those who live without work.

---

5 *Kortárs* (Contemporary) is a monthly literary magazine.
6 *Valóság* [Reality] is a monthly socio-political review.

On Ways of Being a Jew

On Ways of Being a Jew

(Personal Notes in Connection with the Open Letter of *Salom*)[1]

T he idea has been in the air. Since the situation of the Hungarian minorities abroad[2] has made domestic public opinion aware of the problem of minorities in general, it was to be expected that, sooner or later, minority demands would be heard within our borders as well. And indeed, the gypsy intelligentsia is increasingly bold in vocalizing the demand that gypsies should receive minority rights. Ever since attempts have been made to launch independent press, independent social thought, independent peace and environmentalist movements, it was to be expected that there would be those who would enter the public arena as an independent minority group. With its second manifesto, *Salom*—which originally emerged as the "independent peace group of the Hungarian Jewry"—assumed just such a role. Whether the Open Letter will be followed by similar initiatives remains to be seen. One thing, however, is already clear: since its publication the Jewish question cannot be discussed in Hungary in the same way as it was previously.

---

1 *Salom* is an independent Hungarian Jewish peace group. It made its first appearance in 1983 with a statement on the Hungarian People's Republic's Middle Eastern policies. Its most comprehensive statement, an "Open Letter to the Hungarian Jewry and to Hungarian Society," has been published in *Hírmondó* No. 6 (1984), on the 40th anniversary of the Holocaust. On *Hírmondó* see note 4 of "Troops of Weary Seekers . . . " in this volume.
2 See note 1 of "Hungarian Society and Hungarian Minorities Abroad" in this volume.

Not simply because instead of cautious hints it states explicitly that forty years after 1944[3] the relationship of Hungarian Jews and non-Jews is still unresolved. Nor because it points out how the Soviet-styled political regime reproduces the subordinated status of the Jewry (just as it does in the case of non-Jewish communities). All this would be important enough in itself; nevertheless, I see the real challenge of the Open Letter in something else.

Since the time of the emancipation, an ever increasing number of Hungarian Jews accepted the fact that they must assimilate into the majority society. It is true that orthodox groups, at least at the beginning, strongly resisted change. From the beginning of the 20th century Zionism has found followers as well. Between the two world wars yet another aspiration emerged which aimed at the coupling of loyalty to the Hungarian nation, respect for Hungarian culture, and the cultivation of an independent, secular Jewish culture. After the Holocaust and the subsequent Sovietization of the country all this vanished without a trace. The remnants of the orthodox community were forced into joint organization with the reformists. The Zionist movement was liquidated by force. Jewish religious leaders resigned themselves to the fact that the state was willing to acknowledge the Jewry only as a religious denomination, and did not recognize a secular Jewish culture's right to exist. The majority of Jewish non-believers, haunted by the horrors of the Holocaust, was trying to escape from its remaining Jewish identification marks. The position of assimilation which had been dominant earlier now attained monopoly.

From the late sixties and early seventies, however, parallel to the awakening of Hungarian national consciousness (although partially independent of it), there has been an increasing number of young Jews who are ready to accept their Jewishness, who exhibit a sense of community with the Diaspora and the state of Israel, and recognize distinct Jewish traditions as their own. *Salom* articulates their ambition when it breaks with the more-than-hundred-year old principle of assimilation: "While we acknowledge the individual's right to assimilation, concerning the whole of Hungarian Jewry, we profess that it should not assimilate itself to, rather, integrate itself into this country's society." In other words, Hungarian Jewry should strive not for the total obliteration of existing differences between Jews and non-Jews; instead, through the cultivation and further development of Jewish traditions, the separate Jewish minority should find its place in the life of Hungarian society as a whole.

3 On March 19, 1944 the German army occupied Hungary. The mass deportations began in the summer of 1944.

I would like to mention right away that I do sympathize with this aspiration, consider it legitimate, and would be glad to see the realization of even a fraction of it. My personal aspiration, however, is different and, I am convinced, of course, that it is also legitimate. What I really want to write about in these notes is that the Hungarian Jews may choose from various life strategies which are all compatible with the coexistence of Jews and non-Jews, a coexistence which is based on mutual respect.

Can this position be reconciled with the one put forward by *Salom*? In my opinion, yes. *Salom*, in effect, formulates a secular and democratic minority program. It is a fundamental principle of liberal democracy that every individual may choose not only the guiding philosophical and moral beliefs of his life, but also his affiliation with ethnic-cultural communities, if he chooses any such affiliation at all.

Yet the Open Letter contains some assertions which may lead to opposing conclusions. The pivotal "Assimilation or Integration" section argues on behalf of minority separation in the following manner: The Hungarian Jews, as the last remnants of the Eastern European Jewish masses, inherited significant cultural values. This heritage represents an obligation and today when in democratic societies there is a growing realization that minority cultures should not be obliterated because they enrich the majority society, "Hungarian Jewry must also recognize its duty towards itself."

This passage does not lend itself to easy interpretation, since the expression "Hungarian Jewry's duty to itself" is clearly a figure of speech, which, in effect, means the Jewish individuals' duty to the Jewish community. It is not clear, however, who these individuals are: those who consciously identify themselves with Jewry or all those who, on the basis of their Jewish ancestry, can be considered Jewish? "Duty," nonetheless, has a different meaning if we accept the narrow rather than the broad definition of those addressed.

For Jews, conscious of their Jewishness, it means: If you profess to be Jewish, you have to immerse yourself in your traditions, cultivate your past, foster your cultural heritage. For the others it has an additional meaning: If you were born Jewish, it is your obligation to become a conscious Jew.

In the first case the call relies on the notion that those addressed identify themselves with Jewry. Such identification, whether it is based on habit or conscious choice, is associated with personal moral commitment, and it may, indeed, imply duties (although the precedence relationships between such duties and those which we bear on universal grounds are not at all easy to establish). In the second case, however, the call relies on the sole fact that the addressee—according to a certain social assessment—is Jewish by birth.

This fact has nothing to do with the commitments of one's moral personality. If we mandate duties merely from a man's origin, what we really state is this: whoever a man wants to become, he, by definition, sins if he does not become who he is (according to the opinion of others) by birth. This notion was already latently present in 19th century nationalism, and emerged in a particularly repulsive manner in 20th century racism. It is, at any rate, incompatible with liberal democratic principles.

In my view, *Salom* did not fully clarify which interpretation it really stands for. The Open Letter, in a subordinate clause I have already quoted, declares: "We recognize the individual's right to assimilation." From this it should follow that "Hungarian Jewry's duty to itself" may bind only the conscious Jews. The Open Letter, however, contains a few elements which are more consistent with the broad interpretation. The whole letter recognizes only two types of Jewish behavior: the first one is that of the Jew who professes his identity and affiliation with dignity; the other—portrayed with contempt and passionate anger—the Jew who is trying to conceal his origin from his environment, from his children, and even from himself. One might think that the assimilated Jew is not mentioned, since with him *Salom* does not have any problem. But if it is so, then why does the Open Letter criticize the Jewish members of the Party apparatus for representing the official party line towards Israel in spite of their Jewishness? If only identification with Jewry, and not origin, obliges someone to show solidarity with Israel, then these people can be criticized, like everyone else, simply for their acceptance of the Soviet-Hungarian policy on the Middle-East. If, in addition to this, we blame them as Jews too, then we hold them accountable on the basis of "congenital" duties as well.

I think it is obvious which interpretation, as opposed to the one expressed in *Salom*, I would choose. But do I not want too much? Does not it follow from my position that a Jewish minority program can address only the already conscious Jews because propaganda, aimed at the others to awaken their Jewish consciousness, is inevitably intolerant? Not in my opinion. What follows from my position is nothing more than that a tolerant minority propaganda argues not with the individual's *duty*, but with the individual's *good*.

The Open Letter contains this form of argument as well, although it cannot be linked to any particular passage, but emerges from the piece as a whole. I would summarize it like this: Although Hungarian Jews have become almost completely Magyarized, their environment still recognizes and distinguishes them as Jews. For this very reason, to strive for complete assimilation is an idle effort; it can lead only to a compulsion of overcompensation, inferiority complex, and humiliating exposure. We can avoid all these if we accept that we are as they see us: Jews, descendants of a people with a great history and rich cultural traditions. We share something that bonds us together; something we can be proud of. There is no reason to be afraid that the upholding of Jewish identity will stir up anti-Semitism, since it was not the Jews' refusal to blend into the non-Jewish masses that caused anti-Semitism earlier. Moreover, we can be loyal to the Hungarian nation as a separate Jewish minority and could enrich its culture.

I consider this course of reasoning flawless. The problem pointed out by *Salom* does exist. The circle of those who struggle with the problem of self-definition, self-identity, and affiliation is much wider than the group of conscious Jews (the latter have already resolved the problem). The proposed solution is one of the possibilities; it does not exclude either the orderly coexistence of Jews and non-Jews, based on mutual respect, or the possibility that some Jews could choose another solution. The question is: are other solutions conceivable at all?

It is, of course, true that complete assimilation could be realized only through repeated intermarriages for generations to come. A potential increase of mixed marriages would undoubtedly be a sign of society's growing openness. Nevertheless, it would not help the present generations and it is the sort of thing which can be influenced only marginally by individual decision. Between minority separation and complete assimilation, however, there are numerous intermediate possibilities. I cannot provide a survey of all of them, but I would like to mention a few. It is possible for a person not to identify himself with any ethnic-cultural community; to be a loyal Hungarian citizen, but beyond that, to be indifferent to any national and ethnic group (a considerable portion of non-Jewish Hungarians take this position). It is possible for a person to have double bonds: to consider both the Jewish and Hungarian historical and cultural traditions his own, and to exhibit solidarity with both communities. It is also possible for a person to identify himself with his Jewishness without binding himself to the cultivation of Jewish culture and traditions, but instead identifying himself with the historical fate, social role, and status of secularized Jewry. And, finally, it is possible for a person to acknowledge and openly accept his status without identifying himself with it; rather, to consider himself part of the Hungarian nation, a Hungarian of Jewish ancestry.

Personally, I profess as my own this last possibility. I consider Hungarian culture, history, the destiny of Hungarian society to be my own. I do not have a comparable direct relationship with any other culture, history, or people. I come from a family which has been secularized for generations;

the Jewish religous traditions do not occupy me; my lack of religious interest probably explains why I am not drawn to them. I think of my ancestors with love and curiosity, but I do not feel that they are the markers of an ethnic community to which I belong. They themselves were eager to assimilate themselves, and I see myself as somebody near the end of a path which has been leading to Magyarization and one which has also brought special colors to the Magyar culture. The fact that later on my ancestors were artificially forced back into the ghetto (incidentally, as a baby, I was there myself) and that the majority of Hungarian Jews was massacred, fills me with outrage and horror, but does not induce me to accept what they did not want to accept even then.

I am concerned, of course, that the image of the Jew, with whom my environment identifies me, carries a number of prejudices, false beliefs, and reflex-like antipathies. But I do not think that the psychological problems of this origin can be overcome in only one way; namely, by seeking those Jewish values on the basis of which one can proudly accept the role already assigned to him. I do not have the impression that society looks upon me with the biased glance of one collective individual when I am looked upon as a Jew. I do not know anybody who would not use the jewish/non-Jewish distinction. But how many people agree on the question of who is a Jew; what makes him recognizable; whether there are any specific Jewish characteristics; and, if there are, what they are, are they variable and, finally, when is it important in two people's relationship that one of them is Jewish. I have met non-Jews who are barely interested in the whole question, while others are consumed by it. I know of fanatic anti-Semites and partial filo-Semites. Just like any other social role, the role of the Jew is not so unequivocal that it would not leave room for keeping our distance, for our own self-definition. Naturally, the Jew who chooses the Magyars, by the same option also a limited segment of Hungarian society, a limited tradition within Hungarian culture and politics: he chooses the moral community of those people for whom it is self-evident that, in spite of his Jewishness, he can be Magyar just like the non-Jews; he chooses the tradition which recognizes as Hungarians not only those of Petcheneg ancestry but of Jewish origin as well. There are quite a few such people to choose from. Just to mention some great ones of the more recent tradition: István Bibó, Imre Csécsy, Zoltán Szabó, and Gyula Illyés (as he comes through, for the most part, in *The Magyars*).[4] Obviously nobody can think that with this choice he has placed himself outside of the Jew/non-Jew distinction. I would not

4 István Bibó (1911–1979) was a Hungarian political thinker.

consider it proper to behave as if one is beyond it. I am stating something else; namely, that one can oppose anti-Semitism not only as a conscious (Hungarian) Jew, but as a conscious Hungarian (of Jewish origin) as well.

I repeat, all this does not contradict the program of *Salom*; rather, it complements it. Nevertheless, the different approach with regard to secondary issues does lead to conflicting views. At first I will outline these controversies and in the end I will raise an objection which is independent from the difference of perspectives:

- *Salom*'s defense of the Jewish community's right to solidarity with the Diaspora and the state of Israel seems to me to be convincing. *Salom* is also correct in stating that the solidarity among members of the domestic Jewish community is natural and not objectionable. Nevertheless, while warding off the moral accusation of the "cohesion of the Jews," *Salom* fails to notice that it is coming close to dealing with an important sociological problem which cannot be settled with the simple statement that "The 'cohesion of the Jews' does not and cannot mean corrupt fraternization." In our lopsidedly modernized society personal contacts are probably the most important avenues of success. Since these contacts are developed unevenly between Jewish and non-Jewish members of society, the rival cliques of various institutions also frequently divide into Jewish and non-Jewish ones. There are workplaces where a Jew cannot expect good assignments, recognition, nor advancement of his career; other places, to the contrary, are in the hands of Jewish groups. It has to be realized that if a person speaks of the "cohesion of the Jews" he does not necessarily think of the fictitious Jewish world conspiracy (this may not even cross his mind) but of experiences and hearsays related to such Jewish cliques. Just as the Jewish sense of injury is not only nourished by the indigestible memory of genocide and the outrage over official anti-Zionist propaganda, it also is sustained by the multitude of experiences and hearsays related to the non-Jewish cliques' conduct. The mutual prejudices continue to subsist not only because the past was not honestly confronted, but much more so because there are social mechanisms which reproduce them. A solution is possible only in the long run: through institutional pluralism, increasingly market-oriented economy and political democracy. Some immediate improvement is possible, however, if we speak about this phenomenon impartially: if we reveal and articulate the fact that the reproduction of mutual prejudices is fostered by both the existence of separate circles of friendships and by the formation of cliques supported by the bureaucratic system.

• Having taken all this into consideration, I agree that an honest confrontation with the past is also a precondition for clarifying the relationship between Jews and non-Jews. Hungarian society must learn what role the Jewry played in the history of Hungary. But it is not enough to learn, as *Salom* suggests, who was of Jewish origin among the radicals, Social Democrats, Communists, revisionists, and among the populist writers[5] and the authors of *Nyugat*.[6] First of all, it has to be understood that several pivotal processes in modern Hungarian history—such as industrialization, urbanization, the formation of urban culture and intelligentsia—is intertwined with the process of Magyarization and social adaptatin of the emancipated Hungarian Jewry. This connection, with all its entanglements, is a part of contemporary *Hungarian* history; it has left its imprint not only on Hungarian Jewry but on non-Jewish Hungarians as well. All the same, I would take extra care in distinguishing between the actions or works of Hungarian Jews and "the intellectual and political achievements of Hungarian Jewry." Not everything that Jews did in this country is the achievement of the Jewry, only those achievements which were done with Jewish consciousness and/or built on Jewish traditions. Just as the Slovaks rightfully expect that we would not hide the origin of Maria Hruz's son, but cannot demand that "the Hungarians should not expropriate" Petőfi's poetry,[7] the Hungarian Jewry can lay claim, let us say, to Oszkár Jászi[8] only in biographical terms, since his activity is part of *Hungarian* politics.

• In my opinion, the Open Letter is absolutely correct in pointing out that between 1945 and 1953[9] and in 1956-57[10] a lot of Hungarian Jews were carried to the ranks of anti-national and anti-democratic forces by their gut-level dread of the Hungarian people's "Fascist infestation." I also share

---

5 On the populists, see note 20 of "Troops of Weary Seekers . . . " in this volume.

6 *Nyugat* [The West], was a literary journal launched in 1908. The most important cultural magazine of its time, it had an orientation to Western liberalism. In the 1920's, it opposed the semi-fascist, counterrevolutionary regime. It disbanded in 1942 after the death of its last editor, Mihály Babits.

7 See note 1 of "Can 1956 Be Forgotten?" in this volume. Petőfi's mother, Maria Hruz, was of Slovak origin.

8 Oszkár Jászi (1875-1956), a sociologist and historian, founded the Hungarian Radical Party. He was editor of *Huszadik Század* [The Twentieth Century], a progressive socio-political magazine. Cabinet minister during the 1918 democratic revolution, he emigrated in 1919 and from 1925 was professor at Oberlin College in the United States.

9 1945–1953 was the formative period and the pinnacle of the Stalinist dictatorship in Hungary.

10 1956–57 was the period of the bloody suppression of the October 1956 revolution, and of the restoration of the Communist party-state's power.

Salom's view that this fear can be eliminated only through a mutual and honest confrontation with the past. Furthermore I agree with the assertion that this confrontation should entail not only the Hungarians' responsibility for the 1944 persecution of the Jews, but also the responsibility of those Jews who, after 1945, were driven to definitely criminal actions by the haunting horror of the Holocaust. However, it is questionable whether *Salom* is not going too far when it draws a direct parallel between the two responsibilities: "for all this a certain responsibility lies with the Hungarian Jewry," just as "the Hungarian nation does bear responsibility for the destruction of the Hungarian Jewry."

I would not consider the parallel exaggerated if we understood the historical responsibility of a people as a collective accountability of a whole people for the wrongdoing of one segment of it. It would be a valid parallel if all Hungarians should be accountable for the actions of those gendarmes,[11] Arrow Cross party members[12] and their accomplices who collaborated with the SS; and the whole Jewry for acts committed by Jewish Party leaders and AVH members. Our moral sensibility, however, rightfully protests against such an interpretation of collective responsibility. The majority can bear responsibility only for those actions that the majority did do or did fail to do. István Bibó wrote in this regard that responsibility does lie with the Hungarians for 1944, because too few of them knew their duty towards fellow human beings in grave danger: too many looked on the deportation of the Hungarian Jews without compassion, maliciously, or, at best, with pity, but in any case with idle passivity. As a result of this the victims could not feel that society stood behind them and the persecutors did not have to fear excommunication from society.

Is it possible to speak, in this regard, of the Hungarian Jewry's moral responsibility for the Stalinist dictatorship? Up to a certain degree, yes. For whatever opinion a considerable portion of the Jews held about the regime, they accepted it on the grounds that, at least, the persecution of the Jews could not return. This view drove some Jews to a religious identification with Communism, others to a certain conditional sympathy with the regime

11 The Hungarian gendarmerie as a body took an active part in the deportation of the Jewry: In most cases, gendarmes escorted the Jews to the railway station and handed them over to the SS.
12 Arrow Cross Party was the Hungarian equivalent of the National Socialist Party. An outsider in party politics before the March 1944 German occupation of Hungary, it got unlimited power from the German occupiers in October 1944, after the failed attempt of Miklós Horthy to make a separate peace with the Allied Powers. Arrow Cross gangs were responsible for pillaging, manhandling, and massacring thousands of Budapest Jews and soldiers who defected from the army during the winter of 1944–45.

even during its darkest years. Only a relative few were able to keep their distance.

The parallel with 1944 is still somewhat inappropriate, since the Stalinist dictatorship was not a revenge for the persecution of the Jews. The social transformation which was carried out by fire and sword did elevate to new heights masses of people: farm hands, workers, young peasants. The regime had an enormous number of enthusiastic followers among non-Jews as well; among them a multitude of those who in the preceding era had been driven to the anti-Semitic extreme right by their social destitution. It also should be remembered that there had been a large number of Jews among the oppressed, the deprived, and those who were taken to the torture chambers and the scaffold. At the time when the barns of the peasants were cleaned out in the 1950s, small Jewish shopkeepers were also squeezed to the limit by exorbitant taxes; along with the "class enemy" Christian lawyer, the Jewish bank director faced the same forced relocation. The "saboteur" and the "enemy who infiltrated the party" received his 'deserved' punishment without regard for his religious denomination. And there were even those who were beaten to death as "Zionist agents" on the basis of their Jewish origin.

The Jews, if they did take part in this terror, did it, at least partially, for specific reasons, and therefore, they have to face its lessons as well. But they do not have more weighty reasons for soul searching than the non-Jews.

• Although I do not consider it completely fortunate, it is, nonetheless, respectable, that *Salom* is trying to draw a parallel between Hungarian responsibility for the deportations and Jewish responsibility for the tribulations of Hungarian society after 1945. I recognize this attempt, which runs through the entire Open Letter, to measure Jews and non-Jews with the same yardstick. The Open Letter is free from both the Jewish mentality of injury and Jewish superiority. Its point of departure is that Jews and non-Jews are equal human beings and have to arrange their coexistence in this country according to this principle.

There is, however, one point where *Salom* deviates from this principle. It is true, this deviation does not concern domestic Jews and non-Jews, but the Jews of Israel and the Palestinians. The Open Letter demands, with good reason, that anybody who criticizes the wrongdoings of the Israeli governments, should first acknowledge unequivocally that Jews have the right to live in their own state, and that this state, according to the 1948 resolution of the United Nations, is Israel. Since the Hungarian government, guided by Soviet foreign policy, occupies an ambiguous stance in this regard, it is reasonable to stress this demand with a special emphasis.

However, if we attribute such importance to this demand, then we are obliged to extend it to the Palestinians as well. At first we have to make it unmistakeably clear that the Palestinian people also has the right to its own state, and that the same UN resolution which recognizes Israel also assigns a territory to the sovereign Palestinian state which has been occupied by Israel for almost two decades. After this, one can talk about the fact that the very same territory also had been annexed by Arab states for almost two decades; that Palestinian terrorism is an unacceptable method of struggle; that Israel's intransigence is only one of the obstacles to a peaceful solution—the second one is the other sides's unwillingness to recognize the Jewish state. *Salom*, however, is reluctant to apply the same rule to the Palestinians which it established in regard to Israel. I consider this a mistake.

Even if I were right, somebody might object, the whole issue is not that important. Since in relation to the coexistence of Hungarian Jews and non-Jews, what position *Salom* takes on the Palestinian question is a tenth-rate issue, and Salom's position is even less important than that as far as the outcome of the Palestinian question is concerned. This is true. Nonetheless, it is never good to treat our principles in a casual manner when seemingly unimportant issues are at stake. Hungarian society would be put to a test even if only a fraction of Salom's program became realized. Then it would become clear whether Hungarians are able and willing to recognize the same legitmate rights of a minority within their borders that they consider self-evident for Hungarian minorities abroad. But Jews would face a test as well. So it is not worthwhile to appear in advance as somebody who violates in thought the fundamental principle of equality among minorities, nationalities, and nations—a principle, the upholding of which is very difficult anyway.

Letter to the Signatories of the Prague Appeal

Letter to the Signatories of the Prague Appeal

Dear Friends,

The spokespersons of the Charter 77 present your Appeal as a discussion paper, inviting comments from both home and abroad. I am glad to take this opportunity to open a dialogue, one so sorely needed. I ask the Hungarian democratic opposition, lacking any formal groupings, to please read my letter as a reflection only of my own ideas. Such exchanges of personal views can serve best, in my opinion, as a first step toward mutual understanding and an outlining of common perspectives.

Let me begin by stating our main points of agreement. I accept without reservation the suggestion that peace (as distinguished from a mere state of non-war) and evolution towards democracy in the eastern half of our continent presuppose a gradual overcoming of the division into political-military blocs inherited from the late '40s. I also accept the idea that transcendence of the present *status quo* is not to be expected from a return to the Cold War rollback rhetoric, but only from a process of negotiation and mutually-satisfactory compromises. Further, I wholeheartedly support your statement that a rapprochement between the two halves of Europe cannot succeed as the work of only governments and state apparatuses, but that a significant input by independent opinion groups, voluntary associations and social movements is absolutely necessary for its success. These points make up the common ground that I find both necessary and sufficient for a rational discussion. And now I would like to move on to the points in your Appeal which in my view need clarification, supplementing,

247

or correction. For the sake of convenience, I group them under three headings:

1. the problem: how to describe the present European *status quo* which is to be transcended;
2. the aims: how to characterize the situation to be brought about;
3. the means: how this desired state of affairs is to be approached.

1. The problem

I must confess I am somewhat dissatisfied with your description of the *status quo* in Europe. What I miss is the explicit treatment of the fact that the two power blocs are not coalitions of nearly equal partners but each is dominated by a superpower. It is particularly important to investigate those of its characteristics which pose difficult questions for any serious program for Europe. These are as follows, as far as I can see:

a) The very different geographical location of the two superpowers with respect to Europe: the United States is on the other side of the Atlantic from the Soviet Union, a Eurasian great power ("our Russian neighbors", ex-Chancellor Helmut Schmidt was reported to say once, generously neglecting the Poles, Czechs, Slovaks, and Hungarians in between, not to mention the Ukrainians, Belorussians, and the Baltic peoples). As a consequence, it is hard to see how the withdrawal of American troops and missiles from Western Europe would be genuinely counterbalanced by a similar move to the Soviet side.

b) The unequal degree and, in important respects, different types of dominance exercised by the superpowers over their allies: the U.S. is a hegemonic partner with NATO but nevertheless a partner. West European states have considerable maneuvering room in foreign policy, including policies toward the Soviet bloc (e.g., the gas pipelines conflict of 1982), not to speak of the extremely limited capacity of the U.S. government to determine who shall govern the allied countries in Europe. I do not ignore important exceptions such as Portugal in '74-'75. Nevertheless, certainly since the post-war consolidation no West European government faces the threat of being overthrown by U.S. troops as the Dubcek-Cernick leadership was in 1968-69, and even a Jaruzelski-type proxy intervention's likelihood is minimal west of the Elbe. The question these differences raise is the following: Can we reasonably hope that an East-West rapprochement would sever the special ties of dependency linking the East European states to the Soviet Union? Or, more precisely, is this result to be expected for any kind of rapproachement or only from some special types of it (or from no one at all)? And if there are any particular ways of rapproachement which conceivably could lead to the increased independence of Eastern Europe *vis-à-vis* the Soviet Union, how are they to be characterized?

c) Finally, I would like to mention that the differences in the degrees and ways in which the two Europes depend on the two superpowers are clearly linked to differences in their respective political and economic systems. Pluralist democracy-cum-constitutional rights for citizens and the market economy offer some safeguards against external intervention which dependent Soviet-type systems painfully lack. Consequently, no military disengagement by the superpowers can by itself render the unification process of Europe irreversible. There is a need for some internal changes in Eastern Europe with built-in checks and balances against the overwhelming Soviet supremacy in the region. The question is: What kinds of changes seem both necessary and possible and how could these be linked to the rapproachement process? This is not a hollow question, as you know. From the mid-'50s until the end of the '60s the general idea of evolution in Eastern Europe was of reforms generated from above and supported from below. Since the mid-'70s until the early '80s there was the other model of self-limiting social movements organized outside of the official cadres and pressuring governments for meaningful reforms. Both strategies presupposed (the former implicitly, the latter explicitly) that the desired changes could be achieved even if the inter-bloc *status quo* remained. One of the lessons many East Europeans drew from the 1981 Warsaw *putsch* was that there was no chance of success for democratic movements in Eastern Europe without some change in the external *status quo*. That may be true. It does not follow, however, that it is sufficient to substitute a scenario of a gradual dismantling of the two blocs for a strategy of the internal pluralization and marketization of our countries. If it is true that the desired internal changes depend partly on changes in the external environment, the reverse seems also to be true. Therefore I don't see how we can avoid facing the question of strategy (or strategies) for the internal development of East European societies.

All this is commonplace and I am sure you are well aware of it. I can even see strong reasons for not treating these problems explicitly. Those addressing themselves to the public—both East and West—have to consider the fact that among the possible Western interlocutors most easy to reach, that is, within the pacifist and ecology movements, there are very important groups which either accept, or can be won over to, a strictly symmetrical presentation of the two blocs but suspect Cold-War reflexes behind any statement of the difference between them. I may be wrong in thinking that this was the reason for your neglect of the issues I mention. If I am right, I must state my strong disagreement with such a tactic. There are some specific cases on which I am sure it is possible to cooperate even with strict "symmetrists," and such opportunities are not to be missed. But a strategic cooperation can be hoped for only from people who are ready to condemn the repression of *Solidarnosc*, the prison camps, political psychiatry, and the general lack of observance of constitutional rights in the Soviet world system, without feeling the need to add that the miners' union-breaker Margaret Thatcher is just another Jaruzelski, that the (certainly revolting) extradition of Turkish political *émigrés* by West German authorities means the FRG is as oppressive a state as the GDR, and that the oligopolistic structure of the press in some Western countries has the same effects as censorship and hierarchical state control in the East. Rather than catering to anyone who is willing to talk to us, we should try to help such principled attitudes take center stage in West European democratic opinion. This does not mean denying our need to understand the specific interests and sensitivities of the Western public, e.g. the tendency of left-of-center Democrats (mainly in the FRG) to suspect old-style anti-Communism behind criticism of the Soviet Union; their feeling that the Pershing and cruise missiles installed in their countries pose a greater danger than the SS-20s directed at Western Europe and that they serve only to augment U.S. control; the mounting animosity towards the invasion of European cultural markets by American mass culture; the perplexity in face of the revival of racism as a mass response to the problem of guest workers, etc. We need to grasp all this not only in order to be able to translate our message into the political language Western democrats speak and understand, but also, and mainly, because we ourselves face the constant danger of provincialism, of losing the capacity to view our own problems within a wider perspective. One very clear symptom of such provincialism is the tendency to fall back into Cold-War Manicheism. But it is also provincial to think that the only way of avoiding the trap of Cold-War thinking is to accept the symmetrical presentation of the two blocs and two superpowers.

2. The aims

"Our aim is European unification," you write, "an alliance of free and independent nations within a democratic and self-governing all-European community living in friendship with nations of the entire world." Yes, this is the aim democrats should strive for everywhere in Europe. Nevertheless, let me pose some malign questions. What about the Soviet Union? Is it expected to become a member of the future European community or rather an outside power, which Russia was until the Napoleonic wars and Stalin's state was until 1939? What is to become of the empire built by the tsars and then rebuilt by Lenin and Stalin? Should the Ukraine, Belorussia, Estonia, Latvia, and Lithuania regain their independence and enter as sovereign partners the all-European community? And what about the non-European great power engagements of the Soviet Union, i.e. its military and other presence in the Caribbean, the Far East, Middle East, and Africa? Is it to be supposed that parallel to the hoped-for changes in Europe the Soviet Union will disengage itself in these remote regions? If so, are not we supposing too much? If not, then can we realistically anticipate a Soviet state integrated into a democratic and self-governing all-European community of equal, independent states? In the case of a negative reply we must count on the Soviet Union removing itself from the European arena. But what would push or pull it to such a withdrawal? And what would keep it from returning as a dominant continental power, Findlandizing the whole of Western Europe, once the departure of the Americans created a power vacuum on the other side?

One could say that such questions completely miss the point. In opting for the federation of equal, sovereign, democratic states, the Prague Appeal defines very long-term aims and, given that the realization of these depends on too many intermediary changes in the present *status quo*, it is only natural that the details are unpredictable. In other words, the aims stated in the Appeal are not to be read as part of a well-defined policy but as general principles intended to orientate attitudes. I am not sure these are the lines along which you would defend your position, but it is a conceivable line of defense. The difficulty is that the same objections then reappear at another level. Politics is not just principles to be followed, one also needs viable policies. The long-term aims have to be supplemented by closer targets which one can link to practical steps. Such a target is, in the Prague Appeal, the solution of the German question.

I think this is a most important problem and it is your great merit to have stated it. In a sense this is *the* European problem, the key to the denuclearization and demilitarization of the continent, as well as to the dismantling of the bloc system. But it is so deeply enmeshed with powerful and conflicting interests that one cannot expect any change in this domain in the short run. Do consider the fact that not only the Soviet Union's interests militate against German reunification, but also those of the biggest neighbors of Germany to the East and West, i.e., Poland and France. Think also of the statements (by the way, juridically not at all indefensible) of some leading West German politicians to the effect that the treaties of the '70s are binding only on the governments of the present, separate Germanies; a reunified all-German state would be at liberty to ratify the post-war borders or to call for their renegotiation.

Thus, for an immediate start, one needs other targets, ones more directly attainable. You propose one: the withdrawal of foreign troops from the European theater. This can be an interesting domain for proposing intermediate steps in the right direction. But, in my view, you fail to make use of the opportunity. You say, "Let us . . . propose that NATO and the Warsaw Pact enter forthwith into negotiations on the dissolution of their military organizations, on the removal of all nuclear weapons either sited or aimed at Europe, and on the withdrawal of U.S. and Soviet troops from the territories of their European allies." This is a very attractive long-range aim. But as a proposal for immediate talks, it seems void of content. Let us recall that the great powers themselves also make such sweeping proposals whenever they refuse to talk seriously on realistic, short-run goals. In the short run, maximalism means stagnation.

In sum, what I find wanting in your Appeal is neither a clear statement of the ultimate aims or principles, nor some intermediate goals, but those short-term targets which, being attainable in the predictable future, could help activate a process of a gradual overcoming of the present *status quo*. But with this remark we are well into the question I mentioned last.

3. The means

Here you make two interesting remarks, viz., that there should be greater use made of the Helsinki agreements in the interest of overcoming the division of Europe and that "individual citizens, groups of citizens, or nations" should take an active part in this process, taking their own initiatives and campaigning against unacceptable government policies. The second idea, although somewhat vague, does not pose any problem for me, so I shall leave it aside in order to concentrate on the first one.

Although the question is much discussed in Eastern Europe, I don't see any sensible position other than accepting the Helsinki process as a framework for advancing desirable changes in the *status quo*. However, I don't agree with all of your arguments in favor of this position. You affirm rightly that the Helsinki Final Act and the Madrid Final Document are "not just an acknowledgement of the *status quo*, but also constitute a program of European and Euro-American cooperation." (I would add that they reaffirm the main points of the International Covenants on Civil and Political Rights, introducing the theme of human rights into the relationships of European states with each other and with the U.S.). But I don't think it particularly good phrasing to say that in Helsinki "the negotiations have not been conducted between the blocs but between equal partners, a fact which has underlined the independence of all participant states." It was only the Western side which, until the '60s, was unwilling to recognize dependent Soviet bloc governments as legitimate, equal partners in international relations. The Soviet Union always laid great stress on the external appearance of sovereignty on the part of its dependencies. If Helsinki represents a change in this respect, it lies only in the attitude of Western governments which now are ready to treat East European states as if they were sovereign parties to international agreements. That this change of attitude may contribute to greater maneuverability on the part of the latter *vis-à-vis* the Soviet Union is a different matter.

However, this is not my main point. What I would like to stress concerning Helsinki is that shortly after the signing of the Final Act the whole CSCE-process entered a deep crisis. Concerning security matters, there has been complete stagnation since 1975; in cultural contacts, there is even a slight decline, and regarding human rights there is such an outright conflict that at some points even the breakdown of the negotiation structures seemed possible. This is not to be neglected. If you affirm that Helsinki offers a proper frame of reference for those who want to further European unification, you must be able to say why this is so in spite of the well-known facts of its crisis.

Soviet behavior is only one aspect of the problem. There is also another, and as far as I can see, somewhat neglected problem of Western attitudes towards Helsinki. As you know, Western governments lack any unitary approach to the CSCE-process. What is more, none of the often conflicting approaches treat the human rights issue in a constructive way.

The social-liberal and Christian-liberal governments of the FRG reject outright any suggestion of representing the human issue. In their view, there is a trade-off between demanding respect for human rights and improving state-to-state relationships. They clearly opt for the latter. The most they seem prepared to do is intervene, behind closed doors, in humanitarian affairs. They claim that support for independent opinion groups like Charter 77 or social movements like *Solidarnosc* can only create international tensions, destabilize the European situation, and endanger peace and the slowly accumulated achievements of the rapprochement policy. Let us add that the results they point to are real ones, e.g. freer entry for West German citizens into the GDR, freer exit for, at least elderly, East German citizens to the FRG, regularization of the redeeming of political prisoners, etc.

Mostly in the wake of the invasion of Afghanistan and the Polish *coup d'etat*, an alternative attitude was shared by the U.S. administration and some West European governments like Great Britian. It consists in rhetorically condemning human-rights violations by the Soviet Union and its East European dependencies and blocking the normal evolution of ties with almost all of them. At specific moments and towards specific countries such a policy seems to be justified. For example, I think that the ostracism of the military regime in Poland and the sanctions applied against it were not only morally right reactions to Jaruzelski's war against the Polish people but also the best practical policy. If Jaruzelski proved unable to repeat Kádár's or Husak's normalization performance, it was partly due to his susceptibility to Western economic and diplomatic pressure (the main factor being, naturally, the stubborn social resistance within Poland itself). But human rights rhetoric plus sanctions are at best a defensive stance; they react to rights violations but fail to contribute to a process of widening established and guaranteed rights. The blocking of normal relationships creates international problems which, after awhile, call for a change in tactics. As a consequence, most govenments following this line, including that of the U.S., gradually switch to another position.

This consists in repeating the noble principles of freedom and dignity, criticizing government violation of them, and then quickly reverting to business as usual. Such an ambiguity became an especially widespread phenomenon when Gorbachev and Reagan seemed to be opening a new era in Soviet-American relations. I don't think it would be right to condemn this ambiguity as a manifestation of bad conscience. Rather it seems to be a sign of embarrassment *vis-à-vis* the Helsinki deadlock.

It is my considered opinion that the crucial step in justifying the statement that Helsinki can offer a framework for meaningful changes in Europe must be a demonstration of the possibility of a fourth, constructive approach to the human rights issue. Anyone claiming that Helsinki is not doomed to utter failure has to show that the general provisions of the Final Act on human rights and cultural contacts can be translated into specific, practical, and negotiable proposals. Only in this way can we hope to see the dualism of human-rights rhetoric and practical business overcome. Of course, this approach needs imagination. It also needs a clear view as to how and why the Soviet Union can be involved in the negotiations behind present Western attitudes towards Helsinki (I think the key task is to understand the dominant West German position and to explain why a constructive policy concerning human rights does less damage, in the long run, to German interests than the abandonment of East European peoples to their fate). It is a position not easily attained.

My present aim was neither to elaborate on nor to give answers to other questions I have posed in the earlier pages of this letter. What I wanted to do here was only to help clarify the questions we are facing. But putting the right questions means having the way to the right answers, as the young Marx once said.

With fraternal greetings,

Janos Kis   Budapest, December 15, 1985.

Yalta Problem
in the Mid-Eighties

Yalta Problem
in the Mid-Eighties

I n public parlance, the term "Yalta" signifies the division of Europe and the subjection of several Eastern European countries to Soviet occupation. Whoever refers to Yalta will imply that the Western powers have acknowledged Soviet decision-making in respect to the economic, political, and social systems ruling in these countries; furthermore, they have tacitly accepted that the Soviet Union may apply military force to the safeguarding of these systems which are serving its own purposes.

There is little doubt that, in actual fact, these assumptions are more or less consonant with the interpretation of the Yalta agreements and the acceptance of their long-term validity by the leadership of the great powers. It is well known that, in August 1968, Brezhnev put the question, through diplomatic channels, to then-President Johnson: Did the United States acknowledge the unchanged validity of the results arrived at in Yalta and in Potsdam? Johnson's reply—on August 18—confirmed that the agreement stood, as far as Czechoslovakia and Romania were concerned; in the case of Yugoslavia negotiations should take place if necessary. In the dawn of August 21, Soviet troops occupied Prague . . .

If this is the true meaning of the Yalta agreements, then this poses a very difficult political dilemma for all those who have the fate of Eastern Europe at heart. Yalta is also one guarantee of peace in Europe. If either party should declare the Yalta Agreements null and void, the framework of peace in Europe would collapse. Either we accept the premise that our peace depends on the recognition of the Soviet Union as the "gendarme of

Eastern Europe" or we demand that the Western powers denounce the Yalta agreements and countenance the danger of war in Europe.

How can we deal with this dilemma? It would be easiest, of course, just to bypass it, meaning a situation wherein the Soviet state would either desist using its powers sanctified by Yalta or would be forced to renounce these powers. This was the scenario sketched by the spokesmen of KOR in the late seventies: "Let us assume that in one or another Eastern European country a social movement would emerge—well-organized and therefore capable of self-restraint—outside the bounds of the hierarchical order created by the Party-State. A bargain could then be struck whereby the geo-political interests of the Soviet state would be safeguarded in exchange for a limited but sensible pluralism. The alternative, for the Soviet Union, would be to hazard a catastrophe in Eastern Europe. Is it completely out of the question that the Soviet leadership and their local satraps would accept the lesser evil and come to terms?"

In my opinion, the idea of a self-limiting social movement is still a valuable and fruitful concept, even after December 13, 1981 in Poland. The experiences of 1980–81, however, cast light on the shortcomings of this idea too. In relation to our question, they have shown that the emergence of an organized social movement, willing to come to terms, is a necessary but not a sufficient condition for a Soviet willingness to bargain. As long as it remains the accepted practice in the international sphere that—come the crunch—the Soviet Union may use brute force, it is more likely that they would prefer a military solution to an uncertain compromise.

It is very difficult to come to terms with this sate of affairs, especially today. Ever since the coup of Jaruzelski, Eastern Europe finds itself in a blind alley. The situation is inherently unstable, and not only in Poland. There, state power is incapable of liquidating Solidarity which has only been forced underground; Solidarity is equally incapable of enforcing its open recognition. The whole area suffers from an economic crisis; the copious and cheap Soviet raw material and energy reserves are threatened by exhaustion; reserves of manpower are also disappearing; the expenditure on rearmament knows no bounds; competition in the markets of the world is getting sharper and sharper; the cost of environmental damage is becoming manifest. The consequence of all these factors is that the economic structures of Eastern European countries, based on the Soviet model, simply cannot continue the previously experienced economic growth. The need for economic reforms is pressing, but the political conditions of reform are missing. Stagnation, deterioration, and hopelessness are the rule everywhere. Eastern Europe is being threatened with the fate of relapsing among the stagnating regions of the Third World.

It is an oft-repeated commonplace that Yalta brought us to this pretty pass. It is also a commonplace that Yalta cannot be changed. Let us have a closer look at this belief: how far is it true? Let us face up to the dilemma of Yalta. Is it an immutable certainty that by denouncing Yalta we would inevitably destroy the *status quo* in Europe? And, is it also immutable that, by sticking to Yalta, one is handing all power to the Soviets, including the right to military intervention?

A unilateral repudiation of Yalta would doubtless conjure up the danger of war. Of course, if the Yalta agreements could be invalidated by negotiation, by common consent, there would be no danger to peace—but this is not a serious proposition. A whole series of important agreements were built on the conference decisions of Yalta and Potsdam, regulating the relationships ruling today in Europe: the treaties of Poland with both Eastern and Western Germany; the contractual relationship between the two Germanies; the four-power agreement on Berlin; the acceptance of the two German states in the UN; the Helsinki agreement; and quite a few others. There cannot be a responsible power that would endanger all these with a stroke. On the other hand, there seems to be no earthly reason why the Soviet Union would even contemplate a rearrangement of this kind—what prize could it possibly gain in exchange for foregoing the main achievements of its diplomatic efforts pursued for decades? Matters once closed are extremely difficult to re-open without very solid and compelling reasons.

However, there is one question among those thrown up by the second world war that is still unresolved: the victorious Allied Powers have never concluded a peace treaty with the successor states of the Third Reich. Why should this not be the beginning, with every other change ensuing from a settlement of the German question?

The answer is this. It is not an accident that the question of a German peace treaty was carefully avoided in the seventies when the frontiers in Europe were finalized, when the status of Berlin was settled, while the two Germanies were accepted in the comity of sovereign nations. Namely, in the course of drawing up a peace treaty, it would have had to be decided, openly and unconditionally, whether the division of Germany should be a permanent or a transitional state of affairs. I doubt whether the majority of Germans would ever accept a permanent division; indeed,the Basic Law of the Federal Republic of Germany clearly declares the aim of re-unification. A permanent division, sanctified by international law, would assuredly meet a violent resistance. So would reunification: and not only by the Soviet Union. Germany's eastern and western neighbors, first of all France and Poland, would be equally upset by the prospect of this. In conclusion we may say that the solution of the German problem can only be the result, not the starting point, of a comprehensive rearrangement of things in Europe. The peaceful invalidation of Yalta looks therefore to be a very distant prospect. Within the foreseeable future, we shall probably have to accept the framework of Yalta as a fact of life. And this leads to the other horn of our dilemma: is it a certainty, an indubitable fact, that, by the acceptance of Yalta as the basis of a European *status quo*, the Soviet Union has a free hand for everything in Eastern Europe, including the right to military intervention?

The answer to this question is not so self-evident as we might think after forty years' experience. It is true that the Yalta agreements do contain a point that could be stretched to an acquiescence in the use of force; but there is no proof that such an extension was consonant with the explicit intentions of the negotiating partners. Indeed, we may find clearly contradictory statements among the documents of the conference. I refer to the text of the "Declaration about Liberated Europe"; this repeated the message of the Atlantic Charter: the Allies would only recognize the legitimacy of those new governments that came to power via free elections. These transitional governments must ensure fundamental rights of freedom and must include all democratic forces. In the literal sense, this declaration explicitly excludes the right of any of the Allied powers to prevent free elections, to remove freely chosen governments, to bring to power or to maintain in power unrepresentative, not freely established governments. I call this the "Atlantic interpretation" of the Yalta agreements.

It is true that these severe prohibitions were instantly disregarded at the Yalta meeting itself, concerning the first disputed case. This was the question of the recognition of a Polish government by the Allies. The leaders of the United States and of Great Britain argued the legal continuity of the Polish state as it had stood on September 1, 1939; therefore, they considered the Polish government-in-exile in London as the legal and rightful one. The Soviet Union—having participated in the dismemberment of Poland alongside Nazi Germany in 1939—did resume diplomatic relations with the Polish government-in-exile in 1941. In 1943, however, it withdrew its recognition and, once Soviet troops set foot in Poland, established a National Liberation Committee (made up of Communists and fellow-travellers) in Lublin. In 1944, this Committee transferred itself to Warsaw and operated to all intents and purposes as a transitional government.

The Soviet behavior in this case had no standing according to the terms of the Declaration. Stalin, however, did not bother with the principles of democracy or sovereignty. His claims were made on behalf of the security of the Soviet Union. He declared that the Polish government in London was anti-Soviet; the Soviet state could not allow the existence of hostile regimes along its frontiers, especially not in Poland, the classic *glacis* for German attacks against Russia, as had been proven in two world wars.

Stalin's arguments may have gained some moral weight in consideration of the terrible bloodletting suffered by the Soviet Union. The war was still on, and Churchill and Roosevelt could not have remained indifferent to this sacrifice. Nevertheless, realities weighed more in the scales than sentiments (Poland was by then occupied by the Red Army), not to speak of self-interest. Churchill wanted to strengthen the influence of Great Britain in the Balkans, while Roosevelt badly wanted a Soviet entry into the war against Japan. In the end, the two Western leaders gave ground. It is true that they acknowledged the Soviet right to decide the nature of neighboring governments in a limited form only: they refused to accept the Lublin "government" as it stood and insisted on some sort of unification of the two governments. Still, it is an indisputable fact that they gave up the principles of the Declaration. This sorry solution of the Polish problem was the precedent allowing us to make a second interpretation of the Yalta agreements. I would call this the "Lublin interpretation."

At the time this concession may have appeared to be a temporary one. After all, the three leaders agreed that elections would be held in Poland within a few months, following which there would have been no dispute about recognition. Nobody asked the question: if it was possible to withdraw recognition from a government enjoying legal continuity on account of its being a "danger to Soviet interests," what would have prevented a similar veto against a freely and democratically-elected new government? Thus the Yalta agreements took two contradictory stands in the question of Soviet rights in occupied countries: the "Atlantic answer" and the "Lublin answer."

Before going further, we may observe that the two were not mutually exclusive. It was not beyond the bounds of imagination that some kind of governance might be established that would come into being through free elections but at the same time would have been able to satisfy the claims of security demanded by the Soviet Union.

A compromise of this nature, agreed to in Hungary in September, 1945, may have had such an aim: the parties in the temporary government agreed among themselves—and with the Soviet President of the Allied Control Commission—that, albeit free and regular elections would be held, the composition of the government would not depend on the ratio of parties in the new Parliament. In remained an open question how far a discrepancy could be sustained in the power relationships in Parliament on one side and in the civil administration on the other, and how this would affect the stability of the system. In Hungary, conditions seemed reasonably favorable for a solution of this kind; in Romania, Bulgaria, and, particularly, in Poland, the conditions were far from promising. The Allies failed, however, to scrutinize the possibilities of an equilibrium between their compromise of the "Atlantic" and "Lublin" solutions on the one hand, and the social and political situation of the whole area on the other. The two Western leaders did not agree even among themselves.

At the time of the Yalta conference, the anti-Fascist coalition had already arrived at a turning point. The Nazi danger was by then fast disappearing: its threat was not enough to suppress the ideological and political antagonism between the Soviets and the Anglo-Saxons any longer. Real conflicts came out into the open, when the Soviet Union began its reordering of matters in the liberated or occupied countries in Eastern Europe. However, it was felt at the time that a complete rupture might still be avoided—nobody had any inkling, how imminent this already was. In these circumstances, the obvious answer seemed to be the well-worn diplomatic maneuver: whenever and wherever there could be no agreement, the minutes of the conference were clothed in a deliberate vagueness.

All the loose talk about possible solutions favored, of course, the Soviet Union, it being in possession of the ground. In the following months, the Soviet Union extorted one concession after another from the Western powers, almost all of them contrary not only to an "Atlantic interpretation" but also to a "Lublin interpretation," nullifying the supposed limitations of the latter.

In the first instance, the Soviet Union rammed down the throat of its partners its own ideas about the reorganization of the Polish government: instead of a completely new government, a couple of ministers from the London one were to be coopted to the existing Lublin group. Next, it extorted an outcome, favorable to itself, in the crises concerning Romania and Bulgaria. In Romania, the king was forced to withdraw his demand for the resignation of the completely unrepresentative government of Groza, against the concession that two members of the opposition would join the cabinet. In Bulgaria, the Western powers abandoned their objections to elections based on a unitary list, in exchange for a similar face-saving formula.

Sooner or later, however, it became clear that there was to be no end to this blackmail. Consequently, the United States and Great Britain became increasingly reluctant to accept the "Lublin interpretation." From the end of 1945 onwards, the Western powers returned to the use of the Atlantic rhetoric; they levelled accusations against the Soviet Union, charging it with breaches of the Yalta agreement; they pretended that Roosevelt and Churchill had never recognized the right of the Soviet Union to subordinate the principles of the Declaration to its geopolitical interests, as far as the European theater was concerned. The fast-deteriorating relationships, however, did not put a brake on Stalin—far from it. Sensing that a permanent compromise had become impossible, he did not bother any longer to stick even to the "Lublin interpretation." On the contrary: it was he who accused his erstwhile partners of warlike preparations on the pretext of defending the "Atlantic" principles, and of attempting to upset, in a forcible manner, the *status quo* achieved in 1945. The Yalta agreement dissolved into two irreconcilable interpretations—the Cold War broke out in earnest.

This meant that, between 1945 and 1947, no clear and mutually acceptable interpretation of the Yalta agreements had emerged that would have been capable of offering a common basis for a changed relationship once the Cold War came to a close. The empty framework could be equally filled by two scenarios: on the one hand, the return of sovereignty and democratization to the Sovietized Eastern European countries (provided that the Soviet Union would be satisfied with geopolitical safeguards offered by sovereign governments); on the other hand, the wholesale Sovietization of the area, not excluding Soviet military interventions from time to time (the Western powers receiving certain concessions acceptable to them in these conditions).

•   •   •

The real meaning of Yalta emerged only later, in 1956 and in 1968. The defeat of the Hungarian Revolution followed by the occupation of Czechoslovakia proved that no agreement is possible with the Soviet Union, either on the basis of the "Atlantic interpretation" or on the basis of a compromise between the "Atlantic" and "Lublin" concepts. Strangely enough, however, this searing experience has contributed just as much to the start of *detente* as the gradual abolition of the Stalinist terror, the tentative opening up of the Soviet sphere to commercial and cultural contacts, and the emergence of a rough strategic balance. The harsh fact is that 1956 and 1968 stamped paid on any illusions the West may have had about the temporary nature of Soviet rule over Eastern Europe. This opened the door to a clarification of the true contents of Yalta and to a mutually acceptable interpretation of it.

The Western powers acknowledged that the Soviet-type governments of Eastern European countries were legitimate ones; indeed—at least in secret diplomatic contacts—they acknowledged that the Soviet Union was entitled to the use of armed force if any of these governments were threatened. In exchange for this recognition, they attempted to attach a more precise and accountable meaning to the other half of the Yalta agreements, the part that does impose certain limits on Soviet freedom of action in the area. There was no more talk about recognized opposition or about representative government, but it appeared feasible to conclude international agreements safeguarding basic human rights. This did not seem to be in contradiction to a recognition of these Soviet-type regimes. The results of efforts in this field was the International Covenant on Human Rights, as well as the so-called "third basket" of the Helsinki Final Act (setting out agreed rules on the free movement of people and of communications, etc.).

By the middle seventies, we saw the emergence of a unified and mutually acceptable interpretation of the Yalta agreements; I would call this the "Helsinki interpretation."

At first, it appeared that the "Helsinki interpretation" might offer the chance for well-ordered long-term relationships in Europe. The leadership of the Soviet Union was granted the demands originally denied it in 1945: a final settlement of the Armistice frontiers, the recognition of the East European Soviet sphere of influence, and the international acceptance of the Soviet-type governments in the area. A certain insistence on human rights may have seemed an acceptable price—particularly because there were very few, not easily verifiable concessions which they were expected to make. I shall return to these presently.

The Western side may also have felt some satisfaction: the status of Berlin was settled and contacts between the citizens of the two Germanies became regularized, if not fully liberalized. Longer-term expectations seemed even more promising. There was a reasonable expectation that, following international approval of respect for human rights, a gradual opening up of contacts might render life more tolerable in the Soviet-dominated area. Soviet satellite governments then might acquire a measure of legitimacy among their subjects; the lessening of political tension might lead to some let-up in repression; finally, it was hoped that all this might lead towards some kind of more pluralistic economic and political orders. From Henry Kissinger to Willy Brandt, this was the meaning of the "Helsinki bargain" to most leading circles in the West.

Alas, this compromise proved to be no more stable than the previous ones. Many things from outside the European theater contributed to its collapse: the impasse of disarmament, the Soviet invasion of Afghanistan, the Central American imbroglio and many others. But let us not delude ourselves: the Helsinki Final Act was undermined from the very outset. It defined the area of human rights in an extremely liberal manner: freedom of assembly, the right to work, the right to health, even the right to recreation were included in it. This broad spectrum in itself supplied the pretext for any breach of basic rights. No government on earth can render all the solemnly proclaimed good things to its citizens at the same time. So the Soviet Union and its satellites could easily argue that perhaps less had been achieved in the field of negative rights but much more in the area of positive ones. While this was bad enough, it was even worse that light years of distance still existed between rhetoric and realities just like the time of the "Atlantic" interpretation. When the Western powers compelled the Soviet Union to subscribe to basic human rights, they apparently did ont expect the emergence of independent organizations and institutions or of a free press in Eastern Europe. They were looking for more modest results: a somewhat more liberally-handled emigration policy, more movement between East and West, perhaps a few Western periodicals in newspaper kiosks and the like. In all this they could have cooperated with the Soviet Union—give or take the occasional friction.

The sudden birth of KOR, of Charter 77, of Soviet groups for monitoring the Helsinki agreement, the spread of uncensored publications—these phenomena created an unexpected crisis. the Soviet Union behaved in the same manner as in 1945–47; being in possession of the ground, it did not give one jot. The persecution of Soviet dissidents, the brutal behavior of Czechoslovak forces or violence towards Charter members, surpassed anything seen before. And when the KOR movement broadened out into a movement embracing the workers, giving birth to Solidarity, 1956 and 1968 were replayed: Russia confronted the universal will of the people with naked force. The Western powers had no means to prevent all this, but they could not swallow the bitter pill of disappointment either. In consequence, the "Helsinki interpretation" fell apart in the same way as its predecessors: one side flourished the banner of universal human rights, the other side rejected alleged interventions into internal matters.

This is the state of affairs today—forty years after Yalta, ten years after Helsinki.

• • •

Looking back at the dilemma I have initially indicated, we can now state quite clearly that the accepted common interpretation of Yalta led to a false view. The original agreement struck at Yalta contained no clause empowering the Soviet Union to use force to protect the ruling systems of the countries occupied by it. The concession belongs to a later, quasi-historical interpretation of Yalta. Between 1976 and 1981, this interpretation was shaken to its foundations. The future of Europe depends to a large extent on the question: what will replace this interpretation? No one can count on the repeal of the Yalta agreement, but a reinterpretation of it cannot be evaded any longer. Would it be possible to arrive at an interpretation that would not include the right to forcible intervention by the Soviet Union, that would apply more determined measures to safeguard basic human rights?

This is the correct question. A positive answer to this would be the only means whereby the Soviet-type regimes of Eastern Europe might be able to get out of their social and economic blind alley. And—last but not least—the stability of the European *status quo* would also depend on a solution of this problem.

At first glance, the lessons of the Cold War do not seem to offer much encouragement. The Soviet Union, in all likelihood, would react in a very hostile manner if limitations were attempted to be put on its freedom of action in its sphere—limitations it would not introduce of its own free will. It is, of course, self-evident that no solution could be stable without acceptance by the Soviet Union. But we must not assume that the Soviet Union today would refuse everything it rejected forty years ago. Between 1945 and 1948, the Soviet Union was only a regional power: its army was the traditional land-based one; its economy, its cultural and scientific establishment was isolated; it was only for a short period that it was able to support its own development from the material and spiritual exploitation of its newly-acquired domains. Today, the Soviet Union is a world power; militarily incomparably stronger than at the end of the second world war. But by the same token, it simply cannot avoid some kind of accommodation with the United States. It cannot obtain the capital and the technology, indispensable for its economy (as well as for its progress in armaments) from the semi-developed, debilitated, East European countries (themselves regressed through aping the Soviet model). It cannot even produce enough grain to feed its population. A thousand-and-one threads are now tying it to the outside world; a return to self-isolation would lead to unforeseeable consequences.

The lessens of the period of *detente* are more complex. It is true that the disputes about human rights remind one, in an eerie way, of the fruitless rhetoric expended about free elections. But this dispute was not sparked by the Western powers making unrealistic demands on the Soviet Union. They would have been satisfied with quite modest results. It was the East European peoples themselves who rebelled against what they saw as the unrealistically restricted concessions they had received from the attempted concord between the West and the Soviet Union. In the course of the Cold War, totalitarian terror ruthlessly suppressed every kind of local resistance.

However, once oppression became somewhat more restrained and more calculable, it became clear that stability in the region could only be achieved by permanent concessions. Not only are those solutions unstable that do not enjoy the acceptance of the Soviet Union, but anything the peoples of Eastern Europe are not prepared to live with is equally unstable.

Following 1956 and then 1968, the Soviet Union did offer certain concessions that eventually led to a period of peace and quiet in the area. After the Hungarian 1956, they offered more normalcy in everyday life, a second, "small" de-Stalinization and, above all, an economic upswing based on the supply of Soviet raw material. After 1968, they allowed a more relaxed range of economic and cultural contacts with the West, and a further injection of Soviet raw materials and energy products. After 1981, there is nothing the Soviet Union can offer. It is forced to reduce its supplies, it is compelled to raise its prices. It makes every attempt to shepherd the subject countries back into the straightjacket of a self-sufficient COMECON; whenever possible, it tries to make them pay for Western investments required for the Soviet economy. In these conditions, it simply cannot expect to maintain an orderly rule over Eastern Europe. Of course, no one can count on its spontaneous retirement from the area.

For these reasons, the propositions of KOR are still on the agenda. What happens to them will depend on the new meaning of Yalta being developed among the powers whose task it is to maintain the peace of the world.

Volumes Published by Atlantic Research and Publications

"Studies on Society in Change"

No. 1   *Tolerance and Movements of Religious Dissent in Eastern Europe.* Edited by Béla K. Király. 1977.

No. 2   *The Habsburg Empire in World War I.* Edited by R. A. Kann. 1978.

No. 3   *The Mutual Effects of the Islamic and Judeo-Christian Worlds: The East European Pattern.* Edited by A. Ascher, T. Halasi-Kun, B. K. Király. 1979.

No. 4   *Before Watergate: Problems of Corruption in American Society.* Edited by A. S. Eisenstadt, A. Hoogenboom, H. L. Trefousse. 1979.

No. 5   *East Central European Perceptions of Early America.* Edited by B. K. Király and G. Barány. 1977.

No. 6   *The Hungarian Revolution of 1956 in Retrospect.* Edited by B. K. Király and Paul Jonás. 1978.

No. 7   *Brooklyn U.S.A.: Fourth Largest City in America.* Edited by Rita S. Miller. 1979.

No. 8   *Prime Minister Gyula Andrássy's Influence on Habsburg Foreign Policy.* János Décsy. 1979.

No. 9   *The Great Impeacher: A Political Biography of James M. Ashley.* Robert F. Horowitz. 1979.

No. 10 Vol. I*   *Special Topics and Generalizations on the Eighteenth and Nineteenth Century.* Edited by Béla K. Király and Gunther E. Rothenberg. 1979.

* Volumes Nos. I through XXVIII refer to the series *War and Society in East and Central Europe.*

No. 11 Vol. II	*East Central European Society and War in the Pre-Revolutionary 18th Century Europe.* Edited by Gunther E. Rothenberg, Béla K. Király, and Peter F. Sugar. 1982.
No. 12 Vol. III	*From Hunyadi to Rákoczi: War and Society in Late Medieval and Early Modern Hungary.* Edited by János M. Bak and Béla K. Király. 1982.
No. 13 Vol. IV	*East Central European Society and War in the Era of Revolutions: 1775-1856.* Edited by B. K. Király. 1984.
No. 14 Vol. V No 15 Vol. VI	*Essays on World War I: Origins and Prisoners of War.* Edited by Samuel R. Williamson, Jr. and Peter Pastor. 1983 *Essays on World War I: Total War and Peacemaking, A Case Study on Trianon.* Edited by B. K. Király, Peter Pastor, and Ivan Sanders. 1982.
No. 16 Vol. VII	*Army, Aristocracy, Monarchy: War, Society and Government in Austria, 1618-1780.* Thomas M. Barker. 1982.
No. 17 Vol. VIII	*The First Serbian Uprising 1804-1813.* Edited by Wayne S. Vucinich. 1982.
No. 18 Vol. IX	*Czechoslovak Policy and the Hungarian Minority 1945-1948.* By Kálmán Janics, Edited by Stephen Borsody. 1982.
No. 19 Vol. X	*At the Brink of War and Peace: The Tito-Stalin Split in a Historic Perspective.* Edited by Wayne S. Vucinich. 1982.
No. 20	*Inflation Through the Ages: Economic, Social, Psychological and Historical Aspects.* Edited by Edward Marcus and Nathan Schmuckler. 1981.
No. 21	*Germany and America: Essays on Problems of International Relations and Immigration.* Edited by Hans L. Trefousse. 1980.
No. 22	*Brooklyn College: The First Half Century.* Murray M. Horowitz. 1981.
No. 23	*A New Deal for the World: Eleanor Roosevelt and American Foreign Policy.* Jason Berger. 1981.
No. 24	*The Legacy of Jewish Migration: 1881 and Its Impact.* Edited by David Berger. 1982.

No. 25   *The Road to Bellapais: Cypriot Exodus to Northern Cyprus.* Pierre
              Oberling. 1982.

No. 26   *New Hungarian Peasants: An East Central European Experience
              with Collectivization.* Edited by Marida Hollos and Béla C. Maday.
              1983.

No. 27   *Germans in America: Aspects of German-American Relations in the
              Nineteenth Century.* Edited by Allen McCormick. 1983.

No. 28   *A Question of Empire: Leopold I and the War of Spanish Succession,
              1701-1705.* Linda and Marsha Frey. 1983.

No. 29   *The Beginning of Cyrillic Printing–Cracow, 1491. From the
              Orthodox Past in Poland.* Edited by Ludwik Krzyzanowski. 1983.

No. 29a   *A Grand Ecole for the Grands Corps: The Recruitment and Training
              of the French Administration.* Thomas R. Osborne. 1983.

No. 30   *The First War Between Socialist States: The Hungarian Revolution
Vol. X   of 1956 and Its Impact.* Edited by Béla K. Király, Barbara Lotze,
              Nandor Dreisziger. 1984

No. 31   *The Effects of World War I, The Uprooted: Hungarian Refugees and
Vol. XI   Their Impact on Hungary's Domestic Politics.* István Mócsy. 1983.

No. 32   *The Effects of World War I: The Class War After The Great War:
Vol. XIII   The Rise of Communist Parties in East Central Europe, 1918-1921.*
              Edited by Ivo Banac. 1983.

No. 33   *The Crucial Decade: East Central European Society and National
Vol. XIV   Defense, 1859-1870.* Edited by Béla K. Király. 1984.

No. 35   *Effects of World War I: War and Communism in Hungary, 1919.*
Vol. XVI   György Péteri. 1984.

No. 36   *Insurrections, Wars, and the Eastern Crisis in the 1870s.* Edited by
Vol. XVII   B. K. Király and Gale Stokes. 1985.

No. 37   *East Central European Society and the Balkan Wars, 1912-1913.*
Vol. XVIII   Edited by B. K. Király and Dimitrije Djordjevic. 1986.

No. 38   *East Central European Society in World War I.* Edited by B. K.
Vol. XIX   Király and N. F. Dreisziger, Assistant Editor Albert A. Nofi. 1985.

No. 39 Vol. XX	*Revolutions and Interventions in Hungary and Its Neighbor States,* *1918-1919.* Edited by Peter Pastor, 1988.
No. 40 Vol. XXI	*East Central European Society and War, 1750-1920.* Bibliography and Historiography. Compiled and edited by László Alföldi. Pending.
No. 41 Vol. XXII	*Essays on East Central European Society and War: 1740s-1920s.* Edited by Stephen Fischer-Galati and Béla K. Király. 1988.
No. 42 Vol. XXIII	*East Central European Maritime Commerce and Naval Policies,* *1789-1913.* Edited by Apostolos E. Vacalopoulos, Constantinos D. Svolopoulos, and Béla Király. To appear in 1989.
No. 43 Vol. XXIV	*Selection, Social Origins, Education and Training of East Central* *European Officers Corps.* Edited by Béla K. Király and Walter Scott Dillard. 1988.
No. 44 Vol. XXV	*East Central European War Leaders: Civilian and Military.* Edited by Béla K. Király and Albert Nofi. 1988.
No. 46	*Germany's International Monetary Policy and the European Mone-* *tary System.* Hugo Kaufmann. 1985.
No. 47	*Iran Since the Revolution — Internal Dynamics, Regional Conflicts* *and the Superpowers.* Edited by Barry M. Rosen. 1985.
No. 48 Vol. XXVII	*The Press During the Hungarian Revolution of 1848-1849.* Domokos Kosáry. 1986.
No. 49	*The Spanish Inquisition and the Inquisitional Mind.* Edited by Angel Alcala. 1987.
No. 50	*Catholics, the State and the European Radical Right, 1919-1945.* Edited by Richard Wolff and Jorg K. Hoensch. 1987.
No. 51 Vol. XXVIII	*The Boer War and Military Reform.* Jay Stone and Erwin A. Schmidl. 1987.
No. 52	*Baron Joseph Eötvös, A Literary Biography.* Steven B. Várdy. 1987.
No. 53	*Towards the Renaissance of Puerto Rican Studies: Ethnic and Area* *Studies in University Education.* Maria Sanchez and Antonio M. Stevens. 1987.

No. 54   *The Brazilian Diamonds in Contracts, Contraband and Capital.* Harry Bernstein. 1987.

No. 55   *Christians, Jews and Other Worlds: Patterns of Conflict and Accommodation.* Edited by Philip F. Gallagher. 1988.

No. 56   *The Fall of the Medieval Kingdom of Hungary: Mohács, 1526, Buda,*
Vol. XXVI   *1541.* Géza Perjés. 1989.

No. 57   *The Lord Mayor of Lisbon: The Portugese Tribune of the People and His Twenty-four Guilds.* Harry Bernstein. 1989.

No. 58   *Hungarian Statesmen of Destiny: 1860-1960.* Edited by Paul Bödy. 1989.

No. 59   *For China: The Memoirs of T. G. Li, former Major General in the Chinese Nationalist Army.* T. G. Li. Written in collaboration with Roman Rome. 1989.

No. 60   *Politics in Hungary: For A Democratic Alternative.* By János Kis, with an Introduction by Timothy Garton Ash. 1989.